# RACK, ROPE AND RED-HOT PINCERS

*Also by Geoffrey Abbott*

Ghosts of the Tower of London
Great Escapes from the Tower of London
Tortures of the Tower of London and Elsewhere
Beefeaters of the Tower of London
The Tower of London As It Was
Lords of the Scaffold

# RACK, ROPE AND RED-HOT PINCERS

## A History of Torture and its Instruments

Geoffrey Abbott
Yeoman Warder (retd.)
HM Tower of London

Brockhampton Press

The right of Brian McConnell to be identified as the Author of
the Work has been asserted by him in accordance with the
Copyright, Designs and Patents Act 1988.

First published in Great Britain in 1993
by HEADLINE BOOK PUBLISHING

This edition published 1997 by Brockhampton Press,
a member of Hodder Headline PLC Group

ISBN 1 86019 795 7

British Library Cataloguing in Publication Data

Abbott, G.
Rack, Rope and Red-hot Pincers: a History
of Torture and Its Instruments
I. Title
365.6409

Phototypeset by Intype, London

Printed and bound in Great Britain by
Creative Print and Design (Wales), Ebbw Vale

This book is dedicated to my wife, Shelagh, who, despite the subject of the book, encouraged me to rack my brains and hang the consequences!

# Contents

# Acknowledgements

With grateful thanks to all the castle custodians, museum curators and librarians, particularly those of the NATO libraries in Germany, Holland and France during the years 1956–74. Without the shudder-making details they provided, the reader would have been left in blissful ignorance regarding just who had been tortured, exactly by what, and how agonising it must have been!

While every effort has been made to trace copyright to all material in this book, the author apologises if he has inadvertently failed to credit any ownership of copyright.

Photographic work by Steven Taylor, Kendal, Cumbria.

# Introduction

We went to the torture room in a kind of solemn procession,
the guards walking ahead with lighted candles. The chamber
was underground and dark, particularly near the entrance. It
was a vast shadowy place and every device and instrument of
human torture was there. They pointed out some of them to
me and said I should have to taste them. Then they asked me
again if I would confess. 'I cannot', I said.

Those words were spoken by John Gerard, a Jesuit priest accused
of spreading Catholicism in England, contrary to the law. And in
1597 he was captured, brought to the Tower of London and there
'put to the question'.

Whatever the country, whatever the crime, one could see the
authorities' dilemma. Fingers of suspicion, strong or otherwise,
sometimes reinforced by evidence, would point to an individual,
but all accusations would be vehemently denied. Yet the truth
had to be determined. And in an age when social conditions were
brutally harsh, when epidemics of fatal diseases decimated the
population and violence was almost a way of life, what more
natural than to attempt to extract a confession by using force?

Similarly, having proved guilt by one means or another, it followed logically that the criminal should be punished by the
further infliction of pain, the severity of which would depend on
the crime committed.

Torture (from the Latin *torquere*, to twist) has of course been
used in most countries from time immemorial. Its concept is
based on two fundamental facts. First, that we all have imagin-
ations, and secondly, that our bodies are susceptible to pain. In

1

other words we can envisage what's likely to happen, and we don't like getting hurt.

So powerful is the imagination that the first stage in the sequence of torture was, as described by John Gerard, that the victim would be shown the instruments of torture in their terrifying surroundings. In some cases this was sufficient, the result being the immediate submission of the victim and the disclosure of the required information without further coercion.

In many other cases, such as that of Gerard, whose strength of purpose and conviction prevailed over his imaginative powers, the full gamut of torture had to be applied. And he was but one of the 252 Jesuit priests who entered this country during ten years in the sixteenth century, more than half of whom were captured, tortured and executed.

The other factor, that our bodies are so vulnerable to pain, was of course of positive benefit to the dedicated torture-instrument designers of the day. Human flesh, soft and sensitive? Well, let's apply heat to it, cut it, pierce it with needles and spikes, lash it with whips. Limbs were only meant to bend one way? Then let's see how far we can bend them the other way. Shoulder blades, hip and leg joints can only operate when moving smoothly in their sockets? Right, let's dislocate them, then.

Such vulnerability thereby brought about suffering and disablement, mutilation and amputation, some countries inventing their own devices or adopting those of other countries, all designed to bring pain and punishment.

The final penalty, that of execution, was also accomplished in many different ways, tributes to the barbaric ingenuity of those deciding how best to remove heads, squeeze necks, burn bodies, and generally extinguish life from an undesirable member of society, not necessarily painlessly.

Where less serious crimes had been committed, those against the community rather than against the State, a further human susceptibility was exploited. This was the feeling of shame experienced by an offender when he or she was subjected to public ridicule. Although not specifically torture, i.e. painful persuasion, punishments expressly designed to bring about such humiliation were devised and administered to those committing minor offences in contravention of the social code.

2

So they were subjected to shameful ordeals, such as having to sit in the stocks or ducking stool, to wear the scold's bridle or drunkard's cloak, to stand at the pillory or ride the stang; and because these penalties were exacted in full view of abusive or malicious neighbours, they provided an added bonus in that justice had not only been done but was seen to be done – always a prized boast of the English courts, as exemplified by the excellent attendance at public executions.

The art of torture – for it was indeed an art, since an ill-judged turn of the screw or excessive twist of the cord could bring about a victim's premature demise and so deprive one's lord and master of vital information – was legally practised, not only in the East, but also on the Continent. Written into the various legal codes for many centuries, judicial torture was not formally abolished in Scotland until 1708, though the last warrant for torture there was issued in 1690. In Denmark the end of legal torture was enacted in 1771, in Spain in 1790 and in France in 1798. Russia followed suit in 1801, though did employ torture in exceptional cases as late as 1847.

Germany ruled out the practice in 1831, Prussia in 1805, and Japan in 1873, though as is well known, torture in many countries has continued to be used to the present day, some forms being more subtle than others.

In earlier centuries in England, thousands of victims were tortured solely in order to wring confessions from them, or to obtain names of accomplices. But unlike most other countries, torture was contrary to the law of the land. So it must have been with tongue in cheek that Sir Thomas Smith, Secretary of State to Queen Elizabeth, wrote in a book published in 1583:

Torment or question, which is used by the order of the civil lawe and custome of other countries, to put a malefactor to excessive paine, to make him confess of him selfe, or of his fellowes or complices, is not used in England . . . the nature of our nation is free, stout, haulte, prodigall of life and bloud, but contumelie, beatings, servitude and servile torment and punishment it will not abide.

Yet as reported by the historian Hallam, 'The rack seldom stood

3

idle in the latter part of Elizabeth's reign', thereby giving the lie to Sir Thomas's hypocritical words.

That torture took place at all was due to the fact that the monarchs of the day were above the law and so could take any measures they thought necessary to safeguard their own thrones and to subdue unruly elements of society.

To ensure this, Henry VII (1485–1509) instituted his Continual Council, consisting of Chief Justices, prelates and members of the Privy Council. Its task was to judge and pass sentence on those too powerful to be dealt with by an ordinary court, or to decide on cases too complex to be understood by the uneducated juries of the day, and the King himself occasionally presided, frequently taking matters into his own hands and pronouncing judgment.

Because the ceiling of the imposing room in which the Council met was ornamented with gilded stars, it became known as the Star Chamber, and while at first its motives were admirable and well intentioned, it soon evolved into a tribunal which arbitrarily created and defined the offences it punished, handing down penalties ranging from the whipping post to the pillory, the rack to the gauntlets, the branding iron to the slitting knife.

Some terrifying examples were listed by the chronicler Ralph Holinshed in 1578.

If a woman poison hir husband she is burned aliue; if the seruant kill his master he is to be executed for petie treason; he that poisoneth a man is to be boiled to death in water or lead, although the partie die not of the practise; in case of murther all the accessaries are to suffer paines of death accordinglie. Manie trespasses are also punished by the cutting of one or both ears from the head of the offendor, from fraimakers, petie robbers etc., and such as those guilty of the vtterance of seditious words against the magistrates.

Roges are burned through the eares, cariers of sheepe out of the land by the loss of their hands; such as kill by poison are either boiled or skalded to death in lead or seething water. Hereticks are burned quicke, harlots and their mates by carting, ducking and dooing of open penance in sheets, in churches and market places, to put to rebuke.

During the sixteenth century the Star Chamber continued to hold supreme sway, and its overwhelming powers were not challenged until 1628. In April of that year John Felton, a 33-year-old ex-officer, bought a tenpenny dagger at a cutler's shop on Tower Hill and, going to Portsmouth, stabbed the Duke of Buckingham to death. He was seized by passers-by and upon being searched, documents found in his possession showed that the man was a religious fanatic, to the extent that he regarded himself as the champion of God and the Duke as a tyrant to be exterminated.

After his arrest he was interrogated by the Earl of Dorset who threatened him with the rack if he did not name his accomplices. Felton replied, 'I do not believe, my Lord, that it is the King's wish, for he is a just and gracious prince and will not have his subjects to be tortured against the law. But if it is his Majesty's pleasure, I am ready to suffer whatever he will have inflicted on me.' And then he delivered his verbal bombshell, saying, 'Yet this I must tell you, by the way, that if I be put upon the rack, I will accuse you, my Lord Dorset, and none but yourself, as my accomplice.'

As can be imagined, this defiant threat had a devastating effect on the Earl who, taken aback and fearing the possible consequences of such a dire accusation, promptly referred the matter to King Charles, only to be told that the prisoner should indeed be 'tortured to the furthest stretch allowed by law'.

A panel of twelve judges was then convened and, as recorded in *State Trials* Vol.iii, 'Felton ought not by the law to be tortured by the rack, for no such punishment is known or allowed by our law.'

What happened to our ingeniously minded John Felton, you ask? Was he freed by a generous-minded monarch, or perhaps given a nominal sentence for revealing past contraventions of the law? I'm afraid not. On 28 November 1628, before a vast crowd, John Felton was hanged at Tyburn, his corpse afterwards being transported to the scene of his crime. There it was suspended in chains from a gibbet, where it was seen by the diarist John Evelyn, who wrote: 'His dead body is carried down to Portsmouth and hangs there high; I hear it creak in the wind.'

Despite the judges' ruling, one further case of torture by the rack took place in England when, in 1640, John Archer was

5

caught leading a street demonstration in Lambeth, beating a drum. In order to ascertain the names of his confederates, he was 'to be shown the rack and in the event of not answering certain questions to be put to him, should be racked as in the examiners' discretions shall be thought fit'. And so he was. After which he was hanged, dying without knowing that he had the doubtful claim to fame of being the last man in England to be stretched on the rack.

In the following pages you will find described not only the instruments of torture and execution in Britain and many other countries, but also the accounts of some of those who, for their sins, their principles or their beliefs, suffered at the hands of such men as Thomas Norton, Rackmaster of the Tower of London; Richard Topcliffe, Elizabethan torturer of the Jesuits; Charles-Henri Sanson, the French headsman; Tomas de Torquemada, Inquisitor-general of the Spanish Inquisition; Franz Schmidt, Executioner of Nuremberg; and others with similar persuasive equipment and capabilities.

So read on and, should *you* ever be 'put to the question', take my advice; don't wait to be asked . . . don't even hesitate . . . just take a deep breath . . . and confess everything!

# 1
## Durance Vile

Before and after torture, prisoners were strictly confined, usually in locations which were in themselves a passive form of torture. Dungeons deep within castles were obvious choices, as were the cells in the heavily fortified gatehouses positioned at intervals along the walls of ancient cities. Some of these gatehouses evolved into purpose-built gaols, Newgate Prison in London being one of them. That particular gaol stood on the site of what is now, appropriately enough, the Central Criminal Court, known as the Old Bailey.

As the authorities saw no reason to pamper wrongdoers and were motivated in making their lives as unbearable as possible in order to sap their resistance, the prisoners were generally subjected to the harshest conditions imaginable, being incarcerated in cells devoid of heating and with little if any light.

In Britain, perhaps the Tower of London had the worst reputation, mention being made in the old records of The Pit, a noisome dungeon in which one of its many occupants was a Roman Catholic, Thomas Briscous, who was imprisoned there for five months in 1581.

In November 1577 Thomas Sherwood suffered 'in the dungeon among the rats', the earthen floor of which was below the high-water mark of the River Thames. At high tide, therefore, the filthy waters would flood the cell floor, driving before it the hordes of scampering, squeaking rats which infested the river banks.

There is little reason to doubt the authenticity of these reports. The dungeon among the rats could feasibly have been situated beneath the south-west corner of the White Tower, for although that impressive building now stands high and proud, well above the river level, in the Middle Ages the uncontrolled Thames was much wider than it is now.

During excavations in the last century an underground passage-way was discovered, running south from the White Tower. More recently, in the 1970s, another tunnel was found (and inspected by the author) extending in the same direction. These passages, ending at the river bank beneath the wharf, could well have admitted the tide, together with the voracious rodents. In the darkness of the bitterly cold cell, the prisoners would not dare to relax but would need to repel the vicious onslaught as long as their strength held out, a contemporary report stating that 'flesh had been torn from the arms and legs of sleeping prisoners by these ferocious creatures'.

Another notorious cell in that fortress was known as Little Ease. To the undiscerning eye, just a doorway links the eastern chamber with the sub-crypt in the basement of the White Tower, but it is believed that originally it was a stone alcove-like cell secured by a heavy door studded with iron bolts. Its dimensions were about four feet square and nine feet high, making it imposs-ible for the occupant to lie down and rest. In the pitch darkness he could only crouch on the damp earthen floor, gradually becoming disorientated and so more amenable to impending coercion.

It is hard to imagine just what it must have been like, shut away without a glimmer of light. Some idea of the prisoners' plight can be experienced by visiting ancient castles. At Lancaster Castle, for example, visitors are invited to enter the ancient tomb-like cells in the dungeon, cells which it is believed once housed, among others, George Fox, founder of the Quakers, and Margaret Fell, who later became his wife.

Once inside, with the immensely thick door closed, one is in absolute blackness. Not the darkness of a moonless night nor even when wearing a blindfold, but an almost tangible, impen-etrable thickness of heavy nothingness, a sensation akin to being submerged in black treacle.

Starvation also played a great part in breaking a prisoner's morale. This inhuman treatment was decreed during the reign of Edward I in an act of 1275 entitled 'The Punishment of Felons refusing Lawful Trial', which stated:

> It is provided also that notorious Felons which openly be of
> evil Name, and will not put themselves in Enquests of
> Felonies (so that they may be charged) before the Justices at
> the King's Suit, shall have la prisone forte et dure, as they
> which refuse to stand to the Common Law of the Land. And
> let their penance be this, that they be barefoot, ungirt and
> bareheaded, in the worst place in the prison, upon the bare
> ground continually, night and day. That they eat only bread
> made of barley or bran, and that they drink not the day they
> eat, nor eat the day they drink, nor drink anything but water,
> and that they be put in irons.

'Prison forte et dure', strong and hard punishment, was widely
used in prisons. So harsh were the conditions inflicted on a seminary priest, Alexander Bryant, that representations were made to
Queen Elizabeth's minister, Lord Burghley. He adroitly sought
to lay the blame on the priest, alleging that he had brought the
suffering on himself. In a pamphlet issued by him, he stated:

> A horrible matter is made of the starving of one Alexander
> Bryant; how he should eat clay out of the walles, gather
> water to drinke from the droppings of houses, with such
> other false ostentations of immanite; where the truth is this,
> that whatsoever Bryant suffered in want of food, he suffered
> the same wilfully and of extreme impudent obstinacie,
> against the minde and liking of those that deal with him.

His gaolers needed to have a specimen of the priest's handwriting
as evidence against him, and because he had refused to write,
Lord Burghley's statement continued:

> then was it commaunded to his keeper to give unto him such
> meate, drink and other convenient necessaries as he would
> write for, and to forbeare to give him anything for which he
> would not write. But Bryant, by almost two dayes and two
> nightes, made choise rather to lack foode, rather than write
> for the sustenance, which he might readely have had for

writing, and which he had, indede, readely and plentifully, as soone as he wrote.

Women too were subjected to the same barbaric penance. In 1357 Cecilia de Rygeway, indicted for the murder of her husband, was sentenced to prison forte et dure. In this case it was reported to the King that she had lived without food for forty days. True or not, the lady was lucky indeed, for Edward III granted her a pardon, writing:

The King to all his bailiffs and faithful men to whom these presents shall come, Greetings. Whereas Cecilia, lately indicted concerning the death of her husband, was adjudged to the penance . . . and whereas she afterwards sustained life without food or drink, in close prison (irons), during forty days after the manner of a miracle and contrary to human nature, as we have been informed on trustworthy testimony. We, moved by piety, to the praise of God, and the glorious Virgin his mother, from whom, as is believed, this miracle has proceeded, have of especial grace pardoned unto the said Cecilia the execution of the judgement aforesaid, and do desire that she be delivered from prison and be no further impeached of her body.

Being deprived of food was bad enough; being deprived of sleep was a lot worse. John Ogilvie, a Jesuit arrested in Scotland, was charged with treason and 'was convoyit to Edinburgh and there keepit in strait waird, and a gaird of men, by the space of eight dayis, with small sustentation, and compellit and withhaldin, perforce, from sleep, to the great perturbation of his brayne, and to compell him ad delirium'.

Such cruelty was not confined to Britain, of course. France too had its version of the Tower's Little Ease. Towards the end of the last century some of their prisoners were confined in the *souriere*, a cell about three feet square, so small that sitting or lying down was a physical impossibility. *The Times* of 22 February 1893 reported the case of a suspected murderer who was held in the *souriere* for many weeks before eventually being acquitted.

The experience is described in all its horror by a prisoner in a French gaol in the 1920s. He said:

The solitary confinement cells were underground, in the very foundations of the prison. They were damp and pitch dark. The diet consisted of bread and water only for two days, and full diet every third day. For forty days I was confined to the blackness of the underground pit. My only exercise was a walk to the end of the solitary confinement corridor to empty my latrine bucket into the moat. But the bucket was not emptied every day, for sometimes I sat for a week without being able to move my legs.

Worse than the diet, dampness and darkness was the monotony, the indescribable loneliness. Go into a small room, so small that your back is against a wall and your hands can touch the other three. Block up your ears with cotton wool so that you can hear nothing. Tightly close your eyes, Try it for just five minutes. Then multiply those five minutes until they make the 57,600 minutes of forty days.

Prisoners in the Bastille in Paris were also subjected to intolerable conditions. As reported by that indefatigable eighteenth-century prison reformer John Howard, the odoriferous dungeons beneath its many towers crawled with rats, toads and other vermin. Being underground they were dark and foetid, with a noxious ditch running beneath them for drainage. Escape was out of the question, all cells having double doors, the inner ones being plated with iron. Elsewhere in the dungeons were cages, each eight feet by six feet, made of wooden beams also plated with iron.

Some Belgian prisons similarly incarcerated their felons in cages about six feet square, this method being successful in preventing escape attempts, and also eliminating the need for cuffs or fetters. The cages in some Polish prisons were of wire mesh, and were of double construction, a small cage within a larger one, so that the occupant was only visible through multiple trellis work.

In the 1940s in Malmaison prison, Romania, men were locked in cupboard cells measuring seven feet high and two feet square.

Incarcerated in these vertical coffins for up to a month at a time, they were not permitted any exercise, and even their food was passed to them via small openings in the door.

Russia too had its versions of 'Little Ease', the cells in the Secret Police headquarters in Leningrad measuring only seven feet by three and a half, and during the purges of the 1920s, thirteen of these cells held eighty-four prisoners at a time.

Neither was Germany lacking in inhospitality towards its criminals. In some gaols felons were put under upturned casks for up to three days without respite, while the Castle of Konigstein in Saxony incorporated a dungeon hundreds of feet down in the rock foundations, a grim tomb in which was found a skeleton lying on a rough bed.

When John Howard visited the prison in Hanover in 1778, he found each prisoner secured to the walls by chains around their ankles, their wrists manacled to each end of a two-foot long bar of iron. And on going to Munich he inspected La Prison de la Cour. This he found to incorporate fifteen cells, each about twelve feet by seven. An adjoining room was, conveniently, the torture chamber within which, on a raised platform at one end, stood a table draped with a black fringed cloth. Behind the table were placed six black chairs for the magistrates and secretaries, while the rest of the room contained instruments of torture, some stained with blood. Shutters to muffle the victims' cries covered the windows, and two crucifixes mounted on the wall doubtless brought some little solace to those poor wretches being put to the question.

More recently, prisoners in Auschwitz concentration camp could find themselves in the 'standing bunker'. Little larger than a windowless telephone box, five convicts would be forced in, to face exhaustion as the hours passed. The urge to sit down would become desperate, yet to do so could be fateful, risking being trampled on and even suffocated.

Swiss gaols were almost as bad. In 1818 one prison situated on an island housed a solitary prisoner who was visited three times a day by his gaoler, who brought his food and checked the fetters which chained him to his bed. The cell contained no other furniture and was without any means of heating.

Of course it was never considered sufficient merely to immure prisoners behind locked doors and high walls. Only by securing each individual, preferably as uncomfortably as possible, could the authorities assure themselves that their captives would be available for the next torture session or would be detained until completion of their sentence.

## The Bilboes

One method of restraint was known as the Bilboes, which consisted of a long iron bar attached to the floor. Free to slide along the bar were a number of hinged iron rings which were riveted about the ankles of the prisoners, forcing them to sit or lie down until the restraint was released. Some prisons in Britain also found bilboes invaluable for securing prisoners who were being flogged, and indeed the punishment cell in Newgate Prison was given the name of the Bilboe or Bilbow.

The word is a corruption of the Spanish town Bilbao, for when the Armada was defeated in 1588, chests of these shackles were found in the galleons, reputedly to pinion English captives. In actual fact similar devices were widely used for naval prisoners on board ship and the Royal Navy was equipped with them until the eighteenth century. As described by a seventeenth-century naval chaplain, 'the punishment by the bilboes is when a delinquent is putt in yrons, or in a kind of stocks used for that purpose, the which are more or less heavy and pinchinge as the qualitie of the offence is proved against the delinquent'.

Doubtless that was how they found their way to the West Indies, where they were used during the slave trade era. Ten or more slaves would be secured in bilboes, being released each day before being taken to work in the plantations.

## The Fetters

By far the most usual form of restraint were leg-irons, also known as fetters. These took many different forms but basically resembled handcuffs, and were locked around each of the prisoner's ankles and connected to each other by chains or iron links.

To add insult to injury, some prisons, York Castle for instance, actually charged Catholics for their leg-irons. 'At their first

13

committing and entry, every Catholic yeoman shall pay ten shillings, every gentleman twenty shillings and every esquire forty shillings', decreed the York gaoler.

When these were worn for long periods, the rough edges of the iron rings lacerated the raw flesh, making every movement agonising. The Jesuit Gerard, when in London's Counter Gaol, was initially secured with very heavy fetters. Ever one to inject humour into the most appalling predicaments, he described his first weeks under restraint:

When I first had my irons on, they were rusty, but I made them bright and shining by having to wear them every day and moving about in them. Though my cell was narrow and I could have walked across in three paces if my legs had been free, I used to shuffle from side to side with short steps. In this way I got some exercise. Also, and this mattered more, when the prisoners below started singing lewd songs, I was able to drown their noise with the less unpleasant sound of my clanking chains.

Another martyr, Nicholas Horner, was fettered so tightly that 'one of his legs rotted and had to be cut off in the Justice Hall'.

Not only Jesuits were ironed, of course. Common criminals were similarly restrained – the more dangerous the felon, the greater the weight of his 'sute of yrons', some fetters weighing fourteen pounds or more, and were riveted on by the local blacksmith.

Jack Sheppard, a notorious housebreaker who had previously escaped from two London gaols, was eventually recaptured and confined in Newgate Prison. There he was fettered about the ankles, the iron rings being about one inch thick. Connecting the rings was an inch and a half thick bar, fifteen inches long, from the middle of which three large links extended upwards to fasten to a chain about his waist.

Despite these restrictions, their weight of about twenty pounds, and the fact that the crossbar was padlocked to a staple in the floor, Sheppard managed to pick the lock with a nail and snap a link of his chains. Via chimneys and across roofs he made his escape and, hiding in a field near Tottenham Court Road, persuaded a cobbler to chisel through his fetters. Alas, celebratory drinks and over-confidence led to his downfall in more ways than one, for he was hanged at Tyburn on 16 November 1724.

Another infamous criminal of the day was the highwayman Dick Turpin. The fact that he was unable to escape was doubtless due to the fact that, around his ankles, his fetters consisted of two iron rings about five inches in diameter and one inch thick. To each of these was connected a long link or shackle, about ten inches in length and over an inch in diameter. These in turn were joined at their other ends to a small circular link which was locked to a chain encircling his waist. In order to walk, therefore, Turpin would have had to shuffle along, half bent, taking the weight of the long shackles in his hands, the total weight of ironware, thirty-seven pounds, considerably impeding his movements.

Some prisoners were rendered more or less immobile by having an iron belt fitted around their waists. This was in three sections, overlapping at the front and having spaced slots, thereby being suitable for large or small convicts. Once the staple had been inserted in the appropriate slot, a padlock would prevent the removal of the belt.

The man's leg-irons were then attached to the belt, the irons being deliberately short in order to make walking hardly possible, and a ring at each side of the belt facilitated the attachment of handcuffs, should they be necessary.

Different prisons had different methods. In Ely Gaol in Norfolk, felons were pinned to the floor by iron bars which were chained to staples, and in Worcester Castle the sleeping arrangements were similarly conducive to insomnia, its inmates being chained together at night, the chain passing through their fetters and its ends then padlocked to rings set in the floor.

Neither was there a great deal of discrimination shown to women. Mary Blandy, accused of poisoning her father, was suspected of planning to escape from prison and so was put in irons. They were later changed for heavier fetters and these she wore until her trial. Found guilty, Mary was hanged on 6 April 1752. And when the reformer John Howard visited Clare Bridewell in Suffolk in 1779, he found three women heavily chained and two men whose chains were attached to logs of wood.

That leg-irons were used at Salisbury, Wiltshire, became gruesomely evident when archaeologists discovered a skeleton with fetters still attached to the legs. But the authorities of that town must have had a charitable side to their natures, for in the 1770s pairs of prisoners were permitted to walk through the streets, one carrying a sack or a basket for gifts of food, the other with a collecting box for cash donations. Needless to say, the prisoners were chained to each other.

This method of begging was also permitted in Russia in that century. In Moscow, those who had been condemned to long sentences in the salt mines of Siberia were allowed to go chained through the city's streets, three days before their departure, crying out for food to support them on their long journey.

In Moscow's main prison men were held in wooden cages, chained by the neck to the wall, irons about their ankles, while in Dresden, felons wore irons weighing twenty-one pounds around one ankle and had to pay the blacksmith in order to have the fetter transferred to the other leg. There too, women were chained up 'for security, the gaoler often being obliged to be absent, fetching prisoners from the country'.

In other foreign prisons, felons fared no better. In eighteenth-century Copenhagen, some prisoners had light irons on one leg, others had heavy irons on both, while at work they were chained in pairs, the chain being slack enough to permit necessary movement. In Austria, new prisoners taken to their cells were greeted by the sight of chains scattered about the stone floor, a burning brazier, and two blacksmiths who proceeded to rivet a six-inch-wide iron belt about the captive's waist. From the belt a long iron bar hung from a chain, a handcuff at each end, and these were locked about his wrists. To complete the pinioning, a leg-iron was then riveted about one ankle, its chain attached to an iron ring set in the stone wall.

Venetian criminals dragged approximately twenty-seven pounds of iron ballast around with them, but the weight of irons at the ankles of those held in Civitavecchia was gradually decreased year by year as the end of their sentences approached, a weight off their minds as well as elsewhere.

Being marched while ironed was always a hazardous experience, especially in the days when prisoners had to walk, fettered, ten or fifteen miles to the town where they were to be tried. In this century French criminals being taken to ports to be shipped to penal colonies abroad, were chained together by their left ankles. A momentary failure to maintain synchronised step with companions instantly brought disaster, and only strict adherence to the chant of *'un – deux, un – deux'* prevented the agony of a broken ankle or worse.

On the other side of the Atlantic, the equivalent to the medieval ball and chain was the 'Oregon Boot', a heavy iron leg cuff which was secured about the convict's ankle and held in place by a stirrup-like attachment passing under the heel.

## The Iron Collar

As if it were not enough to be weighed down with leg-irons and chains, another even more soul-destroying device was employed at times, to subdue incorrigible rogues. This was known as the Iron Collar or Spanish Collar, its latter name reputedly originating from the devices captured from the Armada galleons.

The collar was about three inches deep and an inch thick, hinged to fit around a felon's neck and either locked or riveted in position. Its weight, about ten pounds, could be increased by filling it with lead, and the strain of supporting it on one's shoulders was exacerbated by the painful chafing of the short sharp studs which lined its inner surface. They were not the only cruel appendages, for more sharp spikes, protruding from the upper surface of the collar, deterred its wearer from allowing his head to sink forward on to his chest.

Many specimens of the collar survive in museums, an example displayed in the Tower of London probably being the one listed in the 1547 inventory as a 'stele collar for a prysonr'.

Similar collars used to punish slaves in Jamaica in the 1830s were even more ruthlessly designed. From the circumference of the collar projected three sharp pointed rods, about eighteen inches long, at equal intervals from each other. These effectively prevented the slave from lying down in anything resembling a comfortable position, for one or more rods would touch the ground, pressing the collar against his neck and causing agony when he turned his head.

## The Strait-jacket

But of course since those days we have become more humane and civilised. Or have we? The iron collar may have gone out of fashion, but in its place the strait-jacket made its appearance as a means of restraint. These were frequently used in English prisons late in the last century as punishment for troublesome inmates.

The prisoner, his arms tied together on his chest, was strapped into the garment, which was a stiff canvas jacket. Its rigid leather collar, three and a half inches deep and a quarter of an inch thick, was then buckled so tightly that it was impossible to insert a finger between the leather and the flesh, and the strait-jacket would not be removed until many hours had passed.

Women convicts were similarly punished, albeit less severely. Those guilty of wilfully tearing their prison clothes were strapped into a dress made of coarse canvas, its removal being prevented by a screw-operated fastening at the back of the belt. For more stringent punishment, another type of strait-jacket existed. Also made of canvas, it incorporated long black leather sleeves, the closed ends of which were fitted with straps. Once donned, the culprit's arms were crossed in front of her, the straps at the sleeves' ends being buckled round and behind her, so rendering her completely helpless.

In the United States of America the strait-jacket was often resorted to. Used as early as 1884 in Folsom Penitentiary, California, it consisted, appropriately enough, of a coffin-shaped piece of thick canvas about four feet long, with brass eyelets down each side, and internal pockets for the prisoner's hands. After the convict had been made to lie face down on the jacket, heavy cords were passed through the eyelets and pulled as tight as possible by two or more warders.

A later version of this, known as the San Quentin Overcoat, was in use well into the present century. One victim's ordeal was graphically described to an investigatory committee in 1912:

> After they put me into the jacket they played tug of war with me. The rope broke and they got another. They lifted me off the floor and let me fall several times. This was to knock the wind out of me and to use my natural weight to tighten the jacket. The pain begins in five or ten minutes. It's a suffering

of the kidneys. It seems as if someone is crushing them in his hands, or as if they were jumping and trying to get away from you. Your hands begin to feel twice their size. The hands and arms all go dead, then come to life with sharp, keen pains. You have sharp pains in your stomach, very sharp pains.

## The Spot

Other punishments meted out in American prisons involved no garments, handcuffs or similar restraints. In 1937 the chief warder of San Quentin Gaol in California devised the Spot. Almost machiavellian in concept, it simply consisted of a circle of grey paint, two feet in diameter, in which the offender had to stand for four hours, twice a day. He was not allowed to move at all, the only relief permitted being a two-minute toilet break, morning and afternoon. Very few prisoners showed any desire to be put on the spot a second time.

## Chloride of Lime Punishment

Another unusual punishment came into use in the Folsom Penitentiary around the turn of the century. This vicious method utilised chloride of lime, the biting, acrid smell of which is familiar to anyone using domestic bleach or bleaching powder.

Prisoners rebelling against discipline were put into the Chloride of Lime Cell, the floor of which had been amply soaked in dampened lime. Within minutes the suffocating fumes affected the prisoner's breathing, burning the sensitive lining of his nose and throat and making his eyes sting unbearably. Only when he showed signs of submitting to prison regulations was he eventually released.

## Cayenne Pepper Punishment

A somewhat similar method was used in London's Pentonville Prison in 1856 to overcome a highly aggressive and dangerous convict who, refusing to come out of his cell, threatened to kill any warder who entered. As related shortly afterwards by a warder to prison visitor Henry Mayhew,

He had made a spring at the nearest warder and would

19

assuredly have bitten his nose off had the warder not retreated up the stairs, so that the man below was all alone, vowing and declaring that he would have the life of the first person that tried to get him up. Well, you see, we knew we could master him directly we had him in the corridor, but as we couldn't take his life, yet he could take ours, he was more than a match for us as things stood.

Accordingly the governor had to devise some means by which to get him upstairs without hurting him, and how d'ye think he did it, sir? Why, he got some cayenne pepper and burnt it in a fumigating bellows, and then blew the smoke down into the corridor where the fellow was. The man stood it for some time, but, bless you, he was soon glad to surrender for, as we sent in puff after puff, it set him coughing and sneezing and rubbing his eyes and stamping with the pain as the fumes not only got into his throat and up his nose, but under his eyelids, and made them smart, till the tears ran down his cheeks as if he had been a little child. Then immediately afterwards we threw ourselves upon him and secured him. Oh no, sir, he never tried the same game again, one dose of cayenne pepper was quite enough for him, I assure you.

## The Treadwheel

The main problem facing the authorities in English gaols during the nineteenth century was exactly what to do with a prisonful of idle convicts. With nothing to occupy their time, the more dangerous among them simply planned riots and fomented unrest, with sometimes disastrous results. It was then, in 1817, that the Science of Absolute Uselessness came to the aid of the perplexed officials, in the form of the Treadwheel.

To savour the full essence of the moment, the circumstances surrounding its conception are worth describing. As explained by Henry Mayhew, during his visit to Coldbath Fields House of Correction,

the machine was the brainchild of a Mr Cubitt, an engineer from Lowestoft in Suffolk. This gentleman, on visiting Bury St Edmunds gaol with a magistrate, remarked upon the large number of prisoners seen lounging idly about in groups, the whole aspect indicating a demoralizing waste of time and energy.

'I wish to God, Mr Cubitt,' said the justice, 'you could suggest to us some mode of employing those fellows. Could nothing like a wheel become available?'

An instantaneous idea flashed through the mind of Mr Cubitt (continued Mayhew's account). And Cubitt whispered to himself, 'The wheel elongated!' And merely saying to his interrogator 'Something has struck me which may prove worthy of a further consideration, and perhaps you will hear from me upon the subject', he took his leave. After giving it due thought, he was able to fashion all the mechanical requirements into practical form, and so invented the Treadwheel, surely the most pointless machine ever devised, yet one which was adopted by prisons throughout the country and used to occupy the time of their inmates.

Mr Cubitt, later Sir William Cubitt, was indeed a gifted engineer. Among his many achievements was the invention of a device to regulate the settings of windmill sails automatically, eliminating the need for the miller to stop the mill and alter them by hand.

He constructed canals at Oxford and Liverpool, designed the South East Railway, and even Berlin's waterworks. All these inspired creations of his fertile brain did *something*. His treadwheel however did absolutely *nothing*, and its operation was in fact colloquially known as 'grinding the wind'.

The contraption first appeared at Brixton Prison in 1817 and was quickly put to use. For the technically minded, the machine consisted of a huge wheel sixteen feet in circumference, similar to a paddle wheel but wide enough to accommodate twenty-four men standing almost shoulder to shoulder. The wheel incorporated twenty-four steps, eight inches apart, and was turned by the action of the convicts 'climbing' the steps, moving their legs as if they were slowly and laboriously ascending a flight of stairs, the steps moving down and sliding away beneath them. As they worked, or rather walked, they supported themselves by holding on to a handrail, their backs to the watchful warders, and to complete their isolation from their fellow hikers, the men were separated from each other by high wooden partitions resembling those in public urinals.

The wheel revolved twice a minute, with a mechanism incorporated to ring a bell at the end of each thirtieth revolution, signalling a change of shift. The men were then replaced by another batch of twenty-four convicts, each man having to complete fifteen quarter-of-an-hour sessions a day, with fifteen minutes' rest between shifts.

It was very hard work, and the hot and airless conditions made the task particularly gruelling. The energy required to avoid sinking with the steps being equivalent to the man's own weight meant that fifteen minutes 'grinding the wind' was sufficient to exhaust the strongest of men, 'climbing', as they had to, 480 feet every session, 2,400 yards a day, on meagre prison rations.

And to what end? Did the contraption (of which there were no fewer than six at Coldbath Fields) power anything, such as a ventilation system or prison workshop machinery? Did it grind flour in the kitchens or rotate the roasting spits? No, although admittedly the authorities did advertise the availability of the treadwheel power to local firms, no response was ever forthcoming.

The end-product of all that utterly exhausting labour was there for all to see, for in the prison courtyard stood a pyramid-shaped structure, from the apex of which protruded a vertical iron shaft. Mounted on top of that was a double, horizontal beam, twenty feet in length. Between the beams, at each end, were three large venetian-blind-type blades, mounted vertically, the angle of the blades determining the resistance to the surrounding air and so acting as a brake on the treadwheel itself, creating an artificial resistance to the efforts of the convicts as they plodded laboriously and uselessly on the treadwheel steps. 'Grinding the wind' was indeed the very epitome of futility.

## The Crank

Inspired no doubt by the sheer uselessness of the treadwheel, and seeing the punishment-value of its basic principle, some unknown genius in 1840 miniaturised it so that it could be operated by an individual convict rather than a team. And so the Crank came into existence.

One version resembled a domestic knife-cleaning machine, comprising a narrow iron drum mounted on legs, with a long handle at one side which, when turned, caused a series of cups inside to revolve. As they did so, they scooped up sand from the bottom of the drum, the sand falling out when the cups reached the top of their revolution. A dial on the front of the machine registered the number of times the Crank handle had been turned, and the usual punishment involved operating it about twenty times a minute, culminating in a total of 10,000 revolutions in eight and a half hours. Should the target not be met on time, the convict received no food until the dial registered the required total.

An alternative version utilised weights instead of sand. Without weights, the pressure necessary to turn the crank handle was seven pounds, the addition of weights ranging up to twelve pounds. Both marques of the Crank achieved nothing at all other than morale-shattering exhaustion for the convict on the handle.

So it would seem that, from the 'dungeon among the rats' in 1577, to the Crank of 1840, the Spot of 1937, or later punitive measures, the exponents of penology haven't a great deal about which to congratulate themselves.

# 2
# Pressed to Reply

It was one thing to catch your criminal and bring him to trial for his misdeeds, yet quite another to have him plead guilty or not guilty, as required by the court. But what did you do if, for whatever reason, he refused to plead? What action could be taken if he just stood in the dock, not saying a word? In such an eventuality, all that could be done was to leave it to the jury to decide whether the accused was 'mute of malice', that is, deliberately silent, or 'mute by the visitation of God', physically unable to speak.

If they came to the conclusion that he was mute of malice, the court was then empowered to offer some incentive to the accused to make him change his mind, by committing him to hard and strong punishment, prison forte et dure, as described in the previous chapter.

However, cases reported in 1406 reveal that prison forte et dure was considered inadequate, and that further pressure should be brought to bear on the prisoner, in more ways than one. And so prison forte et dure was replaced by a far worse form of inducement, one which, although still legally a persuasive measure, was by any standards torture.

## Peine Forte et Dure
This dreaded procedure, meaning 'severe and hard punishment', started with a warning given by the court, and repeated twice, of the consequences should the accused persist in his refusal to plead. He was then allowed a few hours to consider the ultimatum and, if still defiant, Judgment of Penance would be announced.

25

That the prisoner shall be sent back to the prison from whence he came, and put into a mean room, stopped from the light, and shall there be laid on the bare ground without any litter, straw or other covering, and without any garment about him except something about his middle. He shall lie, a stone beneath his back, his head shall be covered and his feet shall be bare. One of his arms shall be drawn with a cord to the side of the room, and the other arm to the other side, and his legs shall be served in the same manner. Then there shall be laid upon his body as much iron or stone as he can bear, and more. And the first day after he shall have three morsels of barley bread, without any drink, and the second day he shall be allowed to drink as much as he can, at three times, of the water that is next the prison door, except running water, without any bread. And this shall be his diet until he dies.

The penalty occasionally varied, the sharp stone under the back was perhaps omitted, but the result was the same. Should the prisoner continue to defy the court, death would ensue. As it did in the case of Walter Calverley who, when accused at York Assizes in 1605 of murdering his wife and two of his young children, remained mute. He maintained his silence to the end, and so was pressed to death. Not quite so stoic, or suicidal, was Thomas Spiggott, a highwayman who, in 1721, also came to the erroneous conclusion that silence was golden.

When he refused to plead, he was taken to Newgate Prison and in the Press Room was subjected to the ordeal. He endured 350 pounds weight for half an hour, lying apparently half conscious, though at times he complained bitterly that the warders were putting weights on his face, doubtless due to the sensations caused by the compression of his blood vessels. With the addition of a further fifty pounds, he surrendered and begged to be allowed to plead. And on 8 February 1721 he was hanged at Tyburn.

Later that year another robber, Nathaniel Hawes, also maintained silence in the dock. He held out in the Press Room until, after seven minutes with 250 pounds of stone piled on top of him, he too relented. And Tyburn took care of him also, on 22 December.

Some felons gave in quickly, others showed remarkable stamina. Barnworth, alias Frasier, who was accused of murder in 1726, endured no less than a total weight of 400 pounds for over two hours before submitting. Despite pleading not guilty, he was sentenced to death and hanged.

Not all who suffered the peine forte et dure were excused the sharp stone in the small of their backs. Nor were they all men. In March 1586 Margaret Clitheroe, or Clitherow, the 'Martyr of York', was accused of harbouring and helping a Roman Catholic priest. At her trial she knew that the jury would find her guilty in order to please the judge, and she wanted to spare their consciences. Accordingly she remained mute, and the Judgment of Penance was announced. Lingard's *History of England* conjures up the horrific spectacle:

After she had prayed, Fawcett (one of the sheriffs) commanded them to put off her apparel, when she, with four women, requested him on their knees that, for the honour of womanhood, this might be dispensed with, but they would not grant it. Then she requested that the women might unparrel her, and that they would turn their faces from her during that time. The women took off her clothes and put on her long linen habit. Then very quietly she laid her down upon the ground, her face covered with a handkerchief, and most part of her body with the habit. The dore was laied upon her, her hands she joined upon her face.

Then the sheriff said 'Naie ye must have your hands bound'. Then two sergeants parted her hands and bound them to two posts in the same manner as the feet had previously been fixed. After this they laied weight upon her, which, when she first felt, she said 'Jesu, Jesu, Jesu, have mercye upon mee' which were the last words she was heard to speake.

She was in dying about one quarter of an hower. A sharp stone as big as a man's fist had been put under her back. Upon her was laied to the quantity of seven or eight hundredweight (nearly 900 pounds), which breaking her ribs, caused them to burst forth of the skinne.

Another woman, Jane Wiseman, was similarly caught in 1598, aiding Catholic priests. Known to succour the poor, she was lured into a trap devised by Richard Topcliffe, the infamous torturer of Elizabeth's reign, of whom more anon. His accomplice persuaded Jane to bandage the injured leg of a friend of his, and upon her agreeing, brought a priest, Father Jones, to her home.

Arrested on a charge of 'receiving, comforting, helping and maintaining priests', she refused to plead and was sentenced to be pressed. However, wiser councils, fearful of public outcry, interceded and Jane Wiseman escaped the peine forte et dure. Her estates forfeited to the Queen, she was imprisoned for life.

There was an interpretation of the law by many accused persons that while their goods and chattels would be forfeit to the king on being executed, nevertheless should they die while being persuaded to plead, their worldly goods would pass to their families, as no death sentence had been passed on them by the court. The historian Holinshead reported it as:

Such fellons as stand mute and speake not at their arraignmente are pressed to death by huge weights laid up on a board that lieth over their brest, and a sharp stone under their backs, and these commonlie hold their peace, thereby to save their goods unto their wives and children; which if they were condemned, should be confiscated to the king.

One man who was prepared to die slowly and painfully rather than deprive his successors of their birthright was George Strangeways, a Royalist major in the Civil War. Rather than have his estate confiscated by the victorious Roundheads, he leased it to his sister Mabellah, with whom he lived. Mabellah however got married, and George, fearing the loss of his possessions to the newcomer, murdered him. Determined to defy the authorities to the bitter end, he remained mute at his trial in February 1658. The court sentenced him to be pressed, but vindictively ordered that the planks on which the victim usually lay should be omitted, so that by lying on an earthen floor, death would be delayed.

The press at that time was a triangular board, the acute angle of which was positioned over the victim's heart, and George Strangeways' suffering must have been extreme, before the merciful end came.

He was prohibited that usuall Favour in that kind, to have a piece of Timber layed under his back to Accelerate its penetration, and the Assistants laid on a first weight, which finding it too light for a sudden Execution, many of those standing by added their own weight to disburthen him of his pain. In the space of eight or ten minutes at the most, his unfettered Soul left her tortur'd Mansion. And he from that violent Paroxisme fell into the quiet sleep of Death.

## Scottish Pressing

Witches too were subjected to being pressed, sometimes with fatal results. In the county of Fife, Scotland, in 1705, Janet Cornfoot was unjustly accused of witchcraft and arrested. After having been beaten with a staff by the local minister she was caught by the mob and, tied and helpless, secured to a rope on the shore and brutally stoned, until she collapsed. Not content with that, the rabble then put a door on top of her and, heaping it with heavy stones, pressed her to death.

Eventually the appalling cruelty of peine forte et dure became increasing apparent, and in 1772 it was decided that a prisoner refusing to plead would automatically be assumed guilty, and without further legal argument would be sentenced to death. But denying a prisoner of any defence was so obviously an injustice that half a century later, in 1827, the law was changed – refusal to plead was considered as one of 'Not Guilty'.

## Irish Pressing

Other countries also employed similar methods to cajole an accused person into speaking. In Ireland, Matthew Ryan appeared at the Kilkenny Assizes in 1740, accused of highway robbery. In prison he feigned madness, refused to put any clothes on, and in court affected to be dumb. The jury duly studied his actions and when asked by the judge to decide whether Ryan was mute and mad by the hand of God, or wilfully mute, the jury brought in a verdict that he was 'wilful and affecting dumbness and lunacy'.

Having pointed out the terrible consequences of his continued refusal, the judge mercifully gave him some days to consider his plight. At the later hearing, however, the robber showed his determination by continuing the charade. Accordingly, the court had no option but to pass the dreaded sentence, and two days later Matthew Ryan was taken under strong escort to the market square in Kilkenny. At this late stage, realisation of the horrors to come dawned on the doomed man and, finding his voice, he begged to be hanged instead. But no dispensation could be given, and as the large crowd watched with horrid fascination, Ryan was spread-eagled and tied down. A square board was then laid on his chest, on top of which were placed weights, increasing in number until the felon died of his intolerable injuries.

## American Pressing
Few instances of peine forte et dure have been reported as having taken place in America, though doubtless they occurred. One incident was recorded in Salem when, in 1692, Giles Cory was charged with witchcraft, and subsequently pressed to death.

## Indian Pressing
A macabre variation of this punishment was practised in India in the nineteenth century. A small sharp stone was tied on top of the criminal's head, and a larger, heavier stone was then secured on top of it. Even weightier boulders were then added, until eventually the combined weight drove the pointed stone into the victim's skull.

# The Boot
Persuasion by means of pressing usually ended in death – hardly desirable in court cases where confessions and names of accomplices were required. However, in the sixteenth and seventeenth centuries, particularly in Scotland and France, a device was used which, while not endangering life in any way, positively

encouraged the unfortunate victim to reveal everything he knew, whether true or imagined. The instrument was known as the Boot.

There were several versions of this device, the variations probably owing to the fact that in those times descriptions were passed by word of mouth rather than by detailed drawings and blueprints. So torture-instrument manufacturers at one end of the country were given a different idea of how the machine functioned than was actually the case. But as long as all the machines caused excruciating agony, there was obviously no need for any standardisation by the authorities.

As its name implies, the boot was designed to torture a prisoner's legs and feet, and the device was so effective that even the early stages of its application caused injuries sufficient to induce a hasty confession.

The most common form of the boot required the victim to sit on a bench, to which he was securely tied. An upright board was then placed on either side of each leg, splinting them from knee to ankle; the boards were held together by ropes or iron rings within a frame.

With the legs now immoveable, the torture started with wooden wedges hammered between the two inner boards and then between the outer boards and their surrounding frame, compressing and crushing the trapped flesh.

An alternative method dispensed with the frame. Instead the boards on each side of the legs were bound tightly together. For the 'ordinary' torture, four wedges were driven between the two inner boards. For the 'extra-ordinary' torture, eight wedges were used, bursting flesh and bone, and permanently crippling the victim. It was described by a seventeenth-century visitor to Scotland as 'four pieces of narrow board nailed together, of a competent length for the leg, not unlike the short cases we use to guard young trees from the rabbits, which they wedge so tightly on all sides that, not being ably to bear the pain, they promise confession to get rid of it'.

In 1681 John Spreull was one of the leaders of a treasonable insurrection and in order to make him admit his complicity he was subjected to the torture, while James Stuart, Duke of York, looked on. This particular marque of the device would appear to have been a single iron boot, into which wedges would be driven downwards between the bare flesh and the side of the boot, and it was reported that with each question by the interrogators, the hangman struck each wedge five times.

With stoic courage Spreull endured the pain, his obstinacy inducing one of his tormentors to claim that the boot, a new one, was inferior to the one it had replaced (a size too large, perhaps?) and demanded that the old one be sent for. Accordingly it was produced, and Spreull's injured leg inserted into it.

Again the hangman bent to his task, driving the wedges deeper into the mangled flesh. The victim, half fainting, continued to deny the charges. Whereupon one of those present, a General Dalziel, doubtless eager to ingratiate himself with the Duke, loudly demanded that the hangman should strike harder with his mallet. Incensed by this adverse reflection on his professional ability, the hangman hotly retorted that he was using all his strength, and if the General thought he could do better, *he* was welcome to have the mallet and take over the torture.

Both Stuart kings, James I and James II, were noted for their sadistic natures. James I often visited the Royal Menagerie at the Tower of London to order fights to the death between lions and dogs, bear baiting and other similar bouts for his entertainment.

When faced with treason in Scotland, he wasted no time in committing conspirators to torture. John Fiennes, a dabbler in witchcraft, was accused of conjuring up a storm at sea with the intention of wrecking the ship taking James on a royal visit to Denmark, and so was tortured mercilessly.

First Fiennes' head was 'thrawed with a rope', bound with cords which were then tightened, and this was followed by the ordeal of the boot, until his legs 'were completely crushed and the marrow spouted out'. Later came the rack, after which Fiennes was taken to Castle Hill in Edinburgh and there strangled and burned to death.

Other witches suffered in the same fashion. Thomas Papley and Alison Balfour of the Orkney Isles were, in 1596, charged with practising black-magic rituals. They endured the agonies of the Cashilawis or Caspicaws, a derivative of the boot, in which the casing incorporated a screw attachment for compressing the leg. For added severity, sometimes the boot would also be heated until red hot while the questioning continued.

Eventually they confessed that they had consorted with the Devil, but not until Papley had 'being keepit in the cashielawis allewin dayis and ellewin nychtis; tuyise in the day, be the space of fourtene dayis, callit in the buitis, he beant naikit in the meane tyme, and skairgeit with towis in sic coirt, that they left naither flesche nor hyde on him.'

Roughly translated this means that for eleven days and nights he wore the boot, twice each day he was subjected to extreme cold, while being naked, and was also scourged with the tawse until he had little flesh or skin left on him.

Apparently Alison did not suffer the boot, but Margaret Wood did in February 1631, when the Privy Council decreed that 'Margaret Wod to be put to the tortour of the bootes, in the morne at ten of the clocke, in the Laich Councell Hous of Edinburgh, and that the whole counsell be present when the tortour be given'.

Not everyone in authority wanted to witness victims being tortured, although James II, when he was Duke of York, seemingly revelled in it. Bishop Burnet, in his *History of his Own Times*, relates:

When any are to be stuck in the boots, it is done in the presence of the Council, and upon that happening, almost all offer to run away. The sight is so dreadful that without an order restraining such a number to stay, the press boards would remain unused. But the Duke of York, while he was in Scotland, was so far from running away, that he looked on all the while with an unmoved indifference, and with an attention as if he were watching a curious experiment. This gave a terrible impression of him to all that observed it, as a man that had no bowels of mercy in him.

A less common method was to encase the victim's legs in crude stockings made out of parchment. These were easy to put on when wet, but then the victim would be held near a fire, the shrinking of the hose causing considerable agony.

## The Boot in France

The French, with whom the Scots were strongly allied at the time, also used the boot for persuasive purposes. Their version involved forcing the legs of their bound victim into high boots made of thick spongy leather. Quantities of scalding water were then poured over the boots, sinking into the leather and literally boiling the flesh within.

For the punishment of Francis Ravaillac, the assassin of King Henri IV of France, a more orthodox form of the boot was employed, known as the 'Brodequins'. This consisted of a thigh-boot shaped wooden box just large enough to contain the victim's legs; wedges were then driven in between his knees. That it was agonising in the extreme is evidenced by this extract from the Registers of the French Parliament of the day:

> Ravaillac was then ordered to be put to the torture of the brodequin and, the first wedge being drove, he cried out 'God have mercy upon my soul, and pardon the crime I have committed; I never disclosed my intention to any one.' This he repeated as he had done in his interrogation.
>
> When the second wedge was drove, he said with loud cries and shrieks 'I am a sinner, I know no more than I have declared, by the oath I have taken, and by the truth I owe to God and the court; all I have said was to the little Franciscan, which I have already declared. I never mentioned my design in confession or in any other way. I beseech the court not to drive my soul to despair.'
>
> The executioner continuing to drive the second wedge, he cried out 'My God, receive this penance as an expiation for the greater crimes I have committed in this world; Oh God, I accept these torments in satisfaction for my sins. By the faith I owe to God, I know no more than what I have declared. Oh, do not drive my soul to despair.'
>
> The third wedge was now driven lower, near his feet, at which a universal sweat covered his body, and he fainted away. The executioner forced some wine into his mouth, but he could not swallow it, and being quite speechless, he was released from the torture, and water thrown on his face and hands. Some wine being forced down his throat, his speech

returned, and he was laid on a mattress in the same place, where he continued till noon.

Subjected to further appalling punishments, Ravaillac was then put to a hideous death by being torn asunder by four horses.

## The Boot in Ireland

Ireland, though not indulging overmuch in torture, nevertheless utilised the boot on occasion. In 1583, during Elizabeth's reign, an Irish priest named John Hurley was captured in Drogheda, carrying secret letters from Rome to Catholic noblemen in Ireland.

In order to extract more information from him, he was threatened with the rack. Unfortunately, or perhaps fortunately for him, Dublin did not have one, so rather than send him to the Tower of London, Elizabeth's Secretary of State Walsingham suggested that Hurley's feet 'should be roasted against the fire with hot boots'.

As it was reputed that melted resin was poured over the boots while they were being exposed to the fire, it is hardly surprising that Hurley's brave resistance crumbled. And although insufficient evidence was found against him for a trial in a civil court, the authorities were determined to crush such conspiracies and so he was tried by military court martial and promptly executed.

## The Boot in Spain

Among the armoury of torture instruments in Spain were two versions of the boot. One type consisted of two thick pieces of board, from the inner surfaces of which protruded iron studs or knobs. The boards were secured each side of the victim's leg and slowly tightened together, causing fracture and even breakage of the leg bones unless a confession was forthcoming.

In the other, the prisoner's feet were inserted into iron boots, into which boiling oil, scalding water or molten pitch was poured. This method was also used by the Austro-Hungarian Empire.

In addition to the Spanish boot, Austria also used an instrument called the 'Shin Crusher', a misnomer really, since it resembled a pair of large iron tongs studded with sharp nails, with which the felon's calves were squeezed and compressed.

35

## The Boot in Germany

More accurately named 'Shinbone Crushers' than the Austrian version, these were used by medieval executioners and resembled bench vices which were screwed on to the victim's ankles and then tightened until the leg joints were reduced to pulp.

Another similar instrument was also designed to grip the leg, this one incorporating a long screw at the back which, when slowly tightened, drove its point with such penetrative force through flesh and muscle that it would even pierce the bone itself.

## German Skull Crushers

As an alternative, German wrong-doers would be subjected to various designs of skull crushers. One marque was known in 1530 as the *Kranz* or *Schneiden*, a strap or straps being fastened around the head and relentlessly tightened.

An infinitely more agonising version consisted of an iron skull-cap held in place on the victim's head by a metal strap secured under his chin. A screw mechanism on each side was then operated, tightening the strap until the victim's teeth were forced out of his jaws and the pressure on his head became unbearable. The suffering could be further increased by the torturer tapping on the skullcap as the questions were being put, thus sending waves of excruciating pain through the victim's body.

## The Brakes

As many would doubtless agree, the dividing line between dentistry and torture is a thin one, so it is hardly surprising that in Tudor times, English torturers realised the immense potentiality of molar extraction as a method of jogging a victim's memory. And so they invented the Brakes. Although no specimen has survived, its design may well have resembled a bridle made of iron, with pincer-like attachments designed to force out one tooth at a time, an incriminating question being put prior to each operation of the machine.

One reported instance of its use occurred when rumours reached Henry VIII concerning the dalliance of his new queen, Catherine Howard, with two of his courtiers, Francis Dereham, the Queen's cousin, and Thomas Culpepper, Clerk of the Armoury and Gentleman of the King's Chamber. Confessions had to be obtained, and so, in December 1541, a third suspect, Damport, was taken to the Tower of London and subjected to having his teeth forced out in the brakes. Doubtless this was sufficient to persuade him to turn king's evidence, for he was later released.

Dereham and Culpepper both paid the price – one was hanged, drawn and quartered, the other decapitated by the axe. Their heads were displayed on London Bridge, clearly visible to Queen Catherine as she passed beneath them six weeks later *en route* to Traitors' Gate and her own execution on Tower Green.

A variation of the brakes could well have been used in the thirteenth century on a Bristol man who tried to defraud King John. When he protested that he was unable to pay the fine of £6,500 levied against him, he was sentenced to have a tooth forcibly removed each day until the fine was paid. A week was sufficient to ensure his compliance.

This practice was also followed in France, where money-lenders who failed to hand over their excessive profits ended up considerably down in the mouth.

## Oriental Leg Torture

But why bother to devise and make all these various torture devices? Why not let the victim's own body-weight, plus a few odd stones, create intolerable pain? That is what the Japanese resorted to with their torture called 'Hugging the Stone'. While being forced to kneel on sharp flints, boulders were piled on the backs of the criminal's legs. And in China the victim was suspended by his thumbs and toes in such a way that his knees rested (hardly the word) on a chain formed of small sharp-edged links.

So using stones and straps, boots and fire, traitors, criminals and witches were persuaded to confess. But for some, inspired by the strength of their spirit and the conviction of their principles, even those methods were not enough to make them yield. For them, then, even worse tortures awaited.

# 3
## Two Persuasive Daughters

Allow me to present two very forceful ladies, one the daughter of John Holland, Duke of Exeter, Earl of Huntingdon, and the other the daughter of Sir Leonard Skeffington, Kt. So captivating were they that once they had you in their grasp, you would not be able to tear yourself away from them. And they are certainly not the sort of girls who would take 'no' for an answer. Actually they were not the type of females you would wish to meet on a dark night – or even on a sunny afternoon. To be more precise, the two ladies in question are more shudderingly known as 'The Rack' and 'Skeffington's Gyves'.

### The Rack
The rack was in common use in many countries in the Middle Ages. Known as the *chevalet* or *Banc de Torture* in France, the *escalero* in Spain and the *Ladder* in Germany, it was reportedly introduced into England about the year 1420 by the Duke of Exeter when he was Constable of the Tower of London and so, with the macabre humour of the times, victims of the rack were said to be 'married to the Duke of Exeter's Daughter' – doubtless a wife they could hardly wait to divorce!

Before becoming Constable of the Tower, the Duke had led an adventurous life, fighting against the French at Caen, Melun and Rouen and where, no doubt, he learned about the rack. Now his remains and those of two of his wives lie in a magnificent chantry tomb within the Chapel of St Peter ad Vincula, only yards from where so many suffered on the device he had brought to the Tower.

As with other torture instruments, there was more than one

version. An early marque consisted of an open rectangular frame, over six feet in length, raised three feet from the floor on four legs. The prisoner was laid beneath it on his back, and his wrists and ankles were attached by ropes to a windlass at each end of the frame. These were operated by levers turned in opposite directions, hoisting the victim until almost level with the frame. The strain of being lifted off the ground in that manner was sufficient to give the victim some idea of what was to come: the stretching of the ligaments, the twisting of the muscles, even the dislocation of the wrists and elbows, the shoulder-blades and ankle joints, accompanied by a never-ending blur of excruciating agony.

This particular type of rack was probably operated by four men, two at each end, each man having a pole which he inserted in holes in the windlass and pulled, keeping the ropes taut while his companion transferred his pole to the next hole at his end of the windlass. In that way the ropes, and the victim's limbs, were always under tension which could be maintained while the damning questions were put.

A later version incorporated a ratchet mechanism which reduced the number of operators to two, and this was superceded in turn by a rack having a central wooden roller with a ratchet at each end manipulated by a control bar, so that only one man was required. Not so much a saving in manpower, but a vital precaution when answers involving treasonable conspiracies were being extracted from the wretch on the rack. This later model was probably the one itemised in the Tower of London's inventory of 1678 as the 'Rack for Torment'.

The official Rackmaster in Tudor times was Thomas Norton, a man who boasted that he had stretched the Jesuit martyr Alexander Bryant 'a foot longer than God had made him'. His assistants in the torture chamber were the author's predecessors, the yeoman warders, and when, in Elizabeth's reign, it was said that the rack seldom stood idle in the Tower, her minister Lord Burghley sought to allay public concern by issuing a statement recorded in State Papers of 1583: 'The Queen's servants, the warders, whose office and act it is to handle the rack, were ever by those that attended the examinations, specially charged to use it in as charitable manner as such a thing might be.'

However, it is impossible to inflict pain painlessly! And, anyway, the official line was that the prisoners deserved to be tortured, for as Rackmaster Norton wrote to Elizabeth's Secretary of State Sir Francis Walsingham on 27 March 1582: 'None was put to the rack that was not at first by some manifest evidence known to the Council to be guilty of treason, so that it was well assured beforehand that there was no innocent tormented. Also none was tormented to know whether he was guilty or no, but for the Queen's safety to know the manner of the treason and the accomplices.'

Deserved or not, guilty or not, in those days of court intrigue, religious persecution and plots against the sovereign, the rollcall of those forced to descend the spiral steps into the bowels of the White Tower – there to be brought face to face with Rackmaster Norton and his blood-chilling array of pain-inflicting machines – seemed endless.

They came from all walks of life. Edward Peacham, Rector of Hinton St George in Somerset, preached a treasonable sermon and was suspected of having like-minded sympathisers. He was taken to the Tower where the Lieutenant reported, 'He was this day racked before torture, in torture, between torture and after torture'. Common robbers such as Nicholls and Pitt were 'to be brought to the rack and to feel the smart there, if the examiners by their discretion shall think good, for the better boulting out of the truth of the matter'. Clement Fisher was 'to be put in some fear whereby of his lewdness and such as he might detect . . . to cause Fisher to feel some touch of the rack'.

Bannister and Barker, witnesses at the trial of the Duke of Norfolk in 1572 were 'to be put to the rack and find the taste thereof'. But after the commissioners had sat by their side, putting the questions as the windlass wrenched their limbs, it was reported by Sir Thomas Smith: 'I suppose we have gotten so mych at this time as is lyke to be had; yet tomorrow we do intend to bryng a couple of them to the rack, not in any hope to get to any thyng worthy that payne or feare, but because it is earnestly commanded unto us', and later 'of Bannister with the rack, and Barker with the extreme fear of it, we suppose we have gotten all'. Only in the orginal phrasing, with its utterly detached, completely dispassionate phraseology, can any indication even begin to convey anything approaching the full horror of the torture chamber.

The Jesuit priest Edmund Campion was racked two days in succession, refusing to yield despite the offer of freedom if he would, just once, attend a Protestant church service. Because his joints had been dislocated, his trial had to be postponed, and when eventually it took place in Westminster Hall, he was incapable of raising his hand to plead, so two of his companions lifted it for him.

The Duke of Exeter's Daughter continued to embrace her unwilling husbands. Sir Francis Throckmorton, a zealous Catholic, plotted insurrection on the Continent and on returning to England to set up communications between Mary, Queen of Scots, and contacts in Paris, was caught. In November 1583 he was racked to make him divulge the names of his fellow conspirators. And as the historian Froude wrote:

Interrogated in the gloomy cell which had rung with the screams of the Jesuits, the horrid instrument at his side, with the mute executioners standing ready to strain his limbs out of their sockets, his imagination was appalled, his senses refused to do their work. He equivocated, varied in his story, contradicted himself in every succeeding sentence. Pardon was promised him if he would make a free confession. He still held out, but he could not conceal that he had much to tell, and the times did not permit humanity to traitors to imperil the safety of the realm.

The Queen gave the necessary authority to proceed with 'the pains'. Her Majesty thought it agreeable with good policy and the safety of her person and throne, to commit him to the hands of her learned council, to assay by torture to draw the truth from him. Again he was proffered pardon; again he refused, and he was handed over 'to such as were usually appointed in the Tower to handle the rack'. His honour struggled with his agony. On the first racking he confessed nothing; but he could not endure a second trial. When he was laid again upon the frame, before he was strained to any purpose, he yielded to confess everything he knew. Sitting in wretchedness beside the horrid engine, the November light faintly streaming down the tunnelled windows, he broke his pledged word, and broke his heart along with it.

His guilt proven, he was delivered to the sheriffs of London on 10 July 1584 and, drawn on a hurdle to Tyburn, he was duly hanged, drawn and quartered. Even those who confessed were not entitled to mercy.

Another dedicated supporter of Mary, Queen of Scots, was one Charles Bailey. Coded letters were found on him, and the Lieutenant of the Tower was told: 'You will ask him for the alphabet of the cipher and if he shall refuse to show the said alphabet or to declare truly the contents of the said letters in cipher, you shall put him upon the rack, and by discretion with putting him in fear, and as cause shall be given afterwards, you shall procure him to confess the truth with some pain of the said torture.' Accordingly he was put to the question, later being escorted back to his dungeon in the Beauchamp Tower 'discoloured and pale as ashes'.

Few people may have heard of Peacham or Fisher, Nicholls or Throckmorton, but that cannot be said about Guy Fawkes. When he was caught preparing to blow up the Houses of Parliament, James I, urgently needing to discover who else was implicated in the plot against him and never reluctant to inflict suffering on his fellow creatures, issued instructions of which the following is a transcript.

Copy of the Interrogatories drawn up by His Majesty King James I to be put to John Johnson, otherwise Guido Faukes, November 6th 1605.

This examinate should now be made to answer to formal interrogaties.

As to what he is? For I can never yet hear of any man that knows him.

Where he was born?

What were his parents' names?

What age he is of?

Where he hath lived?

How he hath lived, and by what trade of life?

How he received those wounds in his breast?

How came he into Percy's service?

What time was this house (adjoining the Parliament buildings) hired by his master?

How soon after the possessing of it did he begin to his devilish preparations?

When and where learned he to speak French?

What gentlewoman's letter it was that was found upon him?

And wherefore doth she give him another name in it that he gives himself?

If he was ever a Papist, and if so, who brought him up in it?

If otherwise, how was he converted, where, when and by whom?

This course of his life I am the more desirous to know, because I have divers motives leading me to suspect that he hath remained long beyond the seas and either is a priest or hath long served some priest or fugitive abroad, for I can yet meet with no man that knows him . . . if he will not confess, the gentler tortures are to be first used unto him *'et sec per gradus ad ima tenditur'* (and so on, step by step, to the most severe) and so God spede your good work. James R.

And 'spede' it they did, taking Fawkes to the torture chamber in the White Tower. As was customary he was first shown the devices ranged around the vault, the very sight of which had proved sufficient for some prisoners, but Fawkes was made of sterner stuff. He was therefore secured to the rack and its levers were turned. Over him bent the questioners, the Secretary of State, the Lord Privy Seal and the Lord High Admiral, for this was the King's business and not to be delegated. No sound escaped through the fifteen feet thick walls to the outside world as the ropes creaked, the ratchets clicked and the incessant voices, demanding answers to James's questions, urged and probed.

For thirty minutes, although it must have seemed an aeon of agony to the tormented wretch on the frame, the interrogators' questions hung unanswered in the cold dank air of the vault. Then Fawkes gasped his surrender. He divulged a few vital facts, then hesitated. Once again the levers were pushed, straining the ropes even tighter around the rollers, stretching Fawkes's sinews to snapping point, forcing his hip and shoulder joints from their sockets. And then, 'when told he must come to it againe and againe, from daye to daye, till he should have delivered his whole knowledge', he blurted his confession.

Names, dates, meeting places spilled forth, damning and incriminating his fellow conspirators; every whispered word was written down by his inquisitors. Later, with a hand literally racked with pain, he could only scrawl his name to his confession, the document which would in effect be the death warrant of so many. Together with seven of his fellow plotters – Bates, Grant, Rookewood, Digby, Keys and the two Wintour brothers – he was hanged, disembowelled while still alive, and quartered.

In Tudor times, sexual discrimination hardly existed – at least where the rack was concerned. It mattered not whether wrists and ankles were slender and feminine, or sinewy and masculine; questions were there to be answered, and the rack was there to persuade and cajole. When Catherine Parr, last wife of Henry VIII, was suspected by her enemies at court of having Protestant inclinations, her companions were taken into custody; for if the Queen could be incriminated, a third royal head might well roll on Tower Green.

One close friend of the Queen was Anne Askew, a highly intelligent and fervent reformer who had sought to convert her royal mistress to her own Protestant beliefs. She was arrested, tried and condemned to death by burning, the usual manner of death for heretics. After her trial she was taken to the Tower to be questioned further about the Queen's involvement by the Lord Chancellor Sir Thomas Wriothesley, Sir Richard Rich, and the Tower's Lieutenant Sir Anthony Knivett. She would volunteer no information and so, in order to terrify her, she was taken to the White Tower and shown the instruments of torture. She refused to be frightened so easily, and the Chancellor then ordered the Tower warders to rack her.

She was tied in position and the levers were slowly operated. The questions came, but no answers. Anne Askew, a strong-willed martyr, was determined to tell them nothing. The Chancellor, equally determined, ordered more pressure on the levers, more agony for his victim, his orders being endorsed by Sir Richard Rich who, eleven years earlier, had perjured himself in order to bring about the execution of Sir Thomas More.

The Lieutenant was appalled by their brutality and ordered his men to release her. Whereupon Wriothesley and Rich seized the levers themselves and, according to Anne's own testimony quoted in Fox's *Book of Martyrs*, 'They did put me on the rack because I confessed no ladies or gentlemen to be of my opinion, and thereupon kept me a long time on it and because I lay still and did not cry out, my Lord Chancellor and Master Rich took pains to rack me with their own hands, till I was nigh dead.' And, as summed up by the historian Bale, 'So quietly and patiently praying to the Lord, she endured their tyranny till her bones and joints were almost plucked asunder.'

At the sight of her suffering, the Lieutenant declared that he would appeal directly to the Monarch – a right, incidentally, which exists to this day. The Chancellor, not to be outmanoeuvred and determined to reach the King first, left the Tower on horseback and headed for Westminster and the royal presence, completely unaware that the Lieutenant's barge lay moored and ready at Tower Wharf. The tide was favourable, and the fast-flowing river was always speedier than the City's muddy and crowded streets.

Gaining the King's audience chamber, the Lieutenant described the woman's sufferings and, his version being accepted, he was ordered to halt the proceedings forthwith. Returning to the Tower, the Lieutenant summoned the fortress's surgeon and the fainting, half-crippled woman was revived. She was, however, still a heretic, and so, in 1546, she was carried, strapped in a chair, to Smithfield, where she was publicly burned at the stake.

It should not be thought, however, that the Tower's rack was the only one in the country. In fact there was actually one installed and in use in a private house. It belonged to Richard Topcliffe, the ruthless priest-hunter described in Chapter 4. He boasted that the Tower's rack was as child's play compared to his, and he used it extensively, although he did not believe in restricting its use solely to Catholics. Gypsies rounded up in Northamptonshire were tortured by him, as were common thieves such as Thomas Travers, guilty of stealing the Queen's standish, her ornamental inkwell.

Eventually even some Protestants recoiled at his savagery, and their protests caused Lord Cecil to imprison Topcliffe for exceeding the authority of his warrant, but this was purely a gesture to placate public opinion, for Topcliffe soon returned to his barbaric ways.

I regret to say that right and justice did not prevail. He was not murdered by an intended victim or stretched on his own rack. For him, crime *did* pay. In 1594 he quarrelled with an accomplice named Fitzherbert who had promised him £5,000 to have his own father and cousin murdered. The accomplice refused to pay up on the grounds that one victim was still alive and the other died of natural causes and not while under torture. Who lost the court case is not recorded, but it certainly was not Topcliffe, for somehow he gained possession of the Fitzherbert estates, and died in the family house at Padley, Derbyshire, in 1604. Paradoxically, earlier this century a direct descendant of Topcliffe became a Jesuit priest!

### The Irish Rack

By the seventeenth century Ireland had its own rack, though it was rarely used. In 1627 the Lord Deputy asked Lord Killultagh whether he had authority to torture a priest named O'Cullenan, to which his superior replied that the man ought to be racked if cause was seen, and hanged if reason could be found.

And in 1628 two criminals were tortured to compel them to testify against the Byrne family of County Wicklow, who were thought to be plotting against Charles I. One was racked in Dublin and the other was burned to death.

### The Spanish Rack

In marked contrast to Ireland, in Spain the rack featured prominently, especially during the existence of the Inquisition. This ecclesiastical tribunal of the Roman Catholic Church had the task of suppressing heresy. Its trials were conducted in secret, and torture was used to force confessions of guilt from the heretics or anyone suspected of being an unbeliever in the Faith. Originating in 1229, it was revived in 1480, when Tomás de Torquemada persuaded Ferdinand and Isabella to ask the Pope to sanction the institution of the Holy Office of the Inquisition, with himself as

Inquisitor-General. Displaying pitiless cruelty, he is believed to have been responsible not only for the expulsion of the Jews from Spain, but also for the torture and death by burning of more than 10,000 people.

Most of the population lived in fear of the Holy Office, since an ill-judged remark or vengeful accusation by an enemy could result in imprisonment, trial and torture.

Just as at the Tower of London, the Inquisition's torture chamber was an underground dungeon, its walls heavily sound-proofed with quilts to keep the outside world oblivious of the suffering within. It was illuminated only by flickering torches, and to increase the horror of the scene, the executioner was clothed in black, his head completely covered with a black cowl, his eyes glittering through the eyeholes.

Many heretics surrendered at the very sight of the torturer and his array of menacing instruments. Others more stout hearted or obstinate were, as described in 1731 by Limborch in his book, *The History of the Inquisition*, made ready for their dread ordeal: 'The stripping is performed without regard to humanity or honour, not only to men, but to women and virgins, the most virtuous and chaste of whom they have sometimes in the prisons. For they cause them to be stripped, even to their very shifts, which they afterwards take off, forgive the expression, even to their pudenda, and then put on their strait linen drawers.'

At that stage the accusations were repeated by the inquisitors, and should the victim not confess immediately, he or she was put to the torture. Many suffered severe injury, Tomás de Leon being racked until his left arm was broken. Some held out longer than others. Maria de Coceicao was racked twice and, when threatened with further racking, vehemently retorted that 'as soon as I am released from the rack I shall deny all that was extorted from me by pain'. Again they racked her and, her resistance holding fast, she refused to confess. For once thwarted, the tribunal sentenced her to a public flogging and banishment for ten years.

Not so fortunate, though, was Jane Behorquia, accused of discussing the Protestant religion. Although pregnant, she was incarcerated in a foul dungeon until after the birth of her child. In her weakened condition she was then racked with such severity that the ropes scythed through the flesh of her wrists and ankles, and the blood gushed from her mouth. Carried back to her cell, she died a week later, the tribunal blandly announcing that she had been found dead in prison, cause unknown.

An Englishman who endured the terrors of the Inquisition was a seaman named Thomas Sturgeon. In 1585 his ship, the *Maria* was attacked by Algerian pirates, and he was taken to Algiers. Escaping from his captors, he managed to get aboard an English ship, but again misfortune struck, for that ship in turn was intercepted off Spain, and the crew taken to Cadiz.

Sturgeon was interrogated by the Inquisitors and ordered to recant his Protestant faith, but he refused to do so. He was then whipped and imprisoned in an underground cell, and his food was lowered to him by means of a basket let down through a stone trapdoor.

During the following ten months he was repeatedly racked and whipped, but his luck dramatically changed when, while the basket of food was being lowered, the gaoler was called away. Sturgeon managed to climb up the rope and, killing the gaoler with his bare hands, he escaped. Travelling across country to the coast, he stole an open rowing boat and set sail. After twenty hours adrift, without food and on the point of complete exhaustion, he was picked up by an English ship and taken to Plymouth and safety. Few victims of the Spanish Inquisition can have been so fortunate.

## The Portuguese Rack

Another type of rack was used in Lisbon in 1753, one of its victims being John Coustos, who was accused of being a Freemason. Refusing to divulge the Masonic secrets, he was secured to the rack by his ankles, a collar round his neck preventing any further movement. Instead of being stretched, ropes were then bound around his arms and legs, passing down through holes in the frame, and drawn tighter and tighter by the torturers. The appalling flesh wounds as the ropes bit through to the bone eventually rendered the victim insensible.

William Lithgow, a suspected spy, was similarly tied down and tortured. The ropes binding his arms and legs were progressively tightened by levers which, passing through loops in the ropes, were twisted, tourniquet-wise. Savage ingenuity was never in short supply during the Inquisition.

## The French Rack

In the neighbouring country of France, different versions of the rack were also widely used. Some types were of the 'standard' pattern – the victim was pulled by ropes attached to both ends of the frame – but by 1765 a small modification had been incorporated into the French model after it had become obvious that a victim could be just as adequately stretched by tying one end of him down and pulling on the other end, as pulling both ends simultaneously. This variation, employed in England somewhat earlier, allowed the French torture-chamber workforce to be similarly halved.

And so it was that in order to extract a confession from a robber Pierre Delluque, he was stripped and laid on the rack. His ankles were secured to an iron hook at the end of the frame, and a rope about his wrists was tied to a ratchet-operated roller at the other extremity. Then, as recorded in the French archives,

> Thereupon, having ordered the executioner to turn three cogs, we the prosecutors interrogated the accused as to all the facts relating to his condemnation. He answered that he had never committed any robbery and had no accomplice, and having ordered three more cogs to be turned, the accused, again questioned, answered that he was not a party to any robbery. Having ordered three more cogs to be turned, accused answered that he had spoken the truth.
>
> Having ordered yet another three cogs to be turned, accused said that if he were released he would speak the truth. Thereupon the executioner, having by our order released the accused, again urged him to tell us what robberies and offences he had committed since leaving the galleys; who were his accomplices; whether he did not steal a mare at Rousset; whether the said mare was not taken by him to the farm of Brousses, near Belfort, answered that he had spoken the truth, had never committed any robbery alone or with any other person.
>
> Thereupon ordered the said executioner to again stretch

the cords to the same point at which they were before the prisoner was released; ordered three more cogs to be turned, and the accused, interrogated, answered that the devil might take him, body and soul, if he had been a party to any robbery. And having ordered three more cogs to be turned, again interrogated the accused as to the above facts but he made no reply.

Thereupon called upon the surgeons who, being sworn after examining the state of the accused, reported that breathing was suspended and he was in danger of suffocation unless released within a few moments.

On this report, ordered the accused to be released, he having regained consciousness by the aid of cordials administered by the surgeons. Interrogated again but still denied being a party to any robbery. Thereupon, having ordered the cords to be stretched to the same point as before, the accused, interrogated again, replied only with loud screams; and having ordered the executioner to turn two more cogs, the accused still gave no reply and the surgeons, having again examined the state of the accused, reported that the movement of the diaphragm was stopped by the twisting of the nerves, and that the thumb of his right hand was torn off, and that he was in danger of losing his life if we did not release him.

Thereupon ordered the executioner to entirely loosen the accused; had him carried on a mattress in front of a fire, where he regained consciousness with the help of the surgeons and the cordials they administered to him. Read over to him the present report, and after interrogating him generally as to all the facts, he again answered that he had not committed any robbery either alone or with accomplices.

Another version of the rack consisted of a large wheel, the victim being strapped to its circumference, with his feet fettered to the ground and his hands bound above his head. The wheel was slowly rotated, stretching his limbs in much the same way as the more orthodox horizontal model.

All these machines made it quite obvious that being racked was a catch-22 situation. If one were innocent, denials brought further torture, possibly permanent mutilation and probably death. Yet if, in the throes of agony, one confessed, truthfully or not, execution automatically followed.

Of the many executioners and torturers in France, probably the most renowned was Charles-Henri Sanson, who reigned on the scaffold from 1754 to 1795. Well-educated and musically talented, he excelled in playing the violin and violoncello, and was always dressed in the height of fashion when not on the scaffold. In any other walk of life he could have risen to an honourable position, but being a member of a family which traditionally provided the executioners of France – seven generations were eventually to serve their country in that role – his career was preordained.

A man of sensitivity, Sanson treated his female victims with as much compassion as he dared, under the hostile gaze of the bloodthirsty mobs gathered around the guillotine, and he was stricken with remorse after beheading King Louis XVI. Far from gloating over his doomed victims, the sheer slaughter involved in executing so many hundreds of victims during the French Revolution sickened him so much that he developed nephritis, a kidney complaint, which forced his retirement in August 1795.

## The Italian Rack
If one had to be racked, probably the country to avoid would have been Italy. With their device, known as the *Veglia*, the victim was secured in a horizontal position, and his wrists and ankles tied to rings in opposite walls. And to ensure that he did remain horizontal, despite the appalling strain on muscles and sinews, a sharpened spike was positioned immediately beneath his backbone.

## The German Rack
The Germans also utilised spikes in one version of their rack. Similar to the standard English rack, it incorporated an extra roller across the middle of the frame, which pressed against the back of the stretched victim. By manipulation of the rollers at each end, the victim could be pulled back and forth across the central roller, and severe lacerations were caused by the sharp spikes which protruded from it.

Their other model was known as the 'Austrian Ladder'. As its name implies, it consisted of a wide ladder secured at an angle of forty-five degrees against the dungeon wall. The victim was laid on his back part-way up the ladder, his wrists tied to a rung behind his back. A rope about his ankles was then tied to a roller at the foot of the ladder, and should confession be slow in forthcoming, the roller would be rotated, pulling his legs and body down the ladder and thereby twisting his bound arms up behind him, straining his shoulder-blades to dislocation-point. And being great believers in multiple torture, the German executioners would simultaneously apply lighted candles, torches or red-hot irons to the victim's armpits and sides, as an added incentive to answer the incriminating questions. Yet another refinement was to subject the victim to the *Kranz*: straps were tightened about his head while he was stretched on the rack.

Charles-Henri Sanson was not the only executioner with a few of the finer feelings left. Franz Schmidt, public executioner of Nuremberg from 1573 to 1617, was another whose sensitivities were in marked contrast to men in the mould of Topcliffe and Torquemada. Admittedly, by virtue of his office, Schmidt had to torture and execute criminals, but this he did strictly in accordance with the sentence of the court, no more and no less.

Unerringly accurate with his decapitating sword, adept with the red-hot pincers, whip and branding iron, nevertheless he was far from being a sadist or a death-dealing automaton. Indeed he was so appalled by the death penalty meted out to women guilty of infanticide – that of being tied in a sack and held under water until drowned – that he persuaded the authorities to replace it with hanging or beheading. A mercifully quicker death, if nothing else.

During his forty-four years of service he executed 360 criminals, forty-two of whom were women. So highly was he regarded that at his funeral in 1634, many of the city's dignitaries attended as a mark of respect.

## Skeffington's Gyves

If all the aforementioned has convinced you that the Duke of Exeter's Daughter is definitely not the girl for you, I should warn you not to be too precipitate in making advances to her companion, Sir Leonard Skeffington's Daughter, until you have read on, and pondered long and hard.

Sir Leonard was Lieutenant of the Tower of London in the reign of Henry VIII, a time when the resources of the torture chamber were occasionally as frequently strained as were its victims. The motive for the invention of his torture device, which was also known as 'Skeffington Gyves' and the 'Scavenger's Daughter', is not known. It could have been a sudden inspiration, for no other country seems to have had an 'engine' of that particular design. Or perhaps it was the solution to a problem which must have bedevilled the Tower authorities over the years.

A prisoner, brought in through Traitor's Gate, would first be taken to the King's House (currently known as the Queen's House) to be booked in, initially questioned and assigned accommodation in one of the many small towers. The predicament arose when the prisoner, after having been tortured in the White Tower, had to be returned to his cell. The journey from one building to another, albeit short, nevertheless exposed the distressed or semi-conscious victim to those living in or visiting the fortress. Not only might the sight upset their sensitivities, but more importantly, it may not have been deemed expedient to reveal just who was being held prisoner at that time, and what had been inflicted on him or her.

The root of the problem was the rack. As already described, this machine was a sturdy rectangular structure, its four legs positioned in sockets in the ground to ensure rigidity while in use. The prisoners' cells were almost invariably approached via spiral stairs, and anyone who has ever attempted to carry a single bedstead up a narrow, right-angled staircase will immediately appreciate the difficulty facing those who, needing to torture a victim in the privacy of his or her cell, tried to get a seven-foot rack up a continuously spiralling stairway. What was required was a more compact, eminently portable device which would be just as – if not more – painfully persuasive than the rack. And the answer was 'Skeffington's Gyves'.

It consisted basically of two halves of a large iron hoop, joined together by a hinge. The prisoner, his hands bound behind him, was made to kneel over one half and, with the executioner straddling his back and pressing down, the other half of the hoop was brought down, a screw mechanism increasing the pressure on the victim's back. It forced his chest down on to his knees, his stomach down on his thighs, his thighs on to his legs, and compressed him into the shape of a ball. Further pressure exerted by the screws crushed his body even more, dislocating his vertebrae, fracturing breastbone and ribs, while blood spurted from his nose and mouth, even from his fingertips and toes.

In direct contrast to the stretching on the rack, the compressive action of this fearsome machine was designed literally to make both ends meet, and few victims could endure more than a few minutes of its torments.

Two Jesuits who suffered in Skeffington's Gyves were Thomas Coteham and Lucas Kerbie. Arrested on suspicion of high treason, they were brought to the Tower on 5 December 1580. Both were clamped in the Gyves; Coteham, it was reported, 'bled profusely from the nose'. After months of harsh imprisonment, as recorded by the contemporary chronicler John Stow,

On the 20th November 1581 they were brought to the high bar at Westminster where they were indicted vpon high treason, for that contrary both to loue and dutie, they forsooke their natiue countrey, to liue beyond the seas vnder the Popes obedience as at Rome, Rheimes and diuerse other places where, the pope hauing with other princes practiced the death and depriuation of our most gracious princess and vtter subuersion of her state and kingdome, to aduance his most abhominable religion, these menne hauing vowed their alleagiance to the pope, to obey him in all causes whatsoeuer, being there, gaue their consent, to ayd him in this most trayterous determination.

And for this intent and purpose they were sent ouer to seduce the harts of her majesties louing subjects, and to conspire and practise her graces death, as much as in them lay, against a great daie, set and appoynted, when the generall hauocke should be made, those onely reserued that joyned with them.

This laid to their charge, they boldly denied, but by a jurie they were approoued guiltie, and had judgement to bee hanged, bowelled and quartered.

And so they were, before a vast crowd, at Tyburn on 30 May 1582.

Not all victims were tortured to such extremes. Some, regarded as minor pawns in whatever conspiracies were suspected, were let off lightly, the authorities believing that little incriminating information was known to the victim. That would certainly account for the survival of one Thomas Miagh, who had been accused of treasonable correspondence with rebels in Ireland, and the Tower bills, the official diary kept by the Lieutenant, showed that on 10 March 1581 he was brought to the Tower of London. He was questioned twice but not at first tortured because they had been ordered to examine him in secrecy, 'which they could not do, because that manner of dealing with him required the presence and aid of one of the warders all the time that he would be in those irons', and also because they 'found the man so resolute as in their opinions little would be wrung out of him but by some sharper torture'.

He was then imprisoned in the Bell Tower and later the Beauchamp Tower, the walls of both still bearing the inscriptions carved by him: 'Thomas Miagh which lieth here alone, that Fayne wold from hens be gone, by tortyre straynge mi troyth was tryed, yet of mi Libertie denied, 1581.' The 'tortyre straynge' was the intimate embrace of Skeffington's Gyves, but it would seem that the ordeal was unproductive, for 'we subjected hym to the tortyr of Skevington's Iron and with so mutche sharpeness as was in our judgement conveniente, yett can we get from hym no farther matter'.

Accordingly, on 30 July of the same year, he was handed over to Rackmaster Norton 'to deal with him with the rack in such sort as they should see fit'. Whether he had nothing more to divulge, or the instigators of the plot had already been rounded up, is not known, but Thomas Miagh was released at the end of 1581 and returned to Ireland.

'Skeffington's Gyves' also materialised in the Royal Navy in the eighteenth century, though not under that name, of course, and without the mechanism. On board warships, the punishment was known as 'Tying Neck and Heels'. The erring seaman would have to sit down on the deck, where a flintlock rifle would be positioned under his knees and another over his neck. The two

56

weapons would then be strapped so tightly together that, in forcing the man's chin down between his knees, blood would flow from his nose, mouth and ears, and even result in fatal ruptures.

## American 'Neck and Heels'
Torment with a similar name was also inflicted on some of the notorious Witches of Salem during their trial in New England, in 1692, when they were subjected to being 'tied Neck and Heels until blood spurted from their noses'.

## Indian Variations
In a like fashion, Indian felons were punished by being sentenced to *Anundal*. This involved them being tied in various positions, the torturer forcing the victim's head down and, passing a rope around his neck, securing it to his toes.

Other unnatural positions were also enforced, the man having to lift one leg as high as possible, to have it then tied as close to his neck as possible. These punishments, applied at the whim of the torturer, had to be maintained for long periods in the heat of the Indian sun, causing excruciating cramp and temporary paralysis of the limbs. No doubt Sir Leonard would have been exceedingly pleased with these Eastern adaptations of his device.

# 4

# A Time of Suspense

In the torturers' world, the weight of the human body was never overlooked. Not so much when executing the victim – that was the hanging side of the business – but during the actual sessions in the torture chamber itself.

The number of different ways in which a human being could be suspended, with the essential accompaniment of coercive agony, was considerable. The Chinese secured their victims by the toes of one foot and the fingers of one hand, the ropes then being passed over a high roller. When hoisted in that manner, the very weight of the victim caused dislocation and even crude amputation of the distended digits.

Another fiendish method employed by their torturers was to pinion the criminal about the ankles and then, suspended upside-down, he would be swung continually backwards and forwards, until dizziness and nausea brought merciful unconsciousness.

## The Gauntlets

By far the usual method adopted by the judiciary of Western countries, allegedly the less barbaric nations, was to suspend their victims by means of iron manacles locked about their wrists.

There were two variations of this, both equally successful in obtaining confessions, with little to choose between them when it came to the agony ratings.

One was to bind the victim's wrists to a beam above his head, then remove the blocks on which he stood so that his feet were clear of the ground. After some little time, partial paralysis of the arms and shoulders, together with searing pains in the chest and stomach, would set in, making him amenable to answering the incriminating questions.

This particular procedure was reportedly introduced into England by Richard Topcliffe, a man born in Gainsborough, Lincolnshire, who became Member of Parliament for the Yorkshire town of Beverley.

He rose to notoriety when, in 1586, he was appointed by Lord Burghley to be one of Her Majesty's servants. His official duties were to track down and arrest Jesuits and Popish recusants, those Catholics who refused to attend Protestant church services, or those who practised their own religion in private. Ironically he himself had formerly been a Catholic.

Topcliffe was further empowered 'to torment priests in his own home as he shall think good', and soon became a feared and hated priest hunter. So ruthlessly and cold-bloodedly did he perform his tasks that 'a Topcliffe custom' became a euphemism for being racked, and to hunt a recusant was known as 'to topcliffizare'.

His brutality spread far and wide, the author Meyer commenting, 'Only a man like Topcliffe was capable of torturing afresh a man who had already been broken on the rack, who had confessed and admitted everything asked of him, and had even renounced his faith. Only a man like Topcliffe was capable of insulting his victim as long as he drew breath and of stifling the last words of farewell and prayer. Had he not been sure of the Queen's approval, the wretch would not have applied his trade.'

Having such royal authority, Topcliffe recruited teams which scoured the countryside, searching for their prey. The incentives were high, for the law offered rewards to any person who supplied information leading to the arrest of a priest for saying Mass or performing any priestly function. These emoluments amounted to a third of the fines levied against those Catholics caught attending the priest, with a top limit of £50 – no mean sum in those days. In addition, the pursuivants, as they were called, though in reality they were little more than bounty hunters, could claim travelling expenses of thirteen pence per mile, paid by the victims rather than by the Civil Service accounts department.

For this lucrative income the pursuivants eavesdropped in taverns, interrogated the servants of known Catholics, and recruited local Protestants to spy on Catholic families and send reports of anything suspicious.

One such report, included in State Papers of 1536, was submitted by a tradesman living near Ufton Court in Berkshire, the home of a Catholic family named Perkins.

There resorteth unto the dwelling howse of the said Fraunys Parkyns, a certain unknowen person which is commonly lodged in a cocke lofte or some other secrett corner of the howse and is not commenly seene abroad, but when comminge abroad he weareth a blew coate. Which person soe unknowen, I vehemently suspecteth to be a seminary priest; for that on divers Wenesdayes, Frydayes and other festivall dayes, I have seen most of the familye, one after another, slipping upp in a secrett manner to a high chaumber in the toppe of the howse and there continew the space of an hower and a half or more, and harkening as neere as I might to the place, hath often heerd a little bell rounge, which I imagineth to be a sacring bell, whereby I conjectureth that they resort to heare mass. Divers other persons resort to the howse in a secrett manner, sometimes by day, sometimes by nighte.

Reports such as this were immediately acted on by Topcliffe's pursuivants. Skilled in their profession, these human ferrets would arrive without warning and, empowered by the warrants which authorised them to search for priestly activities, would proceed to comb the premises. Thorough and well organised, they would count windows outside and in, for a discrepancy indicated a hidden room; the number of chimneys were compared with the number of grates, for a false chimney stack could be a secret priest hole.

They would go into each room ringing a little bell, and by the variation of its sound in the next room, they judged where there could be hollow spaces. They would then tear down walls and panelling, demolish stairways, ransack attics, and if their search proved fruitless, would depart noisily, only to creep back into the house, to proclaim, 'It's all right, they've gone – you can come out now.'

One notorious pursuivant named Fenwick who operated in the

North of England adopted the ruthless strategy of forcing all the residents to leave, and rather than expend energy on wrecking the place, he and his men would surround the house and simply starve any fugitives until they surrendered. And they then handed over their prey to Richard Topcliffe.

Two men whose capture had become an obsession with Topcliffe were the Jesuit priest John Gerard and a lay brother Nicholas Owen, both of whom had miraculously escaped time and time again from the pursuivants. Topcliffe was so determined that the priest in particular should be caught, that he even issued a 'wanted' notice: 'Jhon Gerrade ye Jhezewt is about 30 years oulde, of good stature, blubarde lipps, turninge outwards especially the over lipps, most uppwards towards the noase. In his speetche he slourrethe and smyles much . . . his beard is cut close, saving little mustachios and a little tuft under his lower lippe.'

So it was with sadistic delight, when an informer, John Frank, reported the whereabouts of the wanted pair, that Topcliffe despatched two pursuivants, Newell and Worsley, to arrest them. Without chance to escape, both were captured and brought to the Tower of London for brutal interrogation.

In the same way as the priest hunter had issued a wanted notice for Gerard, so Topcliffe was described by the Jesuit in his autobiography as 'old and hoary, a veteran in evil who thirsted for the blood of Catholics . . . the cruellest tyrant in all England, a man most hateful and infamous in all the realm for his bloody and butcherly mind'. Hardly an understatement, for Gerard had been threatened by Topcliffe: 'I will see you are caught and brought to me and placed in my power. I will hang you up in the air and will have no pity on you, and then I shall watch you and see if your God will save you from my grasp.'

In the White Tower dungeon, manacles were locked around Gerard's wrists and he was made to stand on wicker steps positioned against the base of one of the huge wooden posts that supported the roof. Iron staples had been driven in at the top of the post, to which his manacles were attached by means of a bar and pin.

One of his torturers then removed the steps, only to find that their prisoner, being a tall man, was still able to touch the ground with his toes. Accordingly he scraped away at the earthen floor, until the priest's weight was taken solely by his wrists.

Gerard was then told to confess. Despite the appalling pain sweeping over him, and the feeling that, as he later described, the blood was spurting from his fingertips, he refused to submit. Wise in their ways, his interrogators left him hanging alone but for yeoman warder Bonner who had been detailed to guard him day and night.

Bonner, a compassionate man and thereby quite unsuitable for his job, bathed Gerard's face and implored him to confess, but the priest, not surprisingly suspecting that this was a subtle ploy to dupe him, refused to listen. The pain became more intense, and Gerard fainted several times during the next few hours. Each time he was revived by having the steps replaced, only for them to be removed at the first sign of returning consciousness.

In the afternoon Sir William Waad, the Lieutenant of the Tower – a tyrant described as 'that beast Waad' by Sir Walter Raleigh when he too was a Tower prisoner – returned to his pinioned victim. On being thwarted by Gerard's obstinate refusal to confess, he lost his temper. 'Then hang there till you rot off the pillar!' he shouted, leaving the dungeon again.

When, later, Gerard was lowered from his bonds, he was assisted back to his cell in the Salt Tower by warder Bonner, who nursed him and, because of the priest's grotesquely swollen hands and arms, cut the priest's food into small pieces and fed him.

Further sessions in the gauntlets followed, the torturers encountering difficulties in locking the manacles around the mutilated flesh of his wrists. But Gerard's spirit was undaunted. Despite his sufferings he refused to capitulate and eventually, with Bonner's help, actually escaped from the dreaded fortress, one of the very few to do so (see the author's *Great Escapes from the Tower of London*).

Not so fortunate was Nicholas Owen, 'Little John' as he was known. He had ostensibly been the servant of the Jesuit Father Garnet who, with Father Oldcorne, was later caught at the time of the Gunpowder Plot, tortured, then hanged, drawn and quartered. In actual fact Owen, originally a carpenter and mason, had developed his craft until he had become the supreme architect and builder of priest holes in the large houses owned by practising Catholic families.

Literally scores of priests owed their lives to Nicholas Owen, for so skilled was he at devising and creating his secret hiding-places that they were rarely discovered, and then only by extensive searches by a large number of men.

His designs were elaborate: cavities were dug into the solid masonry of walls and foundations, sometimes linking one with another so that discovery of the first one, being empty, would fool the pursuivants into thinking that their bird had flown. Others would lead, via apparently secret trapdoors, away from the real hiding-places, ending up in attics or roof voids.

Beneath 'hearth stones', in reality planks piled high with kindling, cavities were created, large enough for a fugitive to sit, if not stand, while the interiors of window seats gave access to adjacent hollow panelling. All these he would construct himself, excavatingly slowly and laboriously, working secretly so that not even the servants were aware of his activities. His expertise at Hindlip Hall near Worcester, for example, was such that an eight-day search by a hundred pursuivants eventually revealed no fewer than eleven secret hiding-places.

So it was vital that as much information as possible should be wrung out of Little John, for once in possession of the names of the Catholics for whom he had worked, and the locations of the hiding-places he had installed, Topcliffe's ravening pack would reap a rich harvest of fugitive priests, and be able to destroy scores of refuges.

In the White Tower he too suffered the gauntlets, weights being attached to his ankles to increase the torment. Hour after hour the questions came, the torture increased, but Owen somehow withstood the appalling agonies. Later reports stated that, back in his cell between periods of interrogation, he obtained from his warder a blunt knife with which to cut his meat, and fatally stabbed himself. But this was disputed, for Father Gerard declared that 'under torture his bowels gushed out with his life'. And against the date of 2 March 1606 the entry in the Lieutenant's official record stated: 'The man is dead – he died in our hands'.

Nicholas Owen took his secrets with him to the grave, and

even now, many of the hiding-places he constructed still await discovery. Such was his unflinching spirit and his devotion to his faith, that he was beatified by the Catholic Church earlier this century.

## Squassation and Strappado

Another variation of the gauntlets was introduced when it was decided that even more pain could be inflicted if the victim was suspended with his wrists behind rather than in front of him. And so was born Squassation.

This most unpleasant treatment usually involved a pulley mounted high above the floor, over which the rope attached to the victim's manacles was passed. Pulling on the rope lifted him at least six feet above the ground, forcing his arms upwards and backwards behind him, and putting an intolerable strain on his shoulder-blades and spine.

### Squassation in America

Penologists in the United States realised that, while torture as such was against the law, nevertheless that sort of punishment would be a good way of maintaining order in their gaols. In the 1890s they installed a derrick, a block and tackle, at Folsom Prison, near Sacramento, hanging it from a hook near the punishment cells. The prisoner's wrists, handcuffed behind him, were hauled up by the derrick until he stood on tiptoe, his head tilted down to the level of his waist. No further torture was applied, but docility was guaranteed by the time the erstwhile troublesome convict was released some two or more hours later.

### Squassation in Spain

As practised by the Inquisition, this torture was applied in stages, the first of which entailed the victim being winched up with a weight of 180 pounds attached to his feet. At the second stage, this weight was increased to 250 pounds and a further refinement was introduced. This was *estrapade* or Strappado. The rope from which the victim was suspended was suddenly allowed to slacken for a second before being abruptly jerked taut again, as described by John Marchant, author of *The Horrid Cruelties of the Inquisition*, published in 1770:

65

he is then drawn up on high, till his head reaches the pulley. He is kept hanging in this manner for some time, that by the greatness of the weight hanging at his feet, all his joints and limbs may be dreadfully stretched, and on a sudden he is let down with a jerk, by the slacking of the rope, but is kept from coming quite to the ground, by which terrible shake, his arms and legs are disjointed, whereby he is put to the most exquisite pain; the shock which he receives by the sudden stop of his fall, and the weight at his feet stretching his whole body more intensely and cruelly.

Women too were subjected to *estrapade* by the Inquisitors, whips also being applied while they were suspended in mid-air.

## Squassation in Italy
When John Howard, the prison reformer, visited Rome in 1778, he too found the verb *strappare*, meaning 'to tug sharply', very much part of the current vocabulary, for in the New Prison in that city he inspected the mechanism which was 'used to pull up malefactors by their hands which are tied behind them; after they have been suspended for some time, by being suddenly let down part of the way, their arms are dislocated'.

## Continental Squassation
The 'Torture of the Pulley' was also widely used in France, and the Germans not only adopted it but also added a vicious refinement. Their version, *Aufziehen*, included the mandatory weights about the ankles, but, according to Dr Wylie's description of his visit to Nuremberg, 'There was the iron chain wound over a pulley, which hauled the victim up to the vaulted roof; and there were the two great stone weights which, tied to his feet and the iron cord let go, brought him down with a jerk that dislocated his ankles. While the spiked rollers, which he grazed in his descent, cut into and excoriated his back, leaving his body a bloody dislocated mass.'

# 5
## Cut and Thrust

The human anatomy seems to have been expressly designed to be pierced. Had it been an amorphous mass like that of a jellyfish, or enclosed in a shell, other punitive methods would have had to be devised. As it was, the human body's soft, yielding flesh, with vulnerable parts such as fingers and toes, ears and noses, sticking out, positively invited the attention of the torturers' keen-edged blade and sharpened spike.

That this was recognised as early as the eleventh century is evidenced by an edict of William the Conqueror, ordering the maiming of criminals, while Henry I (1100–135) ordained that those guilty of counterfeiting the nation's currency should be rounded up and taken to Winchester, where they were to have their right hands severed and afterwards be castrated.

Through the centuries that followed, there was no real substitute when it came to punishing forgers, rioters, blasphemers, sheep stealers, Puritans and the like. In 1578 sheep rustlers were sentenced to have both hands amputated, while three years later an author, John Stubs, and his printer, William Pace, also faced the knife. They had been found guilty of publishing a pamphlet insulting the Queen and her intended suitor, the Duke of Anjou. On 15 November 1581 they were taken to Westminster and on a scaffold specially erected in the market place, 'their right hands were struck off and a cleaver driven through the wrist with a beetle (a heavy wooden hammer)'. After the bleeding stumps had been cauterised with a hot iron, William Pace boasted 'I have left here a true Englishman's hand', while John Stubs took off his hat with his sole remaining hand, waved it in the air and loudly proclaimed 'God save Queen Elizabeth'. How patriotic can one get?

Libelling royalty was one thing. Posing a threat to the lives of royalty was another. And so, in 1542, as a necessary precaution, a statute was enacted by Henry VIII declaring that any malicious striking of blows within a royal palace which drew blood would be punishable not only by perpetual imprisonment and a fine, but also by severance of the right hand.

As to be expected, such an amputation would certainly not be the humdrum, everyday surgical operation that was carried out on ordinary criminals, requiring little more than the local hangman, a block of wood and a cleaver. In fact the statute defined the elaborate ritual that had to be adhered to with as much attention to detail as if it were a coronation.

After sentencing, the offender was brought in by the Knight-Marshal and met by the Sergeant of the King's Woodyard who carried a mallet, a large block of wood and some lengths of cord. The offender's right arm was then bound to the block in a suitable position. The King's Master Cook brought in the knife and gave it to the Yeoman of the Larder who positioned it on the wrist joint. The Yeoman of the Scullery had already arranged two benches on which the items of equipment were laid out, and he also tended a fire in which to heat the cauterising irons. Nearby stood a jug of water to quench the irons after use. The cautering, or searing, irons were brought in by the Sergeant Farrier, whose task it was to sear the veins and stump.

The Sergeant Surgeon, using the mallet and knife, performed the operation with the Groom of the Salcery standing by with vinegar and cold water in case the offender should faint. Then the Sergeant of the Poultry brought in a live cock and, using the amputation knife, beheaded the bird. After the offender's wound had been sealed with the hot irons, the body of the cock was wrapped round the injured limb.

The Sergeant of the Chandry and the Yeoman of the Ewry then came forward with basin, ewer and cloths for the surgeon's use, followed by refreshments for all, the offender included. The bread was provided by the Sergeant of the Pantry, and the Sergeant of the Cellar poured out wine, ale or beer as required. As will be seen, each of the thirteen officials had his own carefully delineated task, thereby avoiding any demarcation problems that might have arisen.

This particular penalty was suffered by Peter Bourchet of the Middle Temple in 1573. Bourchet, a religious fanatic, had convinced himself that it was lawful to kill anyone whose views on the Gospel differed from his own, and so he attacked Sir John Hawkins, whom he had mistaken for the Lord Chancellor, Sir Christopher Hatton. While Bourchet was imprisoned in the Tower of London, he seized a block of wood from the fireplace and struck his warder, Hugh Longworth, who was standing by the window with his back turned, killing him outright.

The processes of the law duly took their course, and Bourchet was tried at Westminster on 11 November. He was then taken to be executed at Temple Bar, the place of his assault on Sir John Hawkins. But because of the blows he had struck within the Tower (which incidentally is still a Royal Palace), his right hand was severed in accordance with the statute, and it was then nailed to the gibbet on which he was subsequently hanged.

Some offenders, however, were luckier than others. On 10 June 1541 Sir Edmund Knevet was arraigned before the Officers of the Green Cloth for striking Master Cleer of Norfolk in the tennis court of the King's House at Greenwich. (Doubtless a dispute over whether the ball was 'in' or 'out'!) Found guilty, he was sentenced to lose his right hand and to forfeit all his lands and goods. And so, when the fearsome ritual had been prepared, Sir William Pickering, Knight-Marshal, brought in the prisoner. Sir Edmund confessed his crime and humbly submitted himself to the King's mercy, but begged that his left hand be cut off instead, because 'if my right hand be spared, I may live to do the King good service.' Upon His Majesty being informed of this, he 'of his goodness, considering the gentle heart of the said Edmund, and the good reports of lords and ladies, granted him full pardon'.

Surprising as it may seem, this savage statute was not repealed until nearly 300 years later, in 1820, during the reign of George IV.

Not only hands were amputated, but ears also seemed to hold a peculiar fascination for the judiciary. Such was the puritanical disapproval of adultery during the reign of King Canute, that any man guilty of such immorality was exiled, and his partner was made for ever unattractive to men by having her nose and ears cut off.

Knives were still inflicting the same sort of mutilation five centuries later when, during the reign of Henry VIII, a statute was passed decreeing that 'any valiant beggar or sturdy vagabond shall at the first time be whipped and sent to the place where he was born or has been living for the past three years; and if he continues his roguish life, he shall have the upper part of the gristle of his right ear cut off; and if after that he be taken wandering in idleness, or doth not apply to his labour, he shall be adjudged, and executed as a felon'.

Sometimes the sentences were varied, as in the case of a fraudster who, in 1552, had his ears nailed to a post in Cheapside. After the prescribed time had elapsed, 'he woulde not rent his eare, so one of the bedles slitted yt upwards with a penkniffe to loose yt'.

Another miscreant, overheard speaking traitorously of Queen Jane, even had a musical accompaniment during his surgical operation, for while his ears were being removed, a trumpeter played and a herald recounted his misdeeds.

And for writing treasonable articles, a Dr Leighton was first whipped and pilloried, afterwards having his ears cut off, and both sides of his nose slit open. To complete the mutilation he was then branded on both cheeks.

Being an author was always a risky business, especially where members of the Royal Family were likely to be affronted. In 1632 William Prynne, barrister, Member of Parliament and talented author, wrote a book critical of the theatrical profession. As acting was a favourite pastime of the Queen, King Charles' wrath was unrestrained, much to the delight of Prynne's enemies. After his trial and a year's imprisonment, he was not only fined £5,000 but was also taken to Westminster, where one ear was amputated, thence to Cheapside where he was deprived of the other. As if that were not enough, his nose was then slit by the hangman.

Freed after further imprisonment, in 1637 Prynne wrote more insulting pamphlets, this time attacking the bishops. He was brought to trial before the Star Chamber again, where a member of the court ordered the usher to expose the prisoner's scars. Pushing back Prynne's flowing locks, the official did so, to reveal a stub of flesh still remaining on one side of his head. 'I had thought

70

Mr Prynne had no ears at all, but methinks he hath ears after all,' exclaimed one of his judges.

Fined a further £5,000 and sentenced to lose what was left of his ears, to be branded and then imprisoned for life, he was taken to Old Palace Yard at Westminster, together with one Henry Burton who was also to be mutilated.

The ordeal suffered by the latter gentleman was included in a 1734 account of remarkable trials, and described how Burton, 'when the hangman had cut off one ear, which he had cut deep and close to the head in an extraordinary cruel manner, never once moved and stirred for it. The other ear being cut no less deep, he was then freed from the pillory, and came down, where the surgeon waiting for him presently applied a remedy for stopping the blood after the large effusions thereof.'

After Burton's gory ordeal, it was William Prynne's turn. The public hangman, probably the appropriately named Gregory Brandon, branded 'SL' for Schismatic Libeller, one letter on each of Prynne's cheeks. Unfortunately, in the heat of the moment, he burned a letter in the wrong way round, so had to burn it in again, the attendant surgeon applying a plaster to relieve the pain. The executioner then proceeded to cut off the stub of ear that remained, making so clumsy a job of it that he also sliced off some of Prynne's cheek as well.

The MP was spared life imprisonment, however, for in 1660 he returned to royal favour. Charles II appointed him to be Keeper of the State Records at the Tower of London at a salary of £500 a year, a position where his literary talents could be harmlessly and usefully employed.

Commoners were not the only ones to suffer the loss of their ears. Sir Robert Strange threatened the life of the Duke of Buckingham in 1628 and was not only whipped from Fleet Street to Westminster, but also forfeited both ears and was branded on one cheek.

But ear removals really hit the headlines of the news sheets in June 1731. One of them, *Fog's Weekly Journal*, devoted many column inches to the trial of Sir Peter Stringer, alias Japhet Cook:

who was, some time since, convicted of forging deeds of conveyance of two thousand acres of land belonging to Mr

Garbet and his wife, lying in the parish of Claxton, in the County of Essex, and was brought by the keeper of the King's Bench to Charing Cross, where he stood in the pillory from twelve till one, pursuant to his sentence.

The time being nearly expired, he was set on an elbow chair in the middle of the platform, when the hangman John Hooper (known to the scaffold aficionados as 'Laughing Jack'), dressed like a butcher in a blue apron, came up behind him and, with a knife like a gardener's pruning knife, cut off his ears and held them up so that the mob could see them.

Having handed them to Mr Watson, the Sheriff's Officer, the hangman slit both nostrils with a pair of scissors; all of which Cook bore with great patience, but at the searing with hot irons of his right nostril, the pain was so violent that he got up from his chair. His left nostril was not seared, so he went from the platform bleeding.

It would seem that the now shorn criminal was little the worse for his ordeal, and he was allowed by his escort to have a doubtlessly much needed drink in the nearby Ship tavern, while basking in the congratulations of his cronies over his stoicism. Later he was taken to the King's Bench Prison in Southwark, there to complete his term of imprisonment.

A missing detail in all these reports, except in the case just quoted, is what happened to the severed portions, the 'off-cuts' so to speak. Were they all retained as evidence by the court, sold by the hangman to Surgeons' Hall for anatomical research or simply thrown away? Mystery surrounds their disposal, but the fate of one ear at least is known, for in 1738 the said organ was dramatically produced in the House of Commons by its owner, Robert Jenkins, from whom it had been separated some years earlier.

Master mariner Jenkins, captain of the sloop *Rebecca*, had been trading around Jamaica in 1731 when his ship was intercepted and boarded near Havana by Spanish coastguards. Despite denials of smuggling he was tortured on the orders of the Spanish captain Fandino. He was robbed of his money, 'four British guineas, one pistole and four double doubloons', and even the silver buckles from his shoes, and he was half-hanged from the foreyard of the mast.

Then, as he stated in his deposition to Parliament, his captor 'took hold of his left ear and slit it down with his cutlash, and another of the gang tore it off. He was then ordered to be scalped, but his head being already close shaved, prevented the execution of it.' This incident heightened the already smouldering political tension between the two countries, and resulted in the 'War of Jenkins' Ear' against Spain in 1739. The captain himself did not go entirely unrewarded, for he was subsequently appointed Governor of St Helena.

## Scottish Mutilations

In Scotland, the knife wielders were also in full cry, or rather their victims were. One of them, forger Andrew Drummond, was taken to Edinburgh's market cross in 1556 and had his right hand cut off and nailed to a post, before being banished for life, as was David Fethye for a similar offence in May 1558.

A more dramatic, if somewhat unintelligible, account from Nicholl's *Chronicles of Perth*, gives some idea of the savagery of the punishment:

> . . . last day of September 1652, twa Englisches, for drinking the Kingis helth, war takin and bund to the gallous at Edinburgh Croce, quhair ather of thame resavit threttie-nyne quhipes upon thair naiked bakes and shoulderis, thaireftir thair luggis were naillet to the gallous. The ane haid his lug cuttit from the ruitt with a refour, the other being also naillet to the gibbet haid his mouth skobit and his tong being drawn out the full lenth, was bund togidder betuix twa stickes leard togidder, with ane skainzie threid, the space of half an our or thairby.

Thirty-nine strokes of the whip on bare shoulders and backs; ears nailed to the gallows, one being severed at the root; tongue pulled out and tied between two sticks for half an hour or more – in any language, a very painful experience.

Another Scot, Lamont, wrote a more easily understood entry

in his diary for February 1650: 'Ther was sundrie persons in Edenbroughe that had their eares nayled to the Trone for bearing false witness, and one that had his tongue pearced with a hot iyron.'

And on 9 May 1729, 'a woman was whipt down the city, nailed to the Tron, then had a bit pinch'd out of her nose with a newly invented machine, and was after sent to the House of Correction for thieving, house breaking and other wicked practices'.

## Danish Mutilations

Not that criminals on the Continent fared much better. In the eighteenth century, State offenders in Denmark were, before their execution, allowed eight to fourteen days in which to ponder their fate, the time interval depending on the chaplain's decision. Their execution was also almost invariably preceded by the loss of their right hands.

## French Mutilations

In France, Louis XII, the 'Father of the People', decreed that anyone guilty of uttering eight or more blasphemies was to have his tongue torn out, and in January 1535 a Huguenot, Antoine Poile, had his tongue pierced and attached to his cheek with an iron pin. After that he was burned alive, while the King watched.

Not that French criminals weren't separated from their ears, of course. Laws passed in 1498 and 1534 authorised this form of punishment, known as *Essorillement*, whereby dishonest servants and thieves lost their left ear for a first offence, the other ear for a second misdemeanour, with death as the penalty for a third crime. Even worse than the loss of an ear, felons in medieval France had their feet amputated, the last instance occurring in the reign of Louis IX in the thirteenth century.

## German Mutilations

Together with other drastic punishments, mutilation figured high among the penalties awarded by German judges, and this is best exemplified by perusing a diary compiled by Franz Schmidt, public executioner of Nuremberg from 1573 to 1617.

In 1576 he beheaded murderer Hans Peyhel; 'two years ago I

cut off his ears and flogged him at Herzog Aurach', he recorded. More lopped ears fell, this time of the female variety, when in 1584 Schmidt had to deal with a prostitute Marie Kurschnerin. He had previously whipped her out of town for stealing, but further offences earned her the death penalty, but not before he had deprived her of her ears.

The entry for 19 April 1591 reported the crime of blasphemy against Andrew Brunner who, because a violent thunderstorm raged, called the Almighty an Old Rascal, saying that the noise was caused because He had gambled all his money away and was now trying to win it back by playing bowls. After standing in the pillory, a piece of his tongue was torn off by the executioner as a painful reminder.

Franz also dealt severely with Hans Rossner in February 1599. That gentleman, a known criminal, insulted the local parson, calling him a rogue and a thief, but his ability to make any further abusive signs was sorely limited when the court ordered Schmidt to sever two of his fingers.

Interestingly, some aspects of German criminal law permitted an affluent offender to keep his anatomy all in one piece. In 1577 Peter Kochl beat his father so severely that he was sentenced to have his right hand amputated but, as Schmidt recorded, 'he bought the hand off with a hundred florins'.

## Mutilation in the Middle East

Further afield, in the Middle East, the art of the knife was, and is, part of the judicial system. In Egypt, adultery was punished by mutilation. The offending woman would have her nose cut off. In his *History of Women*, published in 1779, Alexander wrote: 'The chastity of virgins (in Egypt) is protected by a law of the severest nature. He who commits a rape on a free woman has his privities cut off, that it might be out of his power ever to perpetrate the like crime, and that others might be terrified by so dreadful a punishment.'

The Assyrians treated their prisoners of war with unimaginable cruelty, severing their ears and noses, hands and feet, among other torments, as did the Turks in the sixteenth century. On invading Austria, according to Grafton's *Chronicles*, they 'committed such crueltie and tyranny, as never hath bene heard nor written, for of some they put out the eyes, of others they cut off the noses and eares, of others they cut off the privie members, of women they cut off the pappes, and ravished virgins, and of women great with child, they cut their bellies and burnt the children'.

## The Pendulum

A major part of any punishment must be the anticipation of it, when the imagination is given full rein as to the reality of its application. The interval between the sentencing and the penalty itself being put into effect, whether that of losing one's ear or one's head, must be perhaps the most devastating part of the punishment. So possibly the worst torture in that respect was the one invented by the Spanish Inquisition, known as the *Pendola*, and to us as the Pendulum.

This sanity-destroying device consisted of a large pendulum suspended high in the roof of the torture chamber, the bob being replaced by a crescent-shaped blade about twelve inches from horn to horn, and honed razor-sharp. The victim would then be tied down on a bench at right angles to the path of the blade, so that its arc traversed the region of the victim's heart. The pendulum would then be set in motion.

Hypnotised by its rhythmic movement, the victim would not at first realise the full horror of the torture until it became apparent that with each relentless swing, the pendulum blade was almost imperceptibly descending. Mere words can hardly describe the victim's frenzied reactions as the minutes dragged by and the fiendish blade swished nearer and nearer to his palpitating flesh. Suffice it to say that those incredible souls who still refused to recant their heretical beliefs either went out of their minds or died the most hideous death imaginable.

## Spiked Torture in Germany

Not that tortuous ingenuity was the sole prerogative of the Spanish. The Germans were just as adept. If their victim was not sharp enough with his answers, the Teutonic torturers had devices sharp enough to encourage him.

One of them was the *Fass*, a large, iron, bath-sized cradle with spikes protruding from its inner surface. The victim, stripped to the waist and tightly bound, would be lowered into it and then the *Fass* would be violently rocked from side to side, the spikes inflicting countless flesh wounds in a short space of time.

If the torturers' efforts proved unavailing, the victim might well be placed in the German Chair. This piece of furniture was solidly built and secured to the floor so that the victim, in his struggles, could not overbalance – a natural tendency in view of the fact that the chair's seat, back and arms were studded with hundreds of small barbs or spikes, sharp enough to pierce the flesh at the slightest movement.

Once tied in the German Chair, the victim would then be further weighted by a heavy iron collar locked about his neck and boulders piled on his knees, until the pain of the multiple lacerations proved unbearable.

If pressing the victim down on to spikes did not bring about the required results, the Spiked Hare was resorted to, for this device, in contrast, pressed the spikes on to the victim. Simple in construction and operation, it resembled a giant-sized rolling pin covered with sharp spikes and, with the victim in the role of unwilling pastry, a confession was soon extracted.

## The Picquet

In the days when the British Army stationed at the outposts of the Empire lived almost entirely in tented camps, spiked tent pegs provided an elementary but effective form of punishment which, in its final form, took the name of the Picquet or Picket.

First, a long post was driven into the ground, then the recalcitrant soldier would be made to stand on a stool next to it, his right hand secured to a hook at the top of the post. A short length of timber resembling a tent peg would be driven into the ground near the stool, its upper end rounded to a blunt point. The stool would then be removed, the soldier having to rest one heel on the spike. Suspended as he was by one wrist, and with his weight pressing the spike into his bare heel, the most unruly private quickly learnt the error of his ways, especially when, after fifteen minutes, the position would be reversed, his other wrist and heel being subjected to the same agonising treatment.

## The Picquet in Trinidad

The only recorded instance of this torture being applied in non-military circumstances was one which led to the trial in court of Sir Thomas Picton, Governor and Commander-in-Chief of the Caribbean island of Trinidad.

After the defeat of the Spanish, French and Dutch fleets in 1797, Trinidad was surrendered to the English. In accordance with general practice, it was agreed that the inhabitants could retain the framework of justice which had existed under their previous rulers, the Spanish.

In 1801 a young girl, Luisa Calderon, was accused of theft and although she denied it, the Governor of the island, General Picton, ordered her to be tortured until she admitted the crime. She was therefore subjected to a variation of the Picquet, in that her big toe was balanced on a sharp spike of wood and her opposite wrist tied above her head, the rope passing over a pulley. In addition to that, however, her other hand and foot were tied together.

She endured that ordeal for three-quarters of an hour on the first day and for twenty-two minutes on the day following, her positions being reversed. Each time she fainted before being released, and her wrists and ankles remained swollen during the eight months imprisonment which followed.

When, in 1804, news reached London that torture was being officially sanctioned in a British possession, the horrified authorities took action, and General Picton was recalled and put on trial. In court, legal argument was complex and drawn out, for while torture was against English law, Trinidad had been allowed to continue under Spanish law, which did countenance torture in some circumstances.

The legal proceedings dragged on for some five years or more, and in fact were never brought to a final conclusion. In 1809 General Picton went with his brigade to Holland and later to Portugal, distinguishing himself on the battlefield against Napoleon's armies. On his return to England he became a Member of Parliament for Pembroke and was appointed a Knight of the Order of the Bath. Unwilling to settle down to a quiet life, he returned to the war, and was killed at the Battle of Waterloo, winning the accolade of the Duke of Wellington who, in his despatches, praised him for 'gloriously leading his division to a charge of bayonets, by which one of the most serious attacks made by the enemy on our position was defeated'.

A monument to the memory of Sir Thomas Picton was erected in St Paul's Cathedral, London. No one ever said what became of Luisa Calderon, though.

## Spiked Effigies in Sparta

The daughters of the Duke of Exeter and Sir Leonard Skeffington, the Rack and the Gyves, were described in Chapter 3. But there were other *femmes* who were even more *fatale*.

Take for instance Apega, or rather a model of her, constructed on the orders of her husband, Nabis of Sparta. A cruel tyrant, he ensured complete obedience from his subjects by saying, 'If you cannot agree with me, perhaps my Apega can persuade you.' At that, a life-sized automaton would be revealed, resembling a woman clad in voluminous robes. The unsuspecting victim would then be led forward, only to be clasped so tightly by the figure that the sharp spikes hidden in the folds of the robes would impale him.

It is psychologically interesting to note that the male inventors of such instruments of torture gave them female identities. Whether this was from a sense of guilt, a desire to throw all the blame of the suffering to come on to women in general, or just from a warped sense of humour, is hard to say. It could have been that some small solace was achieved by the victims, expiring as they did in the embrace of a woman, albeit a mechanical replica, rather than at the end of an impersonal rope or asexual axe. Be that as it may, instruments of torture endowed with female names were much in use on the Continent.

## Spiked Effigies in Germany

There was no point in claiming to be a misogynist as one was dragged towards the Virgin of Baden-Baden. Ordered to kiss the figure, the trap-door at her feet would suddenly open up, plunging one down on to the spiked wheel rotating below.

Nuremberg too had its *Eiserne Mädchen*, its Iron Maiden or, as it was sometimes known, Virgin Mary. Described in *Archaeologia* of 1838 as a figure constructed of sheet iron on a wooden

79

framework, it had two folding doors at the front. From the inside of one door protruded thirteen quadrangular poinards, the other door had eight. Two more at face-level were clearly intended to pierce the eyes of the unwilling occupant, its design indicating that the victim would have been forced in backwards so that the daggers could do their deadly work.

One legend states that after some time had elapsed, an internal trap-door would open, plunging the mutilated body into a stream flowing beneath the *Falterkammer*, the torture chamber. However Dr Mayer, the nineteenth-century archivist of Nuremberg, believed that the victim's body dropped on to an iron rack which, by activating a pair of counterweights, caused a series of curved blades to interlock scissor-fashion, and so shred the cadaver. The mangled remains would then fall into the stream.

## Spiked Effigies in Spain

A very similar 'lady-like' device was used during the Spanish Inquisition, a detailed description appearing in *The Percy Anecdotes*, 1820–23:

> On the entry of the French into Toledo, during the Peninsular War, General Lasalle visited the Palace of the Inquisition. The great number of the instruments of torture, especially the instruments to stretch the limbs, the drop baths which caused a lingering death, excited horror even in the minds of soldiers hardened in the field of battle. One of these instruments, singular in its kind for refined torture, and disgraceful to reason and religion in the choice of its object, deserved a particular description.
>
> In a subterranean vault adjoining the secret audience chamber, stood in a recess in the wall a wooden statue made by the hands of monks, representing the Virgin Mary. A gilded glory (halo) beamed round her head, and she held a banner in her right hand. It immediately struck the spectator, notwithstanding the ample folds of the silken garment which fell from the shoulders on both sides, that she wore a breastplate. Upon closer examination it appeared that the whole front of the body was covered with extremely sharp

nails, and small daggers or blades of knives with the points projecting outwards.

The arms and hands had joints, and their motion was directed by machinery placed behind the partition. One of the servants of the Inquisition who was present was ordered by the general to make the machine manoeuvre, as he expressed it. As the statue extended its arms and gradually drew them back, as if she would affectionately embrace and press someone to her heart, the well-filled knapsack of a Polish grenadier supplied for this purpose took the place of the poor victim.

The statue pressed it closer and closer, and when, at the command of the general, the director of the machinery made it open its arms and return to its first position, the knapsack was pierced two or three inches deep, and remained hanging upon the nails and daggers of the murderous instrument.

# 6
## All Fingers and Thumbs

Just as Newton is said to have discovered gravity when an apple fell on his head, so it is not beyond the bounds of possibility that thumbscrews were invented by an early torturer who happened to trap his fingers in a door.

In their original form they resembled primitive nutcrackers, but soon evolved into a deadly piece of engineering. Similar to a diminutive ox yoke, the device consisted of two short iron bars of equal length, one having three small rods designed to fit into three matching holes in the other bar. The victim's thumbs or fingers were inserted between the bars on each side of the central rod, which had a screw thread on it. Once positioned over the quick of the nails, the wing nut on the central rod was tightened, forcing the upper bar downwards and so applying the requisite amount of pressure on the victim's nails.

Thumbscrews, or Thumbekins, were referred to in an official Scottish document dated 1684: 'Whereas now there is a new inventione and Ingyne called thumbekins, it is ordained that when any persone shall be put to torture, then the said thumbekins or bootes or both shall be applyed to them.'

Some sources attribute their introduction into Scotland to that extraordinary character Thomas Dalyell, the 'Muscovy General', who had once been a prisoner in the Tower of London. Escaping from the stronghold in 1652, he reached Russia and became a general in that country's army. He instilled strict discipline into the Russian soldiery, leading them into battle against the Poles and the Turks.

A devoted Royalist, he vowed never to shave off his beard following the execution of Charles I, and on the Restoration of the Monarchy in 1660 he returned to Scotland and became Commander-in-Chief, bringing, it is said, some Russian thumbscrews with him.

However the devices had been mentioned in earlier records under a variety of names, 'pyrowykes' in 1397, and as 'pyrewinkes' in 1401. Others were 'pilnewinks' and 'penny-winkis', but although the names may have sounded comical, their effect certainly was not.

Thumbscrews were sometimes used as a means of restraint, tightened just enough to control rather than torture, and were as effective as were handcuffs. John Howard, when inspecting Lavenham Gaol, Suffolk, reported that the magistrates had sent the keeper a number of thumbscrews with which to secure the prisoners. A useful attachment was a chain, enabling the warders to lead the prisoners around as necessary.

When used for persuasive purposes, a violent jerk on the chain would emphasise each question asked, any hesitation being overcome by slowly tightening the wing nut and so causing excruciating agony. Between interrogations the victim could be 'parked' by hooking the chain over a staple set high in the dungeon wall until the next session.

One man who suffered this torture was William Carstares, a Scottish minister who, in 1683, was accused of involvement in a conspiracy to assassinate Charles II and his brother James so that a Protestant monarch could rule the country. The plan was to ambush the royal pair as they were returning from Newmarket races, and the conspiracy was known as the Rye House Plot because the attack was planned to take place close to Rye House Farm, near Hoddesden in Hertfordshire, which lay on the King's route. The intention was to block the road with a cart, then open fire from behind the hedges while others charged their intended victims, but idle talk betrayed the plot and among those implicated was William Carstares.

So vital was it to discover the names of the conspirators that the Privy Council of Scotland passed an 'Act anent Mr William Carstares' Torture', and the report on the interrogation as written by Bishop Burnet in his *History of his Own Time* stated:

The Council called for one of the Bailies of Edinburgh, and

the executioner with the engines of torture being present, the lord chancellor commanded the bailie to cause the executioner to put him in the torture by applying the thumbscrew on him, which being done, and he having for the space of an hour continued in the agony of torture, the screw being space and space stretched until he appeared near to faint; and they drew him so hard that as they put him to extreme torture, so that they could not unscrew them, till the smith that had made them was brought with his tools to take them off.

And Carstares himself later described how the King's blacksmith had produced a new instrument called the Thumbikins, that had never been used before, and that he had endured the torment for more than an hour and a half.

Among the heads that subsequently rolled was not only that of Algernon Sidney, son of the Earl of Leicester, but also of Lord William Russell, who suffered three or four blows by Jack Ketch's axe before succumbing. Some conspirators escaped to the Continent, others were released for lack of evidence, among the latter being Carstares, although he was imprisoned for a year and a half. On his release he went to Holland and became chaplain to William, the Protestant Prince of Orange, his ambitions being realised when, in 1689, James II fled abroad and the Prince of Orange became King William III of England.

Whether Carstares was subsequently presented with the actual thumbscrews previously used on him or not, somehow they found their way back into his possession, and at Court he demonstrated them to the King. His Majesty tentatively tried them on and admitted with a shudder that the slightest pressure would have made *him* confess to anything, without hesitation.

Shortly after the Rye House Plot one William Spence had also been subjected to the thumbscrews, in addition to other tortures. He had been a servant of the Earl of Argyle, who was suspected of conspiring with others against Charles II, and although Spence was offered a pardon if he would confess, he persisted in his obduracy.

After having been deprived of sleep for five nights, and tortured in the dreaded boots, he was handed over to General Dalyell, who promptly produced the thumbscrews. 'Little screws of steel were made use of, that screwed the thumbs with that exquisite torture, that he sunk under this, for he was told that they would screw every joint of his whole body, one after another, till he confessed,' according to Bishop Burnet. The confession came, names and places spilling out, and Spence and his masters duly paid the price of their conspiracy and treason.

In 1690 William III, having previously experienced the efficiency of the thumbscrews at first hand – both hands, to be precise – did not hesitate to order their application to the thumbs of the appropriately named Henry Neville Payne, saying in a letter to his Privy Council,

> Whereas we have full assurance upon undeniable evidence of a horrid plott and conspiracy against our government, and the whole settlement of that our ancient kingdom, for introducing the authoritie of the late King James and Popery in these kingdoms, and setting up an intire new forme of government, whereof there has been several contrivers and managers, and Nevil Pain, now prisoner in our Castle of Edinburgh, hath lykwayes been an instrument in that conspiracie, wee doe require you to examine Nevil Pain strictly; and in case he prove obstinate or disengenious do you procees against him to torture, with all the rigour that the law allows in such cases; and not doubting your ready and vigorous applications for the furder discovery of what so much concerns the public safety, we bid you heartily farewell.

Despite the appalling torture, during which it was reported that he endured two days in the thumbscrews and was later subjected to the boots, it seems that Payne resisted all attempts to extract information, and he was eventually sentenced to ten years' imprisonment.

## Continental Thumbscrews

Of course, the English, the Scots and Russians were not the only ones to have sensitive thumb nails. The Germans elaborated on the standard pattern thumbscrews, modifying them to incorporate spikes which when tightened bored their way into the victim's nails. And in Normandy the torture was phased, the 'ordinary'

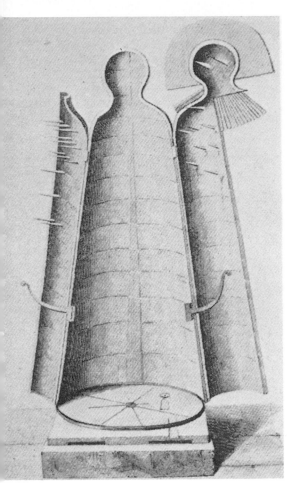
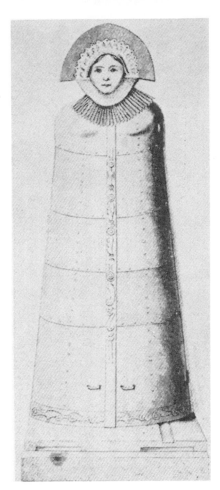

The Iron Maiden or 'Virgin Mary'

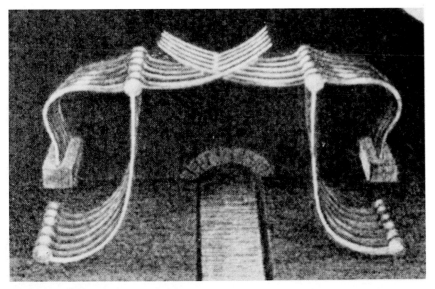

The iron rack in the chamber beneath the 'Virgin Mary'. What was left of the victim's body was shredded between the weighted, curved blades

The Whirligig. A session in this cylindrical caage, which spun round at high speed, left the victim disorientated, dizzy and very sick

A few hours with his head in the jougs, attached by a chain to the church porch or market cross, helped many an offender to see the error of his ways

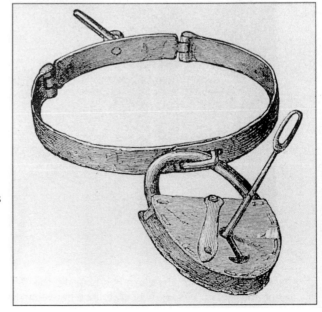

Prisoners at work on the treadwheel and others exercising in the third yard of the vagrants' prison, Coldbath Fields

The Scavenger's Daughter, also known as Skeffington's Gyves

The finger pillory in the parish church at Ashby de la Zouch, Leicestershire, England

The ducking stool sent cold shivers down the spines of nagging wives, shrews, harlots and dishonest tradesmen

Riding the stang

Branding a deserter with the letter D

This brass instrument, used for branding deserters, came into use in the British Army in approximately 1840

A chain has been passed through the hole which has been burned through this disgraced Chinese monk's neck. Another monk follows him through the streets with a whip

treatment consisting of one thumb being compressed, the 'extra-ordinary' treatment bringing pressure to bear on both thumbs.

### Chinese Thumbscrews

The Chinese *Tean Zu* utilised homegrown materials. Lengths of bamboo were splinted around each finger, then bound tightly together. A larger version, *Kia Quen*, comprised three pieces of wood on crossbars, between which the victim's feet were inserted. When they were tightened down in the same way as thumbscrews, the feet were squeezed 'till the heel-bone ran into the foot'. Generally the latter torture was restricted to men, females being subjected to the *Tean Zu*.

### Indian Thumbscrews

India also favoured the bamboo type of thumbscrew in which the fingers were bound together. Hesitation by the victim was overcome by hammering bamboo splints in between his bound fingers. That country also had a larger version, called *Kittee*. Resembling a domestic lemon squeezer, it could be applied with devastating effect not only on hands and feet, but also to a victim's nose and ears, genitalia and breasts.

## *Thumbs Tied Together*

There was of course a much easier way of restraining or torturing a person than by the thumbscrews or pieces of bamboo, and that was simply by tying the victim's thumbs tightly together with a length of whipcord.

This was used as an alternative to peine forte et dure (being pressed beneath weights), used to persuade an accused person to plead guilty or not guilty, and even to coerce a reluctant witness to be more forthcoming with evidence.

At the Newgate Assizes in 1663 it was recorded that 'George Thorely, being indicted for Robbery, refused to plead, and his two Thumbs were tyed together with Whipcord, that the pain of that might compel him to Plead, and he was sent away so tied, and a minister perswaded to go to him and to perswade him; And an Hour after he was brought again and pleaded. And this was said to be the constant practice at Newgate.'

Women too suffered in the same way. In 1721 Mary Andrews

refused to plead, and the hangman, whose duty it was, tightened the cord so much that it snapped. Still obdurate, Mary endured a further three attempts before capitulating.

At times tragi-comedy entered the proceedings as when, in 1734, a deaf and illiterate man, John Durant, stood in the dock. When asked how he pleaded, he made no reply. The judge angrily warned him, threatening to have him pressed, and as an intermediate measure ordered the executioner to tie the prisoner's thumbs together. This was done and, doubtlessly utterly bewildered and in considerable pain, Durant protested vociferously that he was deaf and had been for many years.

Undeterred by the fact that the man could possibly have been speaking the truth, the executioner continued to tighten the whipcord, until the judge eventually told him to desist, and went on to warn the accused again of the dire fate that awaited him.

Durant was returned to the cells and, upon having the situation explained to him by a more sympathetically inclined person, later pleaded not guilty to the charge.

Early in the eighteenth century it became the practice for the executioner to tie the prisoner's thumbs together in order to indicate to the watching public that the sentence of death by hanging had been passed on the felon. This was equivalent to the much older custom in which, where beheading was the penalty, the edge of the axe was turned towards the condemned man during the journey back to the Tower.

This latter tradition still pertains, albeit with less sinister implications, at naval courts martial, when a verdict of guilty is indicated by placing a sword so that its point is directed towards the accused sailor.

The custom of the hangman tying the condemned man's thumbs together was unexpectedly reversed when, in 1718, it was the hangman's thumbs which were secured in that painful manner! The crime which gave rise to that unusual occurrence was the murder committed by none other than the reviled and despised public hangman, John Price.

Price, a brutal and coarse man, spent much of his off-scaffold time in taverns, and some months in prison for debt. And while on a drunken spree near Upper Moorfields in London, he attacked Elizabeth White, an old woman who sold nuts, apples and gingerbread from a stall.

So badly was she injured, her arm broken and blinded in one eye, that she died four days later, and the murderer was tried at the Old Bailey. John Price was found guilty, and his thumbs were promptly tied together by the new executioner, Banks.

While Price languished in the condemned cell, a previous executioner, ex-blacksmith William Marvell, was employed to make a 'suit of irons' – a close-fitting cage of metal strips – for the condemned man, and after John Price had been hanged, his corpse was inserted in its cage, to swing from the gibbet until the bones rotted away.

Tying a criminal's thumbs together had other uses, of course. The cord could be twisted, tourniquet-fashion, to expedite a confession, and could also be used, as were thumbscrews, to secure his bonds to a hook set high in the wall, so that his full weight was taken by his thumbs. A similar punishment in the Royal Navy involved piling muskets on the erring sailor's shoulders, the number of muskets depending on the severity of his crime.

In the New World, Sing Sing Prison adopted the idea, records showing that during 1874, seventy-two convicts were disciplined by being strung up in this way in darkened cells and left standing with their toes barely touching the floor.

## The Arrow

Apart from these standard tortures, there was always scope for the more imaginative official to invent his own device. This certainly seems to have been the case when a deacon of the Protestant faith, Cuthbert Sympson, was arrested in 1557. At that time during the reign of Bloody Mary, Edmund Bonner, Bishop of London, was taking an active part in the persecution of Protestants. Sympson was a popular and energetic preacher who always attracted large congregations; if he could be forced to divulge the names of his flock, the Bishop had ways of dealing with such heretics.

The Lieutenant of the Tower, Sir Richard Blount, firmly believing that old favourites are best, proceeded to marry the deacon to the Duke of Exeter's Daughter – the rack. Despite three hours of appalling pain, Sympson refused to submit. Sir Richard, while doubtless impressed by the man's fortitude, was determined to carry out Bonner's orders, and forthwith devised a torture known as the Arrow. Sympson's forefingers were bound tightly together and a barbed arrow was pulled rapidly backwards and forwards between them until the flesh tore away and the arrow snapped.

Still Sympson proved obstinate and, at the failure of the arrow, the Lieutenant subjected him to the crushing embrace of the Scavenger's Daughter, thereby doubtless making him eligible for inclusion in the Tudor equivalent to the *Guinness Book of Records*, by having been stretched on the rack and compressed in the Gyves!

Little is known of Sympson's fate. The fact that Bishop Bonner personally questioned him later implies that the brave deacon kept the names of his flock to himself. It is known that Bonner placed the Pope's curse on Sympson, but he also conceded that the deacon had been the most patient sufferer of all who had come before him.

The fate of Sympson's inquisitors is, however, well known. Sir Richard Blount, the Lieutenant, died in 1564, and is commemorated by a kneeling effigy in armour in the superb alabaster and marble monument erected to his memory in the Chapel Royal of St Peter ad Vincula in the Tower. Bishop Bonner, secure as only a Catholic bishop could be in Queen Mary's reign, fell from grace when Protestant Elizabeth came to the throne. He was deprived of his bishopric in 1559, and died ten years later, a prisoner in London's Marshalsea prison.

## Needles under Nails

Fingers are obviously vulnerable to barbed arrows. Fingernails are even more sensitive to needles inserted under them. This was the torture which the Catholic priest Alexander Bryant was subjected to in March 1581.

Previously having been so starved that he had had to eat the clay from the walls of his cell, as related in an earlier chapter, he was racked and then endured the agony of having needles forced under his fingernails.

On 1 December 1581 he was hanged, disembowelled and quartered at Tyburn. Nearly 400 years later, on 25 October 1971, Alexander Bryant was canonised, a martyr to the cause.

The needle torture was also employed in Russia during the 1917 Revolution. In a report submitted to the British War Office, General Knox stated that 'At Blagoveschensk officers and soldiers from Torbolof's detachment were found with gramophone needles thrust under their finger nails, their eyes torn out, and the marks of nails on their shoulders where shoulder straps had been worn.'

## Finger Pillory

While not exactly a judicial punishment, mention must be made of the Finger Pillory, a restraining device which utilised the fact that, if one's finger is secured while bent at the second joint as if in an L-shaped tube, it is impossible to withdraw it until released.

A more detailed description of the finger pillory installed in the parish church at Ashby de la Zouch in Leicestershire appeared in *Notes and Queries* of 25 October 1851. The device consisted of two lengths of oak, each three feet eight inches long, four and a half inches wide and two and a half inches deep, hinged together at one end, the lower board being attached horizontally to the wall.

In the lower board were a number of hollows varying in size, and at the inner end of each hollow a vertical hole had been drilled downwards. Corresponding hollows had been shaped in the upper board, matching those below when the boards were closed. The culprit's fingers were then placed in the hollows of the lower board and the ends of his or her fingers were inserted into the holes up to the second joint. The upper board was then lowered and padlocked into position, trapping the immovable fingers between the two boards.

Many churches used finger pillories to punish those who had caused disturbances during church services, and they must have been extremely effective. Other models were more portable, the device being mounted on a heavy wooden pedestal about three feet high. Rich carving and decoration made it a handsome piece of furniture, though disobedient children or servants would hardly agree!

Wealthy families also found a use for them. The *History of*

*Staffordshire* published in 1686 related that in Beaudesart Hall was 'a piece of art made for the punishment of disorders that sometimes attend feasting in Christmas time etc, called the finger stocks, into which the fingers of all such persons as committed misdemeanours were put, servants and others of promiscuous quality, the device being divided in the same manner as the stocks for the legs, and having holes of different size to fit scantlings of all fingers'. And in an account of the fifteenth-century customs of an Ashton-under-Lyne manor house, it is reported that there were frequently introduced a diminutive pair of stone stocks of about eighteen inches in length, for confining within them the fingers of the unruly.

# 7

# Burning to Answer

The strongest person is susceptible to heat, and so it was employed as a test of guilt or innocence by the Anglo-Saxons. Ordeal by fire was almost a religious ceremony, and was based on the theory that if a person was innocent, God would not allow him or her to be injured.

Accordingly, before undergoing the ordeal, the accused had to be cleansed spiritually by attending church services on three successive days, eat nothing other than onions and salt, and drink only water.

At the trial, he had to take a red-hot bar of iron weighing about three pounds from a brazier and walk three steps before dropping it. A priest then bandaged the wound with a linen cloth, and this was left in place for three days. If at the end of that time the wound had healed, the accused was declared not guilty, but 'a blister half as large as a walnut' sufficed to prove the person guilty.

A variation consisted of having to step on nine red-hot bars of iron, bare-foot, while blindfolded, and the same test of healing was applied afterwards.

Such ordeals were used into the thirteenth century, one of the last cases being that of a suspected sorcerer, Gideon, who, after trial 'by the judgement of iron', was acquitted.

## The Ordeal in France

In medieval France, the practice was widespread. As in England, it consisted of holding or walking on heated irons, even noblemen and priests having to submit to it.

After fasting for three days the accused attended Mass, and

was led to the part of the church where the ordeal was to take place. There he took the iron, which had been more or less heated according to the gravity of the crime, he raised it two or three times, or carried it whatever distance had been specified by the sentence. Then his hand was thrust into a bag, which was sealed for three days, after which, if it showed no sign of scarring, he was declared innocent.

An alternative, even more unbearable method, was to make the accused put on a red-hot gauntlet or, if having to tread on hot irons, twelve bars would be substituted for the usual total of nine.

The emphasis in both countries on the number of multiples of three, as applied to the days of worship, the number of steps carrying or walking on the bars, and the number of bars involved, was obviously of great significance, and probably associated with the Holy Trinity.

By the thirteenth century, however, France too came to the conclusion that the Almighty did not work miracles in order to prove the innocence of accused men and women, and so such ordeals were abandoned.

## Branding

To be a man of letters generally indicates one to be a person of much integrity and rectitude. But when the letters are not printed after one's name, but are branded with a red-hot iron upon one's cheeks or hands, the very reverse is indicated.

Branding, from the Teutonic word *brinnan*, to burn, was first used by the Anglo-Saxons and continued until the nineteenth century. Even the Romans had a word for it, or rather a letter, recaptured slaves being branded with the letter 'F' for *Fugitivus*.

The instrument itself generally consisted of a long iron bolt with a wooden handle at one end and a raised letter on the other. An excellent example has survived in Lancaster Castle and was frequently used in the law court there. After sentencing the prisoner had his left hand secured in the 'holdfast', two iron grips attached to the wall of the dock. The heated iron was then pressed against 'the brawne of the thumbe' – the fleshy base of the thumb – and the hangman, after inspecting his handiwork, would call loudly to the judge, 'A fair mark, my Lord!'

That particular iron was used until 1811, although as recently as 1826 prisoners at the bar were required to hold up their hands so that any previous convictions would be evident.

The branding iron letters varied according to the crime committed. For instance, the Statute 1st Edw VI, in 1548, enacted

> that every person not disabled, aged or sick, found loitering or wandering, and not seeking work, or leaving it when engaged, shall be a vagabond; and every such person, on being apprehended by his master, and convicted before two justices, shall be marked, by means of a hot iron, with the letter 'V', and be compelled to serve his master two years.
>
> During that period his master would have to provide bread, water and small drink, and poor meat, and cause him to work by beating, chaining or otherwise. If he absented himself for fourteen days or more during his two years servitude, he shall be again marked, in like manner, with the letter 'S' for slave, and be his master's slave for ever. A third offence would be punishable by death.

These particular penalties were not abolished until 1636.

That there were many crimes on the early statute books is evidenced by the number of different letters available to judges. Thieving was extremely prevalent, so the letter 'T' branding irons rarely had the chance to cool down, and by an Act of 1698, concealment of one's criminal record by keeping one's hands in one's pockets was rendered futile, for those guilty of petty theft and larceny were to be burned in the most visible part of the left cheek, nearest to the nose, the burning to be done in the court in the presence of the judge.

Luttrell, the annalist and bibliographer, records that at the sessions following the Act, two men were burned in the cheek, and at the next session eighteen were so branded. But, he said, 'the innovation did not prove successful, for the said offenders threatened retaliation, saying that whatever house they break into, they will mark the persons within, on the cheek, to prevent distinction!'

The prospect of having the general public, whether innocent or guilty, all branded on the cheek, was too much for the government to contemplate, and in 1706 the provision was repealed, and burning in the hand was reinstated.

Coin clippers were punishable by a heavy fine plus branding, and those holding extreme religious views not only had to sport the letter 'B' for blasphemer on the forehead, but because it was their tongue that had uttered the blasphemous words, that too was punished by being pierced with a red-hot skewer.

Publishers of seditious libels were branded 'SL', and those who sowed sedition had 'SS' burned into their cheeks (usually one letter on each side of the nose).

This latter brand was employed in 1628 when Alexander Leighton, a Scottish preacher, was charged with 'framing, publishing and dispersing a scandalous book directed against his King, peers and prelates'. In court he was told that he had narrowly escaped being charged with treason, and he was sentenced to be fined £10,000, to be pilloried at Westminster, there to be whipped, to have one ear cut off, his nose slit, and his face branded with 'SS'.

A week later he was to be whipped again, this time at the pillory at Cheapside, to lose his other ear, and then to be gaoled for ever.

Having been degraded from his ecclesiastical office, he appeared at the pillory and declared, 'All the arguments brought against me are fines, whips, knives, brands and prison.' Later, scarred and mutilated, he was taken away to serve his sentence, but surprisingly he gained his freedom, and became Keeper of Lambeth House.

An ear was also forfeited by anyone using weapons to fight in church. A repeat of such sacrilege cost the offender the loss of the other ear, plus the letter 'F' for fraymaker branded on the cheek. Malefactors, man slayers, got a letter 'M' on their thumb, a second offence bringing a sentence of death. Rogues got the letter 'R' burned into the hand, and the foreheads of perjurers were decorated with the letter 'P'. Interestingly, in the reign of Henry II, heretics were branded on the face, not with a letter, but with the mark of a key.

Regrettably, women were not exempt from such disfigurement. A Statue passed by James I in 1624 declared

96

by reason whereof many women do suffer death for small causes; be it enacted by the authority of this present Parliament, that any woman being lawfully convicted by her confession, or by the verdict of twelve men of, or for the felonious taking of any money, goods, or chattels above the value of twelve pence, and under the value of ten shillings; or as accessory to any such offence; the said offence not being burglary, nor robbery in or near the highway, nor the felonious taking of any money, goods or chattels, from the person of any man or woman without his or her knowledge shall, for the first offence, be branded and marked in the hand, upon the brawn of the thumb, with a hot burning iron, having a roman 'T' upon the said iron; the said mark to be made by the gaoler openly in the Court, before the Judge; and also to be further punished by imprisonment, whipping, stocking, or sending to the house of correction for so long (not exceeding the space of one whole year) as the judge before whom she shall be convicted shall in his discretion think meet, according to the quality of the offence.

Among those who suffered was Lydia Adler who, no longer able to tolerate her brutal husband, killed him in June 1744. Because her neighbours testified in her favour, she was found guilty only of manslaughter and was 'burnt in the hand'.

Another woman, Sarah Swarton, was accused in 1619 of uttering slanderous statements against Lady Exeter. She was sentenced to be whipped through the streets, branded 'FA' as a false accuser, and imprisoned for life. And in Scotland, poor Janet Robertson, prone to profanity was, on 22 October 1648, 'cartit and scourged through the town, and markit with a hot iron, and banished from the paroche'.

A rather strange alternative, amounting to a symbolic punishment, was devised in the eighteenth century. A tourist, Zacharias von Uffenbach, visited the Old Bailey sessions in 1710 and after protesting at having to pay an admission fee of one shilling for a seat, went on to describe the scene:

First some twenty men and females were convicted of theft

and other petty crimes and condemned to be branded either with a red-hot or cold iron. This is not done, as in other countries, on the forehead or the back, but on the ball of the right-hand thumb. Here the letter 'T' is branded, signifying Thief. In cases of petty crime they are only touched with a cold iron as a warning, and to put them to shame.

It is most diverting to observe how some do not heed because of their terror whether the executioner is taking the iron out of the fire or from the ground, and accordingly set up a great screaming. But when they perceive that the iron is not hot they become silent all in a moment; this is most often the case with the females.

And in 1726, prisoners who could demonstrate their ability to 'read like a clerk' were not treated as common criminals, but had the right to be cold-ironed. On payment of 13½ pence, the branding iron was plunged into cold water before being pressed against their palms.

## Military Branding

Although branding ceased to be a penalty in civilian courts after 1829, the military insistence on absolute discipline demanded its retention after that date. Just as their civilian counterparts had their tongues mutilated for blasphemy, so did the soldiers. A private of Colonel Okey's Regiment was sentenced to having his tongue bored through with a red-hot iron, in July 1750, for uttering blasphemous words, 'he being at the time in a ranting humour with drinking too much'. Even officers were liable to such penalties, and this was not removed from Army Regulations until 1710.

The method of branding, however, was very different to that endured by civilians. Not for the soldier the searing heat, the smell of scorched flesh. Instead he was tattooed, the commodities so abundant in the Army, namely ink and gunpowder, being used.

The fact that the tattooing was almost painless was not a humanitarian decision on the part of the Army Council, for the stigma lay in the disgrace of the punishment. In keeping with the precepts of the Service, in which ceremony is its very life-blood, branding had its own distinctive ritual.

After the entire regiment had been drawn up in a hollow square on the parade ground, the prisoner was marched on and then stripped to the waist. Watched intently by his hundreds of comrades, he then had to raise his left arm, so that the Drum Major could mark the position of the tattoo. This the SNCO did, using a fine paintbrush dipped in thick black ink to trace the one inch high letters – 'D' for Deserter, 'BC' for Bad Character – about two inches below the armpit.

Then with a three-sided, serrated saddler's needle, the Drum Major laboriously proceeded to pierce the skin, causing scores of minute punctures through which the blood started to flow. The SNCO then rubbed in gunpowder with his fingers so that it penetrated every tiny wound, ensuring that the symbol of disgrace would remain indelible for all time.

This was part of the sentence passed on Private James Light, found guilty of desertion in 1820, who was 'to receive eight hundred lashes and to be marked on the left side, two inches below the armpit, with the letter "D", such letter not to be less than half an inch long and to be marked on the skin with ink and gunpowder, so as to be visible and conspicuous and not likely to be obliterated'.

After years of misshapen letters drawn on quivering flesh by semi-illiterate Drum Majors under the concerted and disconcerting gaze of whole regiments, the powers-that-be decided to standardise the calligraphy. In 1840 the saddlers' needles were superceded by a surgical type of instrument resembling a baton, the flat top of which housed about thirty sharp needles in the form of the required letter. Like multiple hypodermic needles, they penetrated the flesh to a depth of a quarter of an inch, into which the gunpowder was then rubbed. And even after branding ceased to be a penalty in civilian courts, instructions on tattooing methods continued to be included in the relevant Army manuals as late as 1858, the punishment not being finally abolished in the Service until 1879.

## Branding in France

The French method combined both red-hot iron and gunpowder. Once the branding iron had done its work, an ointment of gunpowder and lard or pomade was applied with a piece of wood padded with leather. By this means it was hoped that the brand would be indelibly black, but it was not entirely successful because the burn formed a scab on healing and when this came away, the new skin was usually white.

The brands were applied to the shoulder, and in medieval times all felons had but one mark, the fleur-de-lys. Later, however, distinction between crimes was introduced. Forgers sentenced to imprisonment or hard labour received the letter 'F', while those sentenced to penal servitude for the same crime were branded 'TF', *travaux forces* (hard labour). Murderers and armed robbers, whose crimes warranted penal servitude for life, bore the letters 'TPF', *travaux à perpétuité*, while other criminals had 'T' for time servers and TP if serving a life sentence.

Not only did some French criminals have letters burned on them, but numbers as well. These, one inch high, identified the *département* (district) in which the convict was imprisoned, and were burned in beneath and slightly to the left of the letter or letters.

Most branding was administered by the public executioner, who had to provide the branding irons, fuel for the brazier, shovel, tongs and bellows out of his own resources, together with the lard and gunpowder, an expenditure over which he was constantly at odds with the Ministry of Justice. Eventually, on 11 March 1813, the Ministry issued a scale of payments covering all the executioner's tasks and requirements, in which that of 'exposure and branding of a prisoner' earned him FF 2.55.

Branding took place on the scaffold, in full view of the public, and while the irons were being heated, the victims' heads were shaved to prevent them hiding their faces from the crowd during their humiliating punishment.

The reformer John Howard, when visiting the galleys (prison ships equivalent to the 'hulks' used in England) moored off Toulon in 1779, remarked on the 1,600 prisoners housed therein. Each had to wear a bonnet or cap on which was fixed a tin plate with a number on it. The caps were grey, green or red, to distinguish deserters, smugglers and thieves. The latter category, he reported, were always branded at the prison in which they had been sentenced, some with 'GAL' (*galères*) or 'V' (*voleur*).

Despite the high regard in which Frenchmen usually held their womenfolk, members of the fairer sex were also disfigured by the branding iron. The most famous instance of this occurred in 1786 when the Affair of the Diamond Necklace provoked a *cause célèbre* among fashionable French society.

The necklace in question, its 647 diamonds totalling 2,800 carats, had originally been ordered by Louis XV as a present for Mme du Barry. But when he died, the jewellers were unable to sell the magnificent piece of jewellery, priced as it was at 1,800,000 livres.

Then the Comtesse Jeanne de la Motte Valois appeared on the scene. Imperious and aristocratic, claiming descent from Henri II, she duped her lover Cardinal de Rohan to obtain the necklace on behalf of Queen Marie Antoinette who, explained Jeanne, wanted to avoid the inevitable publicity. And when he handed it over to her to deliver to the Queen, Jeanne sold the precious gems for a vast sum of money.

The scandal broke, however, when the jewellers submitted the bill to the Queen. The plot was uncovered, de Rohan accusing Jeanne Valois and her accomplices of fraud and theft, and at her trial she was sentenced to *amende honorable*, to be beaten and birched naked, having a rope about her neck, and then branded on both shoulders with the letter 'V' (for *voleuse*, thief).

The public executioner, Charles-Henri Sanson, more accustomed to delivering an exact number of strokes of the whip to a felon's back rather than an unspecified birching of a nude woman, nevertheless arranged to administer the punishment as discreetly as possible.

By 6a.m., hopefully before many spectators would have gathered, a large platform with a bench on it had been positioned in the courtyard of the Palais de Justice. The Countess, wearing a silk boudoir gown with brown and white stripes decorated with small nosegays of roses, was awakened and informed of her sentence. At this her haughty demeanour entirely deserted her. Protesting frenziedly, she struggled so violently that she had to be tied up before being half-carried to the scaffold-like platform.

Once there, in full view of the crowds already assembling, she continued to struggle wildly as Sanson and his assistants untied her and, in accordance with the court's ruling, deprived her of all her clothing. Held face down on the wooden bench, she had to

101

submit to being birched to the deafening chorus of jeers and obscene insults from the mob.

Even as the birching came to an end, Sanson took the branding iron from the nearby brazier and pressed it against the shoulder of the sobbing woman. At the searing pain she fell to her knees on the planks; then, as Sanson attempted to brand her other shoulder, she wildly twisted away, with disastrous results, for the red-hot iron came down, not on her shoulder, but on her breast instead.

Publicly degraded and humiliated, Madame la Comtesse Jeanne de la Motte Valois was then taken to serve a life sentence in La Salpêtrière Prison. Ten months later, thanks to the efforts of her husband, men's clothing was passed to her by a sentry patrolling outside her cell window, and she daringly escaped. She joined her husband in London, where she lived until her death in 1791, at the age of thirty-five.

Branding continued to have a place in French statute books, the differing letters eventually being replaced by one brand, that of 'TF', *travaux forces*. All branding was however abolished by law on 28 April 1832.

## Branding in Holland
Both men and women suffered this mutilation. John Howard visited the *Tucht-Hus* (House of Correction) on the ramparts of the city of Zwolle in November 1781 and found nine women in the spinning and knitting rooms, all of whom had been branded.

## Branding in Germany
Although few instances are on record, it would seem that some criminals were branded on the cheeks with the initial letter of the city in which they were sentenced. That women were also branded was recorded in his diary by Master Franz Schmidt, Nuremberg's executioner.

Margaret Schreimeri, a sixty-year-old beggar with a lifetime of crime behind her, continued to deceive people into giving her money and clothing by pretending to be of considerable, though temporarily inaccessible, means. Her luck ran out when she importuned the citizens of Nuremberg, and on 23 February 1609

her arms were pinioned behind her on the scaffold while Franz
Schmidt branded her on both cheeks as a swindler.

## Red-hot Pincers

History does not reveal why this particular punishment was rarely
inflicted in England, but other countries certainly employed it.
After all, there were few torments as painful as being nipped with
red-hot tongs. Scotland realised its potentialities as early as 1437,
when James I was assassinated. His murderer, the Earl of Athol,
was taken to the traditional place of execution, the Cross in Edinburgh, where his flesh was torn with hot irons, and he was
crowned King of Traitors with a metal crown similarly heated.

### Pincers in Germany

Germany's approach to the method was rather more technical.
They devised sharp claw-like instruments for pinching and
squeezing the flesh, and spoon-shaped tools to plunge into ears
and eye sockets. But they did not neglect the well-proven torture
of the glowing pincers, as one George Taucher found out to his
cost.

Taucher, guilty of murdering an innkeeper's lad with a knife,
paid for his crime in April 1579 by being nipped twice on the arms
with red-hot tongs and then had his limbs shattered on the wheel.

Two other men who failed to take note of Taucher's fate were
Jobst Knau and George Hornlein. Both multiple murderers and
robbers, they were eventually caught and so accompanied the
executioner in his tumbril to the scaffold. As straightforward
execution obviously was not considered sufficient to expiate their
sins, the tongs were taken from the glowing brazier and after their
flesh had been seared and pinched, their right arms and legs were
broken. Both men were then put to death on the wheel.

### Pincers in Holland

In the neighbouring country of Holland, the authorities found
pincers extremely useful, especially when punishing assassins. In
1584 a Dutchman Balthasar Gerards murdered William I, Prince
of Orange, by firing three poisoned bullets at him. Pursued
and captured, he was later severely flogged and racked. After

suffering repeated knife wounds, he was immersed in salt water, then wrapped in a cloak which had been soaked in vinegar and brandy. Finally the red-hot irons were brought into play with his flesh being systematically torn from his body until he died.

### Pincers in France
The French called the method *Tenaillement*, a melodic-sounding word for a hideous punishment, for not content with tearing the victim's flesh with heated tongs, hot wax or lead would then be poured into the wounds.

This was part of the torture endured by Francis Ravaillac who, as described in a previous chapter, suffered in the 'Boots' for the murder of Henri IV of France in 1610. After having his right hand burned, he was torn with red-hot pincers, scalding oil and molten lead was then applied. The end came when he was torn asunder by four horses, and his remains were burned to ashes by the vengeful mob.

Sometimes suggestions for punishments came from the kings themselves. Louis IX, for instance, ordered that blasphemers should be branded on the forehead, and as was the custom in England, to have their tongues skewered with a red-hot rod. As if that were not enough, he further decreed that their lips should also be burned, and proceeded to invent a spoon-shaped iron for that very purpose.

## *The Brazen Bull*
This was probably the most bizarre, the most fiendish instrument of torture ever devised. Imagine a full-sized replica of a bull, made of brass, with a trap-door in its back to allow access to its hollow interior. The victim would be locked inside it, and a fire then lighted beneath the belly of the 'beast'.

But that was not all, according to the fevered brain of its inventor, an artist named Perilaus, as he proudly displayed it to his master Phalaris of Sicily. For the reeds he had installed in the bull's nostrils would convert the screams of the tormented victim into a musically pleasing lowing sound.

But Phalaris, harsh ruler that he might be, decided that the Brazen Bull was too abominable even to consider using. Not only that, but Perilaus should be punished in the most appropriate

104

manner possible for conjuring up a device of such nightmarish proportions. And in his own words, as recounted in Lucian's *Works*,

> 'Well now, Perilaus,' I said. 'If you are so sure of your contrivance, give us a proof of it on the spot; mount up and get in and imitate the cries of a man tortured in it, that we may hear whether such charming music will proceed from it, as you would make us believe.'
>
> Perilaus obeyed, and no sooner was he in the belly of the bull, than I shut the aperture and put fire beneath it. 'Take that,' said I, 'as the only recompense such a piece of art is worth, and chant us the first specimen of the charming notes of which you are the inventor!'
>
> And so the barbarous wretch suffered what he had well merited by such an application of his mechanical talent. However, that the noble work should not be contaminated by his dying there, I ordered him to be drawn out while still alive, and thrown down from the summit of the rock, where his body was left unburied.

It would seem that the Bull remained intact, if not utilised, for a number of years, some authorities declaring that Phalaris himself met his end within its brazen interior in 563 BC.

News of the Brazen Bull spread throughout the western world, and present-day visitors to the Tower of London can see the horse-armour of Henry VIII, which is superbly engraved with scenes from the lives of St George and St Barbara, both of whom were reputedly put to death in the persecution of Maximilian in AD 303. One engraving in particular portrays a brazen bull in which, in the aperture in its back, kneels St George. Beneath the effigy, executioners keep the fires blazing with faggots and bellows, while above an angel hovers, symbolically waiting for the soul of the doomed saint.

## The Gridiron

Encyclopedias tell us that St Laurence or Lawrence, a deacon of Rome, was challenged to produce the treasures of his church, and proceeded to infuriate the authorities by displaying the beggars in his charge. In 258 BC he was condemned by the Romans for his religious beliefs, and put to death by being broiled alive on a gridiron, a low bench of parallel metal bars beneath which a fire had been lit.

As the cruelly slow grilling took effect, it was reported that the saint, with defiant humour, called out to the executioner, 'This side is roastyed enough, oh tyrant great; decide whether roastyed or raw thou thinkest the better meat!'

On 10 August, St Laurence's Day, in 1557, Philip II of Spain achieved a great military victory over the French at St Quentin, and in honour of the saint to whom he attributed his success on the battlefield, he built the Escurial, a complex of buildings north-west of Madrid, which incorporated a royal palace, a college, a mausoleum and a monastery. It took twenty-four years to complete, its construction costing £8 million.

The recurring theme of the Escurial was the gridiron, symbol of the martyr's death. The ground plan was that of a gridiron: the buildings were the bars, the palace was the handle. A statue of the saint, holding a gridiron, stood at the approach to the Escurial, and throughout the palace gridirons predominated. Made of wood and metal, plaster and pigment they decorated the rooms, positioned over doors and windows, in stables and galleries, halls and bedchambers, a constant reminder of St Laurence's agonising death.

## The Spanish Chair

This was a variation of the gridiron, and was used by the Spanish Inquisition. As its name suggests, it was a heavy iron chair somewhat resembling a garden lounger in which the victim was secured by straps around his neck, arms and upper legs. Integral with the end of the chair was a pair of iron stocks, in which the bare feet of the heretic were secured.

But unlike a garden lounger, in which the occupant is exposed only to the warmth of the sun, the heat experienced by the Inquisition's victim came from a glowing brazier placed by his feet. And to make sure that the roasting process was not too precipitate, his tormentors continually basted his feet with lard or oil.

French criminals suffered a similar torture, especially in

Brittany, where the pan containing the white-hot coals was brought nearer and nearer with devastating slowness until the confession had been extracted.

In Italy any attempts by prisoners of war captured by Ferdinand VII to claim the protection of the Geneva Convention were wasting their breath. For the King carried around with him a portable Chair for just such interrogations. Made of iron, it had a pan beneath the seat which when required contained the persuasive fire.

# 8
## Torture on Tap

### *Ordeal by Boiling Liquids*

When, in the old days, the threat 'You'll be in hot water over this' was made, it was meant literally, and usually ended in injury or death. Recorded as being in use as early as the reign of Ine, King of the West Saxons from 688 to 726, ordeal by boiling water, like that of the alternative ordeal by fire, had its own specific ritual.

It too was performed in a church, and the accused was escorted by two men to an iron or brass pan of water. The men had to confirm to the presiding priest that the water was boiling and that an object – a coin, a ring or a stone – rested at the bottom of the pan.

If only a single accusation had been made against the offender, he had but to plunge his hand in up to the wrist to recover the object. If, however, a threefold accusation had been made, a deeper pan was used, necessitating an immersion up to the elbow.

The congregation were required to fast before the trial in order to sanctify themselves, and were sprinkled with holy water by the priests. After everyone had kissed a crucifix, they watched as the man withdrew his arm from the scalding water, and priests bandaged the injured flesh. As in the fire ordeal, the accused would be adjudged innocent if the limb healed within three days, but found guilty if the flesh was still raw.

### Boiling Water Ordeal in France

We have it on the authority of no less than that of Henri Sanson, last of the hierarchy of French executioners, that a similar ordeal was practised in that country. It too took place in a church, a cauldron full of water being placed over a large fire. When the water was in a state of ebullition it was taken off the fire, a rope was tied above the cauldron from which was suspended a ring or other object, and this was lowered into the water to a predetermined depth.

At the first ordeal the accused had only to plunge his hand in, to catch hold of the object; at a second ordeal he had to plunge the arm up to the elbow, and for the most serious offence, all his arm would have to be immersed.

When the ordeal had been accomplished, the sufferer's arm was inserted in a bag on which the judge imprinted his seal, which was broken three days afterwards. If any mark of burning was still apparent, the accused was declared guilty, otherwise he would be absolved.

## Boiling Oil Ordeal in India

In that country, oil scarred and disfigured victims until well into the nineteenth century. The *Bombay Gazette* of July 1867 reported the prosecution of a camel driver for theft, who was promptly subjected to the ordeal of boiling oil.

Again a strict religious ceremony was observed, involving dung from the cow, the animal venerated by the Hindus. This was spread on the temple floor, preparatory to lighting the fire. The jar of oil, after being consecrated, was then placed on a stand over the fire and heated, prayers being said as the heavy liquid seethed and bubbled.

As the chanting voices reached their crescendo, the accused had to plunge his hand and arm into the oil and retrieve the ring from the bottom of the vessel. And as in other countries, the same test applied.

Some did indeed miraculously escape injury, but whether this could be attributed to some yoga-like power of the spirit, or the prior application of a heat-resisting unguent, will never be known.

## *Ordeal by Cold Water*

One might venture to think that, given the choice, cold water torture would be more endurable than boiling water, and infinitely preferable to boiling oil. If so, one would be very wrong.

The ordeal is believed to have been originated by an Italian gentleman named de Marsilis, who happened to observe that drops of water falling on to a surface slowly wore a hollow in the material, no matter how hard it was. He therefore experimented on the human body with, to him, most gratifying results.

The prisoner was strapped down so that he could not move a fraction of an inch, and water was allowed to fall, drop by drop, on to a selected part of his body. The vessel from which the drops fell was in full view of the sufferer, so that he could see each drop coming.

From his experiments de Marsilis found that the most deadly torture resulted from selecting the forehead as the point of impact. Applied over a longer or shorter period, it eventually drove the prisoner out of his mind.

Worse than the de Marsilis method, if possible, was the continuous-stream variation. In this, a flow of water falling from about six feet on to the forehead of the victim quickly reduced him to a state of absolute surrender within seconds.

## Cold Water Ordeal in America

This method was employed in prisons in the United States to deal with recalcitrant convicts and was known as the 'cold shower'. An understatement if ever there was one, for the inmate, strapped naked to a ladder, was subjected to a high-pressure jet of water delivered by a one and a half inch hose fitted with a three-quarter inch nozzle.

Completely vulnerable to the liquid onslaught, hardly able to see or breathe, the victim was extensively bruised by the force of the jet and his heart beat was caused alternatively to speed up and retard so violently that blood flowed from his eyes and ears, and unconsciousness quickly followed.

An alternative was to lock the convict in an ordinary shower-bath – ordinary except that the controls were outside the cubicle. Any extended length of time under the fine spray of icy water effectively subdued the most mutinous prisoner, but sometimes had fatal results. In 1858 an inmate of Auburn Prison in New York State collapsed and died after half an hour under the shower's jets, and in 1882 all such cold water torture was abolished in US prisons.

## *Submersion by Keelhauling*

With seamen of the Royal Navy being literally surrounded by cold water, what more natural than to use the stuff to punish wrongdoers? And rather than simply dunking them into it from deck level, why not drop them from a greater height, for instance from the end of the main yard-arm, the great wooden crosspiece positioned at right angles to the main mast?

The details of the punishment were formulated as early as 1634, Captain Butler RN describing them in his book as

> The ducking att the maine yarde arme is, when a malefactor by having a rope fastened under his armes and about his middle, and under his breech, is thus hoysted up to the end of the yarde; from whence hee is violentlie let fall into the sea, sometimes twise, sometimes three severall tymes one after another; and if the offence be very fowle, he is alsoe drawne under the very keele of the shippe, the which is termed keel-rakinge; and while hee is thus under water, a great gunn is given fire unto righte over his head; the which is done as well to astonish him the more with the thunder thereof, which muche troubles him, as to give warning untoe all others to looke out, and to beware by his harmes.

Sometimes keelhauling had disastrous results. Impact with the sea, lengthy submersion, and enforced contact with the sharp-shelled barnacles and marine growth which encrusted the under-sides of the old wooden sailing ships, frequently caused injury and even death, but those risks did not deter the naval captains of the day from employing it as a punishment.

Even ships' chaplains considered it a commonplace penalty. Henry Teonge, of HMS *Assistance*, jotted down in his diary against 31 October 1676 that 'One Arrowsmith, for staying ashore without leave, was ducked today at the yardarm.'

On rare occasions mercy was shown to deserving offenders, Chaplain Teonge recounting how, on 28 September 1675,

> This morning one of our men, viz Skinner, a known cuckold, for going ashore without leave, had his legs tied together, his hands tied to a great rope, and stood on the side of the ship

to be hoisted up to the yardarm, and from thence to drop down into the water three times; but he, looking so very pitifully, and also by the gentlemen's entreaties to the Captain for him, who alleged that he had injuries enough already, as having a wife a whore and a scold to injure him at home, ergo had the more need to be pitied abroad, was spared.

So lightly was the practice regarded that, like the not so ancient ceremony of Crossing the Line, whereby those whose first time it was to sail across the Equator were ducked with mock ritual in the ship's swimming pool, so those entering the Mediterranean for the first time had a similar forfeit to pay King Neptune.

This latter was the practice in the seventeenth century. Those first-timers passing between Ape Rock on the African Coast and Gibraltar (then still a Spanish possession) had to 'pay his dollar or must be ducked at the yardarm'. Hardly an attraction to feature in a modern cruise ship's holiday brochure, though.

## French Water Tortures

The de Marilis method of water droplets was adopted by France, the water dripping relentlessly on either the stomach of the bound victim, or on his shaven head, both having dire results.

Straightforward drowning was the punishment inflicted on witches and sorcerers, but King Philippe Auguste later extended this to any 'untitled people who should swear blasphemously'.

As in the Royal Navy, so in the French Navy, the Gallic *La Cale* being not unlike keelhauling. A marine equivalent of Strappado, described earlier, this consisted of hoisting the matelot to a considerable height, then letting him fall. In *Cale Humide* he fell into the sea; in *Cale Sèche* his fall, if nothing else, was broken by the deck.

## Prolonged Immersion

Brief periods under water was used to punish sailors for their misdeeds, but if one needed to prove that a woman was a witch or that a man was a wizard, much longer submersion was necessary.

The test, much favoured by James I and strongly sanctioned by the Church, was based on the belief that those who consorted

113

with the Devil were lighter than water, and so would float.

The method was simple. Once a witchfinder, like the notorious Matthew Hopkins, had identified a witch by 'pricking' her, finding by means of a needle that at least one place on her body was insensitive to pain, she would be 'swum' to confirm her guilt.

The near-naked woman was trussed crosswise, left thumb tied to right big toe, right thumb to left big toe, and then tied in the centre of a long rope about her waist. With a man at each end of the rope, one standing on each bank of the river, stream or village pool, the suspect would be 'swum' – immersed in the depths.

If she sank, she was adjudged innocent, though for this to be unmistakably evident she had to be beneath the surface of the water for a number of minutes, by which time she would probably have drowned. If in sheer self-preservation she struggled to stay afloat, her apparent buoyancy was a sign of guilt. The odds were loaded against the suspect anyway, since the two men controlling her could ensure that she did not sink, by keeping the rope taut.

The method was employed all over Europe as recently as the early 1800s. Among the scores of cases in this country was that of a couple, John and Ruth Osborne, who were immersed at Tring in Buckinghamshire in 1751 by a mob led by one George Colley. Ruth Osborne was drowned, but justice prevailed, for Colley was tried for murder and perished on the gallows.

## The Drinking Torture

The responsibility for the introduction of this inhumane torture can be more or less blamed on the Spanish Inquisition, the influence and practices of which spread from Spain to encompass France, the Netherlands, Portugal and Italy. Known as *Tormento de Toca*, it involved the victim being forced to drink quantities of water, sometimes through a piece of gauze, with horrific results.

During the torture, the heretic had of necessity to be rendered incapable of movement, and in the Netherlands this was achieved by means best described by Ernestus Eremundus Frisius in his seventeenth-century book *The History of the Low Countries' Disturbances*.

There is a bench, which they call the wooden horse, made hollow like a trough, so as to contain a man lying on his back

114

at full length, about the middle of which there is a round bar laid across, upon which the back of the person placed, so that he lies upon the bar instead of being let down into the bottom of the trough, with his feet much higher than his head.

As he is lying in this posture, his arms, thighs and shins are tied round with small cords or strings which, being drawn with screws at proper distances from each other, cut into his very bones, so as to be no longer discerned. Besides this, the torturer throws over his mouth and nostrils a thin cloath, so that he is scarcely able to breathe thro' them, and in the mean while a small stream of water like a thread, not drop by drop, falls from on high, upon the mouth of the person lying in this miserable condition, and so easily sinks down the thin cloth to the bottom of his throat, so that there is no possibility of breathing, his mouth being stopped with water and his nostrils with the cloth, so that the poor wretch is in the same agony as persons ready to die, and breathing out their last.

When this cloth is drawn out of his throat, as it often is, so that he may answer to the questions, it is all wet with water and blood, and is like pulling his bowels through his mouth.

The Italians used the same method. The amount of water that was poured on to the gauze covering the heretic's mouth was limited to five litres for the 'ordinary' torture and twice that amount for the 'extraordinary' torture.

The executioner Henri Sanson, writing in 1876, described how in France the criminal, after having his sentence pronounced, sat on a stone stool, with his wrists attached behind his back to two iron rings placed wide apart. Rope was twined around his body and limbs and pulled as tightly as possible, and he was then lowered backwards on to a trestle, whereupon the interrogator inserted a horn into the felon's mouth. Water was poured into this funnel, and the victim was induced to swallow it by having his nostrils pinched. Again there were two stages to the torture: *Question Ordinaire*, requiring four pints of water to be swallowed and, if a confession was not forthcoming, *Question Extraordinaire* brought a longer drink of eight pints.

These tortures required the victim to be in a horizontal position, but in the 1600s the Dutch authorities in the East Indies devised a water torture of a slightly different kind. There the victim was bound immovable to a vertical board, and cloths were wrapped tightly around his neck and piled high about his face and head. Into this funnel-like receptacle water was slowly poured, soaking into the cloth and mounting higher and higher until it covered his nose and mouth. Half-choking, unable to breathe without taking more and more water into his lungs, the torment continued until the victim showed signs of imminent death by drowning. Only then was he temporarily released, and urged to confess.

## The Ducking Stool

At a more domestic level, and light years away from barbaric religious tribunals and torture chambers, the Ducking Stool had its place in the life of many a village community. Innocuous as the words may sound, nevertheless its name sent cold shivers down the spines of nagging wives, shrews, harlots, strumpets and, rarely, dishonest tradesmen. The device took many forms, and was generally governed by such deciding factors as whether the village had a deep river nearby, a muddy stream with or without a bridge, or just a pond.

One type of stool was described as an armchair mounted on an axle fixed between the ends of two parallel beams fifteen feet in length. Such a design permitted the chair to remain horizontal even when the beams, balanced on a post by river or pond, were raised and lowered like a seesaw.

Another model consisted of a tall vertical post with a swing arm at the top. From one end of the arm was suspended a chair; a rope at the other end allowed the chair, duly weighted by a scold or suchlike, to be lowered into the river. The vertical post was either fixed in the river bank or mounted on a small wheeled trolley, and this type was known as a treebucket or Trebuchet because of its resemblance to the immense catapult of that name anciently used to hurl boulders over castle walls.

In villages situated near rivers, the chair was suspended from a pulley attached to a beam in the centre of the bridge arch, thereby being always ready for use. Yet another type of stool was known as a tumbril or scolding cart, for it comprised a pair of fifteen-foot long shafts, with two wheels on an axle fixed about three feet from one end. On the short end was mounted the chair, and to the other end long ropes were attached.

With the scold in the chair, the tumbril (ominously named after the cart used by French executioners) was pushed into the water. The operators, still on dry land, would retain their hold on the ropes but would release the shafts, thereby plunging the woman backwards into the pool as the shafts flew upwards. After a suitable period of immersion the ropes would be pulled, bringing the shafts down and lifting the spluttering and soaked occupant out of the water. One such tumbril existed at Wootton Bassett, Wiltshire, and bore the date 1686 on its oak frame.

Different villages, different counties had, hardly surprisingly, different names for their proud possession: tumbril, timbrell, treebucket, gumstole, and erroneously, coqueen stole or cucking stool. Some ducking stools were wooden, intricately carved with devils, scolds, poetic quotations, while others were of elaborately shaped wrought iron.

There being no government specification for a standardised model, village councils manufactured their own, based on the designs of models inspected in neighbouring towns, and limited only by the resourcefulness of their own carpenter or blacksmith. An eighteenth-century visitor to Derby noted that 'there is a curious and very useful machine, viz. a ducking stool, here for the benefit of scholding wives. A plan of this instrument I shall procure and transplant to Berkshire for the good of my native county.'

Research into parish accounts reveals the cost of these 'engines of punishment'. When Southam in Warwickshire had to instal one in 1718, a man who visited Daventry to draw a copy of that town's chair charged 3s 2d. The carpenter asked for £1 1s 8d for material and labour, and the painter wanted 10s for his artistic designs. The ironwork was made by the blacksmith for 4s 6d, the fee for carrying it to its final site was 2s 6d, and last but not least a further 9s 6d had to be expended to deepen the village pond to the necessary depth.

These devices, once installed, were put to frequent use, as the records show. In 1534 two women were expelled from the town of

Sandwich for immorality, and were warned that if they returned, one would be set in the ducking stool, and the other in the stocks, with an allowance of only bread and water. After that, she would have to sit in the stool and 'be dipped to the chin'.

At the Leeds Quarter Sessions in July 1694, it was ordered that Anne, wife of Philip Saul, being a woman of lewd behaviour, be ducked for making daily strife and discord among her neighbours. Similar orders were also made against Jane Miller and Elizabeth Wooler.

Far from attracting only a few onlookers, some duckings mustered a goodly audience, one being reported in the *London Evening Post* of 27 April 1745 when 'a woman who keeps the Queen's Head alehouse at Kingston was ordered by the court to be ducked for scolding, and was accordingly placed in the chair and ducked in the Thames under Kingston Bridge, in the presence of 2,000 to 3,000 people'.

Katherine Hall and Margaret Robinson were ducked at Wakefield in 1692 'by reason of their daily scolding and chydering, the one with the other'. Also in that town's Sessions of 5 October 1671, there appears 'Foreas much as Jane, wife of William Farrett, shoemaker, stands indicted for a common scold, to the great annoyance and disturbance of her neighbours. It is therefore ordered that she should be openly ducked, and ducked three times over the head and ears by the constables of Selby, for which this call be their warrant.'

One husband in Kirkby, Yorkshire, got a nasty surprise when he applied to the magistrates to have his wife punished. The official decided that both were equally to blame and so, back to back, husband and wife were chaired by the constable, cheered by the onlookers, and plunged into the cold waters of the pond.

It was not always a quaint village custom. Old scores were settled, and panic could follow indignity as the chair and its occupant were held under longer than was safe. Indeed on rare occasions deaths did happen, as at Nottingham in 1731. The chair in that town consisted of a box large enough to accommodate two offenders at once, their heads protruding through holes in the sides. On this occasion a 'female of bad repute' was installed in it and, left to the mercy of the mob, was ducked so severely that she drowned. The mayor was later arrested and prosecuted, and the ducking stool demolished.

The last recorded case in which a ducking stool was used in England was in 1809 at Leominster, Herefordshire. Jenny Pipes, alias Jane Corran, was first paraded through the streets on the ducking stool, a singularly fine machine mounted on a trolley which ran on four-inch wheels. On the centre post, three feet high, was fixed a seesaw-like twenty-six-foot long beam, ensuring deep water for the culprit and dry feet for the constable.

After the well-attended procession, Jenny was trundled to the river near Kenwater Bridge and soundly soaked. It seems not to have had the immediate remedial effect, for the bailiff reported that her first words after her release were oaths and curses directed at the magistrates!

In 1817 Sarah Leeke, also from Leominster, occupied the same chair as Jenny and would have suffered the same fate, but when the parade reached the river's edge, it was found that the water level was too low.

Such rural punishments gave rise to many a ribald verse. One, composed by Benjamin West in 1780 read,

> There stands, my friend, in yonder pool,
> An engine call'd a ducking stool;
> By legal pow'r commanded down,
> The joy and terror of the town.
>
> If jarring females kindle strife,
> Give language foul or lug the coif,
> If noisy dames should once begin
> To drive the house with horrid din,
> Away, you cry, you'll grace the stool,
> We'll teach you how your tongue to rule.
>
> The fair offender fills the seat
> In sullen pomp, profoundly great,
> Down in the deep the stool descends,
> But here at first we miss our ends.

She mounts again, and rages more
Than ever vixen did before.
So throwing water on the fire
Will but make it burn the higher.

If so, my friend, pray let her take
A second turn into the lake;
And, rather than your patience lose
Thrice, and again repeat the dose.
No brawling wives, no furious wenches,
No fire so hot but water quenches.

A rare instance of a prison being equipped with a ducking stool was reported by John Howard, while on a visit to Liverpool in 1779. In the Bridewell there, he reported

In the courtyard is a pump, to which the women prisoners are tied every week and receive discipline. There is also a bath, with a new and singular contrivance. At one end of it was a standard for a long pole, at the extremity of which was fastened a chair. In this all the females (not the males) at their entrance, after a few questions, were placed, with a flannel shift on, and underwent a thorough ducking, thrice repeated – a use of a bath, which I dare say the legislature never thought of, when they ordered baths with a view to cleanliness and preserving the health of prisoners, and not for the exercise of a wanton and dangerous kind of severity.

Scotland did not overlook the excellent corrective potentialities of the ducking stool. Nor did the United States of America, as the Common Scold Law was part of the judicial cargo imported there by the Puritans and other settlers. Doubtless there were many who were dipped, among them being Mary Davis, who was publicly ducked for nagging in 1813, and in 1889 another Mary, Mrs Mary Brady, who was indicted by a Grand Jury in Jersey City as a 'common scold'.

On referring to their law books, incredulous lawyers found that scolding was still an indictable offence in New Jersey and the

120

ducking stool was still available for use, as it was not abolished when new statutes were adopted.

And in Canada Miss Annie Pope was charged with a similar offence, even though apparently unmarried. As the magistrates had no ducking stool available, she was remanded to the assizes, and was ducked at Ottawa in 1890.

# 9
# The Agony of the Lash

Hangman, I charge you to pay particular attention to this
lady. Scourge her soundly, man, scourge her till her blood
runs down. It is Christmas, a cold time for madam to strip.
See that you warm her shoulders thoroughly.

These words, uttered in 1685 by Judge Jeffreys, the hanging judge
of the Bloody Assizes, vividly conjures up the most frequently
administered punishment of this and indeed most other countries,
a punishment without regard for mercy, for compassion or even
sexual consideration.

In 1530 the Whipping Act ordered delinquents 'to be tied to the
end of a cart, naked, and beaten with whips through a market
town till the body be bloody by reason of such whipping'. It was
not until the reign of Elizabeth I, in 1597, that some decency
eventually prevailed, whereby culprits were required to be naked
only from the waist up. From that time too, the whipping post
came into use for the majority of cases, instead of the back of a
moving cart. It is doubtful whether the victim benefited from this
change, however, as it is easier to hit a stationary target than a
moving one.

So easy was a whipping to administer, so obviously the deterrent it was thought to be, that it became the judicial panacea for
most minor crimes. Rufflers and vagabonds, rioters and
drunkards provided a rich harvest for the flailing lashes, as were
those who obtained goods by false pretences.

In Devon, mothers of illegitimate children were punished in
this way in the sixteenth century, as were the reputed fathers.
Scottish pedlars who deprived English shopkeepers of their

rightful trade, thieves and pickpockets all received the whip. Eleanor Wilson, a Durham woman, was publicly flogged in the market place for an hour, in April 1690, having been found drunk on a Sunday. Similarly chastised was a girl of nineteen who was found guilty in 1769 of obtaining goods under false pretences. She was stripped to the waist and whipped on market day.

Deranged people were whipped for being deranged, ill people for being ill. In Constable's *Account of Great Straughton*, in Huntingdonshire, appears the entry in 1690: 'Charges paid in taking up a distracted woman, watching her and whipping her the next day . . . 8s 6d.' And one Thomas Hawkins received the sum of 8d in 1710 for whipping two people who had the smallpox, probably under the delusion that such treatment would knock spots off them. It was obviously payment by results, as a bill submitted in 1632 shows: 'To Edward Wood, for the whiping of three wanderers sent to his house by Sir George Plint . . . iiijd'.

Blasphemers were as usual constant targets. Samuel Johnson, rector of Corringham, distributed a tract exhorting soldiers not to be 'unequally yoked with idolatrous and bloody Papists'. This, in 1686, when a Catholic King sat on the Throne, was hardly diplomatic, to put it mildly, and it brought down both the wrath of the courts on his head and the whip on his back. On 22 November of that year, as recorded in the House of Commons *Journal*, 'the judgement in the King's Bench was executed with great Rigour and Cruelty, the Whipping from Newgate to Tyburn (now the Old Bailey to Marble Arch) being with a Whip of Nine Cords, Knotted, shewed to the Committee; and that Mr Rouse the Under Sheriff tore off his Cassock on the pillory and put a Frize Coat on him'. There was, however, a somewhat happy ending, in that three years later, on the accession of the Protestant William III, the judgement, if not the pain, was annulled by Parliament.

A more remarkable case was that of Mary Hamilton, alias Charles Hamilton, alias George Hamilton, alias William Hamilton. This curious multiplicity of names belonged to a woman who, in the guise of a man, married no fewer than fourteen women! Her last 'bride' appeared in court and testified that having married Charles (or George, or William), they lived together for three months, she unsuspecting that her partner was anything other than male. Later, however, 'she became mistrustful and, comparing certain circumstances with her neighbours Mr and Mrs Goody, realised that her spouse had indulged in vile and deceitful practices'. The 'certain circumstances' compared were, regrettably, not revealed.

The sentence of the court is worth repeating in all its mind-boggling entirety:

> That the he, she, prisoner at the bar, is an uncommon notorious cheat; and we, the Court, do sentence her or him, which ever he or she may be, to be imprisoned six months, and during that time to be whipped in the towns of Taunton, Glastonbury, Wells and Shipton Mallet, and to find security for good behaviour as long as they, the learned judges aforesaid, shall or may, in their wisdom and judgment, require.

Accordingly, Mary Hamilton was imprisoned and whipped, in the bitterly cold winter of 1746.

There was little doubt that some wrongdoers thoroughly deserved harsh punishment of some description, such as those responsible for the ghoulish discovery, reported in March 1776, of twenty dead bodies found in a shed in Tottenham Court Road. The cadavers had been secretly exhumed from cemeteries for sale to surgeons to use in their anatomical lectures. For crimes such as this, two men were arrested, John Holmes and Peter Williams, both well equipped for body snatching, being grave diggers by profession!

The court showed little mercy. The men were sentenced to six months in gaol and 'to be whipped twice, on their bare backs, from the end of Kingsgate Street, Holborn, to Dyot Street, St Giles, being half a mile'. And so they were, with great severity, through crowds of approving spectators.

Even those called to the Bar were called to account. James Bainham was a barrister accused of heresy in 1532. On the orders of the Bishop of London, he was put in irons and then the stocks. Still obstinate, he was taken to the Chelsea home of the Lord Chancellor Sir Thomas More, where he was tied to a tree in More's garden, a tree the Chancellor called 'the Tree of Life'. There Bainham was severely whipped and interrogated, but he still refused to yield and was sent to the Tower.

125

Sir Thomas, usually a humane and compassionate man, described himself as 'the scourge of heretics'. He had Bainham racked, and in that way persuaded him to recant his religious opinions. Later, Bainham regained the strength of his convictions and rejected the Catholic arguments. He was burned alive at Smithfield, two years before Sir Thomas More himself was imprisoned in the Tower and beheaded.

Because of the supposed value of punishment as a deterrent, most whippings were a public spectacle, and large crowds gathered around the hangman's cart or whipping post. Market places were the best venues, and occasionally the culprit was not only whipped there but also flogged out of town. In January 1812 a man was whipped through Kendal, Cumbria, for fighting, and a few days later a sailor was similarly lashed out of the parish for causing an affray during a church service.

Not every chastisement ended with the victim being scourged, however. At Olney in Buckinghamshire, in 1783, a man was accused of stealing ironwork during a fire in the town, and was sentenced to be whipped. As he was being tied up, he pretended to resist, and the charade was continued by the beadle who wielded the whip with his right hand, pulling the thongs through his left hand between strokes.

Whether through bribery or sympathy, the 'blood' which drenched the culprit's shoulders, however, was the red ochre previously smeared in the beadle's left palm. The constable, present to verify the correct number of lashes and the severity of the punishment, realised the subterfuge and, in order to stop the pretence, promptly set about the beadle with his cane of office.

At this point a young lady burst forth from the crowd and, to defend the beadle, belaboured the constable about the head and shoulders. And so, as described by the poet William Cowper, at that time a lay preacher at Olney, 'the spectacle was such that I could not forbear to relate how the beadle thrashed the thief, the constable the beadle, and the lady the constable, and how the thief was the only one who suffered nothing!'

In London there was, not surprisingly, much more entertainment of the same kind, especially for fashionable City gentlemen who, as a change from riding in Rotten Row or gossiping in the coffee houses could stroll elegantly along to Blackfriars and into the Bridewell Prison on Wednesdays, there to watch the women convicts being whipped before the Board of Governors. The President of the court, Sir Robert Jeffries (no relation to the hanging judge), sat with a wooden hammer in his hand, while the prisoner, stripped to the waist, was tied to the post.

The whipping continued until thought sufficient by the President, and he would then bring down the hammer. The victim and her waiting companions would beseech incessantly, 'Oh, good Sir Robert, knock; pray, good Sir Robert, knock!' An account by such a victim in 1703 describes how 'my hands were put to the post and Mr Hemings, the Whipper, began to noint me with his Instrument and had, I believe, about a dozen strings knotted at the end, and so with that I had Thirty-Nine Stripes. I confess I could not forbear bawling out, but good Sir Robert knockt at last and I was freed from the post'.

Such diverting spectacles were eventually denied the London dandies and other sadistic spectators when, in 1791, the whipping of female vagrants was declared illegal, and all women were spared similar indignity and pain by the passing of the Whipping of Female Offenders Abolition Act in 1820.

The last recorded instance was in 1817, when an Inverness woman was whipped through the streets for drunkenness, and the last man to be whipped at the cart tail occurred in Glasgow on 8 May 1822, shortly before all such public floggings were abolished.

But even into the 1930s, punishment by the whip continued to be administered to men in English prisons. The whip used was a cat-o'-nine-tails, which consisted of a wooden handle nearly twenty inches long, with nine tails of whipcord, each about an eighth of an inch thick, thirty-three inches long, but free from knots. The ends of the cords were bound with silk thread to prevent fraying.

The convict sentenced to receive the punishment was tied with outstretched arms to a triangular frame, so that he could neither move nor see what was happening. Protective pads were fixed over his kidneys and neck to prevent serious injury, and he had previously been examined by the prison doctor to ensure that he was fit enough to endure the coming ordeal.

The cat was wielded by a turnkey, a warder, using both hands, the tails being shaken out after each blow, and the number of the stroke was called out as he did so. Although the pain was severe, a report covering the years 1931–5 found that, contrary to popular belief, blood did not flow during the whipping, probably due to the fact that the tails were not knotted, that convicts did not lose consciousness, and rarely was there any need for prolonged hospitalisation.

Youthfulness was no excuse. Wandsworth prison had a whipping post to which, in 1856, juvenile offenders were secured. This was a ten-foot high rectangular frame fitted with straps which buckled around wrists, waist and ankles. The cat-o'-nine-tails was considered too injurious, so they were beaten with a birch rod, a long handle to which a bunch of long birch twigs was attached, so designed to cause stinging pain over as wide an area as possible.

## Military Whipping

That the seventeenth- and eighteenth-century soldier was uncouth, uneducated and inherently unamenable to any kind of discipline, is beyond doubt. As the renowned military leader and tactical genius the Duke of Wellington remarked of his men, 'They are the scum of the earth – I have no idea of any great effect being produced on British soldiers by anything but the fear of immediate corporal punishment!'

Flogging having been authorised by the Mutiny Act of 1689, punishments of a thousand lashes or more were commonplace under his command, yet without such barbaric discipline it is unlikely that he, and therefore Britain, could have achieved the victories in battle which altered the very course of our history.

The range of punishments available to members of courts martial were harsh in the extreme. Deserting during action brought 900 lashes, deserting when on guard duty, 1,500 lashes. Deserting a second time resulted in 900 lashes and transportation as a felon for life, and even deserting and enlisting in another regiment carried no reprieve, a penalty of 800 lashes and a branding with the letter 'D'.

Military archives record, to the point of mental saturation, case after case of appalling flogging. On 10 October 1731 Robert Blackman, a soldier stationed in Berwick-on-Tweed, was court-martialled for making traitorous references to the King. He was sentenced to receive one lash from each member of his regiment and then drummed out of town. A member of a Guards regiment, absent from his place of duty in the Tower of London, was punished with 300 lashes, and a dragoon belonging to Lord Cadogan's Regiment at Nottingham not only received 300 lashes, with a further 300 at Derby, but was also drummed out of his regiment with a halter about his neck for drinking the Pretender's health. A high price to pay for fealty.

The roll-call numbs the mind as much as the whip did the shoulders. 'November 1810 Private Crooke, for assaulting Sergeant Hethershaw with his bayonet – 1,000 lashes on his bare back with a cat-o'-nine-tails; December 1816 Sergeant Major Whiting, for striking his commanding officer – reduced to the ranks and awarded 1,000 lashes. July 1823 Private Renwick, for stealing from the Pay-Sergeant, 620 lashes.'

Punishments like these were sanctioned, not by choleric or sadistic colonels of regiments, but by the very top. In January 1807 King George III promulgated a court-martial sentence of 1,500 lashes on a soldier, though added, 'It appearing to His Majesty, that a punishment to the extent of one thousand lashes is a sufficient example for any breach of military discipline, short of capital punishment; and as even that number cannot be safely inflicted at any one period, His Majesty has been graciously pleased to express his opinion that no sentence for corporal punishment should exceed one thousand lashes.' One hopes that the soldier was duly grateful for the royal reduction.

The general procedure required the man to strip to the waist in front of the assembled regiment, and be secured by the wrists and ankles to a tree, ladder or three sergeants' halberds tied together to form a triangle, hence the colloquialism 'going to the halberds'.

In his book *A Historical Sketch of Military Punishments* published in 1840, Henry Marshall describes the train of events.

The culprit having been secured, the requisite number of Drummers, who have previously been detailed by the Drum-Major to inflict the punishment, commence their operations by each taking off his cap, coat or jacket. The Commanding Officer then says 'Drum-Major, see that the Drummers do their duty.' The Drum-Major gives the time to the

Drummers, audibly calling out, 'one', 'two', 'three' etc., in slow time.

When the first Drummer has inflicted twenty-five lashes, the Drum-Major calls out in a loud voice 'Stop, twenty-five' and then orders a second Drummer to take the place of the first. When another twenty-five lashes have been inflicted, the Drum-Major again calls out 'Stop, fifty' and so on until the punishment is completed.

It is the job of the Adjutant, who stands near to the triangle, to record the number of lashes inflicted. Water is always at hand for the delinquent to drink or to restore him, should he faint, by sprinkling a little on his face.

The first stroke of the cat occasions an immediate discoloration of the skin from diffused blood, the back appearing as if it was thickly sprinkled with strong coffee even before the second stroke is inflicted. Sometimes the blood flows copiously by the time the first fifty or one hundred lashes are inflicted; at other times little or no blood appears when two hundred lashes have been delivered.

During the first hundred and fifty and two hundred lashes, a man commonly appears to suffer much, considerably more, indeed, than during the subsequent part of the punishment, however large it may be. The effused blood in the skin or, perhaps, the disorganisation of the nerves of sensation, seems to occasion a blunting of its sensibility, and thereby lessening the acuteness of the pain arising from the application of the cat.

Left-handed Drummers, whose blows are therefore directed to an area of sound skin, and Drummers who have not been sufficiently drilled in flogging, spread the lashes unnecessarily, and cause an unusual degree of pain.

The sensations experienced by the victim can hardly be imagined, one describing each lash 'as though the talons of a hawk were tearing the flesh off his bones'. And when it is remembered that each tail of an army cat had three knots in it, a thousand lashes therefore meant that he had to endure the impact of 27,000 knots cutting into his back. Even more agony could be caused, if that were conceivably possible, by the practice by some regiments of not cleaning the cat after it had been used, the dried blood stiffening the tails. Other regiments soaked their cats in brine, and dipped them in salt and water during the punishment.

After the flogging the soldier, bleeding profusely and semiconscious, would be escorted to the sickbay, there to have his mutilated shoulders and back covered with cloths wetted with a dilute solution of sugar of lead. These were held in place by a wide bandage known as a 'saddle' or a 'wrestling jacket'.

This savage punishment was gradually phased out, but even as late as 1881 floggings were administered within military prisons, and the 1914 Army Regulations still permitted provost marshals to apply up to thirty strokes for certain offences. Instances of the latter occurred in Mesopotamia, now Iraq, in 1917, to would-be deserters among Indian regiments as the alternative punishment of dismissal from the Service would have delighted, rather than punished, the culprit.

## Naval Whipping

As would be expected in the days of 'pressed' seamen, brutal discipline was considered essential, and was administered almost daily. Flogging the last man up and the last man down the rigging might have encouraged them not to dawdle; it certainly did not guarantee that they had performed their duties aloft in a satisfactory manner, and it could even result in seamen losing their footing in the scramble, with dire results.

The weapon used in the Navy was as awe-inspiring and fearsome as its Army counterpart. Comprising five feet of rope, the thickness of a man's wrist, three feet of which formed the handle, the remaining strands were twisted into thongs and knotted along their length, a 'rope's end' capable of inflicting extreme pain and frequent injury.

Being beaten while spread over a ship's gun was a regular chastisement, this 'Kissing the Gunner's Daughter' being a far from sought-after embrace. A more formal whipping was known as 'Flogging at the Grating', the preliminaries requiring two large gratings to be positioned, one flat on the deck, on which the culprit stood, the other at its end, at right angles.

Tied in a spread-eagled position, the seaman had to wait until the assembly was complete; the officers in full, resplendent uniforms, the marines with loaded weapons, the ship's company drawn up to witness the punishment.

The Master-at-Arms was the master of ceremonies, ensuring that when the offender had been stripped to the waist and the charges read out, the flogging would begin. The officers present removed their cocked hats and the Sergeant of Marines wielded the cat-o'-nine-tails, usually timing his blows every quarter minute with the aid of a sand glass.

After every twelve lashes another NCO took over, until the required total had been delivered, or the Captain, out of the goodness of his heart or the pitiable state of the victim, suspended further punishment.

While not suffering to the same extent as their army counterparts, nevertheless the number of lashes per victim was formidable. In 1759 John Gazard was sentenced to 600 lashes for refusing to obey orders, while James Mansfield received 400 lashes for stealing. Thomas Golden deserted and when caught earned 350 blows with the cat, and Midshipman Francis French took 350 strokes across his shoulders 'for scandalous actions'.

Without doubt the most feared punishment of all was that of 'Flogging round the Fleet', whereby all ships in port took part in a bizarre ritual. At the time designated, the culprit, stripped to the waist, was secured to a wooden frame in a launch, accompanied by the Master-at-Arms with sword drawn, the Surgeon's mate, a drummer and a fifer.

At the head of the floating procession was a small boat, the dispatch boat, which announced the approach of the offender, and a third craft carrying the Lieutenant and the Surgeon.

On the arrival of this small flotilla alongside one of the ships in harbour, the crew of which had already been paraded on that side of the deck, the sentence was loudly proclaimed, this being the signal for two Bosun's Mates from that ship to be rowed out. Boarding the launch, they delivered the number of lashes apportioned to them, the total number of lashes having been divided by the number of HM ships anchored there.

Throughout the funereal proceedings the fifer played a tune 'The Rogue's March', to the accompaniment of a muffled drum, and after each beating, the flotilla moved on to the next ship where the procedure was repeated. And in the days when Great

Britain was a truly maritime nation, with hundreds of ships in its Navy, scores of vessels would be moored in any one port, the punitive ceremony of 'Flogging round the Fleet' thereby taking several hours to complete.

In 1761 John Rookey, guilty of mutinous behaviour, received thirty lashes alongside each ship in commission in port, plus twelve months in prison, while seaman Robert Taylor earned twelve lashes by the bosun's mates of every ship in Portsmouth harbour, for thieving, these being only two of the many thousands listed in Naval records.

As an Awful Example to one's shipmates, accompanied by humiliation and agony, no doubt flogging round the fleet had its place in the naval discipline considered necessary to control men of that calibre. Whether it was effective is anyone's guess.

In 1871 it was decreed that only mutiny or offering violence to a superior officer were to carry a sentence involving corporal punishment, and in 1879 even that punishment was limited to twenty-five lashes.

By 1881 flogging could only be awarded with Admiralty concurrence, but it was not until 1949 that all corporal punishment was finally and officially abolished. Caning of boy seamen was however retained, not being done away with until some years later.

## Whipping in France

The official instrument of punishment in that country was the whip, expertly wielded by the executioner, and in one much publicised case early in the eighteenth century it was used with devastating effect on the bare shoulders of a beautiful woman named Antoinette Sicard.

The mademoiselle was in love with a Baron von Schlieban, a conspirator in a plot to murder the Regent, Philippe d'Orleans. One evening a furious row developed between the couple, attracting the attention of neighbours, who promptly broke in and endeavoured to separate them. In the mêlée that followed, the Baron managed to escape before the police arrived, and Antoinette, rather than disclose the identity of her partner and thereby possibly incriminate herself in the assassination plot, declared that she was a prostitute and did not know her 'client'.

133

Found guilty of being a harlot and creating a public nuisance, she was sentenced to thirty lashes, to stand in the pillory for one hour, and to serve an indefinite period in prison. Antoinette was taken to the Halles pillory, adjoining the executioner's house and there, before an avidly watching crowd, she was stripped to the waist, her wrists being secured to rings set in the wall.

Charles Sanson, the executioner, ordered one of his assistants to grip the woman's ankles while the other assistant commenced to whip the now weeping and struggling woman. To an accompaniment of abusive and obscene comments from the mob, Antoinette Sicard endured the thirty strokes of the whip.

But even though the whip descended for the last time, her ordeal continued. Charles Sanson released her from her bonds and allowed her to replace her upper garments, only to lead her to the waiting pillory, there to lock her pretty neck and wrists immovable in its wooden grasp, before escorting her to prison.

Instruments other than whips were occasionally used to flog offenders. Even in the 1920s the prison guards in the French penal colonies used long, supple riding whips with which to control the convicts, lacerating blows being delivered for the slightest infraction of the rules.

But without doubt the most horrific weapon, for weapon it was, was the *Battoir*. In 1818, during a period of intense religious conflict, the Protestants suffered appalling maltreatment at the hands of the more numerous Catholics, persecution verging on massacre.

The history of the persecution, written by Mark Wilks in 1821, describes how peaceful scenes of rural domesticity erupted into bloodbaths within minutes, by the use of otherwise innocuously shaped pieces of wood resembling battledores.

This household implement, part of every French woman's laundry equipment, was used by her to beat the sodden clothes when washing the family linen at the village fountain or river bank. But this simple paddle was converted into a weapon of terrible mutilation by the fanatical Catholics when they attacked the Protestant communities. In Wilks's words

The Catholics vented their fury on the wives and daughters of Protestants by a newly invented punishment. They turned their victims' petticoats over their heads and so fastened them as to favour their shameful exposure, and their subjection to chastisement; and nails being driven into the wood of the battoirs in the form of a fleur-de-lys, they beat them until the blood streamed from their bodies, and their screams rent the air.

Often was death prayed for by their victims, as a commutation of this ignominious punishment; but death was refused with malignant joy; murder was to perfect, and not prevent the obscene and cruel sport. To carry their outrages to the highest possible degree, they assailed in this manner several who were in a state of pregnancy.

Madame Rath, when near her confinement, was attacked by about sixty of the Catholics, armed with knotted cords, battoirs and stones. It was with difficulty that she escaped instant death, and only by extraordinary skill that her life was preserved in premature childbirth, though her babe just breathed, then expired.

Madame Gautiere and Madame Domerque, in a similar critical period, were treated with the same indignities. Madame Reboul died in a few days of the injuries she had received, her young daughter Benouette being beaten and torn with nails by the inhuman rabble of both sexes.

The *battoir*, with its fleur-de-lys of nails, was never a judicial instrument, and it reverted to its commonplace use when religious harmony of sorts was restored in later years. The official whip, as an instrument of punishment, was abolished in 1789, but continued to be used in the French Navy until the Provisional Government of 1848 finally suppressed its use, other than in the prison hulks.

## Whipping in Denmark and Holland

Eighteenth-century Danish and Dutch inhabitants were left in no doubt as to what awaited them, should they transgress; the whipping post was prominent in Dutch gaols, and put to frequent use; in Denmark those guilty of infanticide were imprisoned for life and were whipped annually on the anniversary of and at the place where they had committed the murder.

135

Visitors to most Danish towns were greeted by a conspicuously sited whipping post surmounted by a figure of a man, a whip in his right hand, a sword slung at his waist. Such threatening symbols and their implied punishments obviously met with the approval of the man who became the inspiration behind the Howard League for Penal Reform, John Howard. He went even further, recommending more drastic measures:

> Would not some public intimations of the punishment to follow crimes be useful also in England? Notwithstanding the numbers of fishermen and loose boys about Amsterdam, the Hague and Schevelin, their public walks and beautiful plantations remain uninjured; which is owing, partly to the strictness of the police, and partly to the warnings given by placards painted on boards and hung up in different places, with representations of whippings, cutting off hands, etc.

Hardly a policy to be advocated by his twentieth-century disciples!

## Whipping in Germany

The early Teutonic whip consisted of a short wooden handle from which protruded iron cords, each with a spiked circle at its end, the better to ravage flesh and sinew.

A more conventional, though still extremely painful type of whip was used in the seventeenth century as retribution for many minor crimes, one of which was that of perjury. Unlike its present meaning – lying while under oath – in those days it applied to those who, after conviction, breached their vow to keep the peace, sought revenge on officers of the State, or returned to the town from which they had been banished. For them, a broken promise meant broken skin on their bared back.

Husbands and wives also felt the kiss of the lash should they practise infidelity, for bigamy and polygamy carried the penalty of being flogged out of town, a long and painful journey. Despite there being no marriage ceremony or vow-taking as such, the authorities frowned on a partner who reneged on the verbal contract and took others in matrimony.

Thieves and swindlers, adulterers and witches received neither mercy nor lessons in social adjustment. Town councils did not waste ratepayers' money on imprisoning them, but simply ordered the executioner to use the whip while escorting them to the city limits, there to tell them to keep walking – or limping.

So it was in December 1588 when Ann Pergmennin was caught stealing. Unable to follow up her boast that because of the powers she possessed, she would escape by flying away on a pitchfork, she remained earthbound long enough to be whipped to the boundary and banished.

Cheating at backgammon brought no profit to Hans Gessert, and Hans Spiss had a similar unavoidable appointment with the executioner when, instead of intercepting a wanted murderer, he ran the other way.

A blackguard who richly deserved his fate was Stephen Reutter who, in 1599, got his girlfriend into trouble after having promised marriage. As a remedy for her unfortunate condition, he brought her some *Juniperus sabina* and helped her mother to brew it, but the concoction was not successful. Later, as recorded by the executioner, 'Reutter had four times lain with the mother in her bed, wearing only his shirt, the daughter and nurse being privy to the fact. For which reason, as a favour, I merely flogged him out of town.' As such an event was usually punishable by decapitation, it was a favour worth accepting.

## Whipping in Russia

Knout, Knoot or Knut; the spelling might be different but the result spelt only one thing – insufferable agony which all too frequently culminated in death.

Ever since it was introduced into Russia by Ivan III in the fifteenth century, there were various designs of the knout, and different ways of administering it.

The common knout had a wooden handle about a foot long, its thongs being plaited together to give a two-foot lash. At its end was fastened a further thong, eighteen inches in length, tapering to a point. This latter extension could be detached and replaced by another, for despite being soaked in milk and frozen, it soon became softened by the victim's blood.

This type of knout was at one time administered with the offender stretched over the back of one of the executioner's assistants. Extra punishment was inflicted by incorporating a whipping with that of strappado – the victim was hoisted by his wrists, his hands behind him, the whip compounding the pain caused by dislocated shoulder-blades.

Another version bore thongs of leather interwoven with wire cords, bare wire protruding from the extremities. But the really fearsome brute was the Great Knout. Mounted on a nine-inch wooden handle was a single leather lash, sixteen inches in length. A metal ring at its end permitted the attachment of yet another lash of nine inches length. And at the extremity of that one was a further attenuated one of hard leather, having a metal hook at its tip.

We are fortunate indeed to be able to refer to the detailed and factual reports of John Howard, who was one of the few if not the only Englishman to have visited and inspected so many national and foreign prisons during the eighteenth century. No naive do-gooder, no protesting campaigner, he had known prison conditions from the inside, for in 1756, while on a voyage to Lisbon, the ship had been captured by a French privateer, and Howard found himself imprisoned at Brest.

His account therefore of a flogging he witnessed at St Petersburg on 10 August 1781 owes nothing to journalistic extravagance and everything to the discerning eye of an experienced observer. He said,

I saw two criminals, a man and a woman, suffer the punishment of the knoot. They were conducted from prison by about fifteen hussars and ten soldiers. When they arrived at the place of punishment the hussars formed themselves into a ring about the whipping post, the drum beat for a minute or so, and some prayers were repeated, the populace taking off their hats.

The woman was taken first, and after being roughly stripped to the waist, her hands and feet were bound with cords to a post made for the purpose, a man standing before the post to keep the cords tight. A servant attended the executioner, and both were stout men.

The servant first marked his ground, then struck the woman five times on the back. Every stroke seemed to penetrate deep into her flesh. But his master, thinking him too gentle, pushed him aside and took his place, giving all the remaining strokes himself, which were evidently more severe.

The woman received twenty-five, the man sixty strokes; I pressed through the hussars and counted the number as they were chalked on a board. Both seemed but just alive, especially the man, who yet had strength enough to accept my small present with some signs of gratitude. They were conducted back into the prison in a little wagon. I saw the woman in a very weak condition, some days after, but could not find the man any more.

That the great knout, wielded by an expert knout master, could kill, was confirmed in another of Howard's reports, this time from Riga.

while inspecting the prison there, the head knoot-master was brought from St Petersburgh, who being with two other knoot-masters at a public house, they happened to quarrel. He immediately struck off the head of one of them; the other, seeming to resent it, he dexterously decapitated him also.

As no crime, not even one of shedding blood, is punished in Russia by death, this man received two hundred and seventy strokes of the knoot, the executioner from Moscow being brought for that purpose. And being condemned for life, was branded accordingly.

In Riga prison he met several of his former acquaintances to whom he had given the knoot, and on being asked in how many strokes he could kill a man, he said, if a strong man, he could in five and twenty, but if not strong, in twenty strokes.

Not that the knout was restricted to common criminals. Alex, son of Peter the Great, was reportedly flogged to death by his father, and the Empress Eudoxia, suspected of infidelity, broke down on hearing of her fate and confessed to every accusation made against her. But her admission came too late, and after being knouted, she was incarcerated in prison.

Eventually, after 400 years of inflicting mutilation and death, the knout went out of use. In 1845, during the reign of the Emperor Nicholas, it was abolished and was replaced by the triple-thonged *pleti*, a somewhat less lethal instrument of punishment than its predecessor.

## Whipping in the Middle East

Still carried out to the present day in many of these countries, the earlier, more barbaric punishments included being rolled in thorns and torn with sharp reeds. In Egypt offenders were stripped and flogged on their backs, women while they knelt, men while lying prone, up to 1,000 lashes being administered. Persia, now Iran, favoured the *bastinado*, where the victim was almost gently and rhythmically beaten with a lightweight stick or bamboo on the soles of the feet. Continued for any length of time, this usually resulted in uncontrollable hysteria and eventual mental collapse.

The *bastinado* was also used in Turkey to punish shopkeepers who swindled their customers. In the eighteenth century, police would carry out surprise checks, arresting in particular bakers whose loaves were underweight. Offenders were taken to prison and there they would be bastinadoed. Turkey was not the only country whose bakers feared retribution for that offence, even though punishment did not come via the *bastinado*. In English bakeries, rather than run the risk, bakers sold loaves in batches of thirteen instead of the usual twelve, thereby originating the phrase 'a baker's dozen'.

In Smyrna's gaol, John Howard saw a prisoner who had been bastinadoed so severely that he was swollen from head to foot, and advised him 'to bathe in the sea and to apply salt and vinegar plasters to the throbbing soles of his feet. The addition of two doses of Glauber's Salt (crystallised sodium sulphate) would prove a considerable amelioration, which indeed it proved to be.'

## Whipping in the Orient

True masters of whipping using the bamboo, the Chinese developed it to a fine art. As an alternative to the soles of the feet, the bare buttocks were the target for incessant, featherlight

140

blows, the same devastating effect as that of the *bastinado* being produced within a matter of minutes. Similar results were achieved by using a split bamboo on the upper thighs, the knife-like edges lacerating the flesh with every blow.

But perhaps the most fiendish torture was that devised during the Manchu dynasty, where victims were flogged by 'lictors' wielding long thin canes. So adept were they that they could strike hundreds of times without lacerating the flesh, or draw blood with three blows. If the court decreed extra severity, the lictors would flick the bamboo so that it tore off the flesh in strips.

Such expertise was achieved only by constant practice on a block of bean curd, a substance resembling thick custard. Perfection was not reached until they were able to strike repeatedly without breaking the surface.

As in England, where it was considered too indelicate to sentence a woman to be drawn and quartered, so in China women's modesty was equally respected. They were allowed to retain their lower garments, but were punished by being caned on their mouths or hands, or by having their breasts pierced by hot irons.

In Japan, too, the bamboo industry prospered. That country's instrument consisted of three lengths of split bamboo bound together, up to a hundred or more blows being delivered to the back and buttocks, the multiple edges of the bamboo causing extensive lacerations. The Japanese authorities did not hesitate to use this implement in the countries they had invaded, such as Korea and Formosa, and although judicial torture was officially abolished in 1873, many Allied prisoners of war during the Second World War would emphatically refute this.

## Whipping in the Philippines

In complete contrast to the customary wielders of the whip, executioners, prison warders and the like, the Filipinos received their floggings at the hands of the Roman Catholic priests. From the early days of Spanish rule in the sixteenth century, to the turn of the present century, the friars subjugated the natives. As reported in a Senate investigation in 1900, the Commissioner quoted a priest as saying, 'The Filipino must be given bread with one hand and a rattan beating with the other.'

Another witness stated in his testimony that

> The principal cause for the hostility against the friar curates in the said provinces has been egotism, unbridled license, ill-treatment, and contempt for the Philipino.
>
> As a sample of what a displeased parish priest is capable of, I shall relate what I witnessed about the year 1867 or 1868 in Rosales on a feast day after high mass at the very moment in which the people were leaving the church. The curate of this pueblo, Fr Raimundo Gallardo, a Franciscan, with his sleeves rolled up, was in front of the principal entrance to the church belabouring the shoulders of a man standing, though strongly tied to a step ladder, with a rattan. I left that repugnant spectacle, which lasted, I subsequently learned, until the curate no longer had strength to continue.

The instrument of punishment, the rattan, was a part of an East Indian climbing palm, the name being derived from the Malay *rotan*. This plant has many thin and pliable stems which, being cane-like and flexible, could almost have been designed for chastisement purposes.

## Whipping in Australia

Just as English law prescribed the whip for lawbreakers and prison inmates, so the same applied to convicts while in seaborne transports *en route* to Australia and also when they had landed in what was at that time virtually a penal colony. Medieval Germany flogged its unwanted criminals out of town; England flogged its criminals out of the country, and then continued to flog them. An investigation by a House of Commons committee, undertaken before transportation to New South Wales ceased in 1840, uncovered many cases of brutality.

Twenty-five lashes were the norm for stealing, Richard Johnson receiving that number in April 1823, for acquiring a pair of blue trousers, the proceeds of a robbery. John M'Clutchy escaped from his working party and, recaptured, was promised twenty-five lashes each day until he informed on those who had sheltered him.

Whereas a once-for-all punishment was soon over and done

with, this instalment system was deliberately devised to prey on the convict's nerves, thereby sapping his morale. So James Blackburn, caught gambling in April 1822, was sentenced to twenty-five lashes every morning until he gave the names of his fellow gamblers, and Thomas Smith looked forward with less than relish to being flogged every second day until he told the authorities where he had hidden the goods he had stolen.

There were, of course, far more serious crimes, such as that committed by one convict who, on passing a magistrate in the street, failed to doff his cap. For that he received fifty lashes.

## Whipping in Mauritius

Wherever slavery flourished, so the whip was the instrument of subjugation. And in countries where the supply of slaves was virtually inexhaustible, it mattered not whether excessive flogging resulted in a high death rate, for fatalities were easily replaced. To put it succinctly, slaves were always on a hiding to nothing.

Mauritius, a beautiful island in the Indian Ocean, was occupied by the Dutch in 1598 and later, in 1715, by the French. In 1814 the territory was ceded to Britain, and although by then slavery in the British dominions had been abolished, it made little difference to those landowners who maintained large labour forces.

The absence of any controls gave them an unfettered hand to administer unlimited floggings, the victim, male or female, either being tied to a triangular framework or to a ladder lying flat on the ground. After the flogging, which usually consisted of a hundred lashes or more, salt or a similar irritant was rubbed into the slave's mutilated back, intensifying the agony and retarding the healing process.

## Whipping in Jamaica

Inhumanity on a vast scale was the unavoidable lot of the slaves in Jamaica. First brought over from Africa in 1563, their numbers increased until by 1825 there were no fewer than 314,300, providing cheap labour to the plantation owners. Purchased for about £30, a slave became the sole property of his owner and was subjected to whatever punishment his master wished.

The usual weapon was the cart whip, its lash, mounted on a two-foot handle, sometimes being twelve to fifteen feet long, and tapering to a vicious point. Wielded by a practised hand, it could cut a slave's back to ribbons within seconds and disable him or her for life.

Although the number of blows by an overseer was limited to thirty-nine for one offence, this was circumvented by accusing the slave of several offences, thereby permitting a flogging of greater severity, sometimes as many as 300 strokes being given. Or after thirty-nine blows, the whip would be exchanged for a tamarind switch – a thin flexible cane from the tropical fruit tree of that name. An exotic title for a fearsome instrument.

The ubiquitous cat-o'-nine-tails was also popular with planters, some of whom were so sadistic as to flog women in the presence of their children or, worse, to force their husbands to administer the thrashing. In the *Anti-Slavery Monthly Reporter* of 1829, the Reverend Peter Duncan reported: 'In the year 1827 I knew of a married negress having been flogged in the presence of her fellow slaves, and I believe her husband too, for it was her husband and herself and other slaves who told me the circumstances. Merely because this negress would not submit to satisfy the lust of her overseer, he had flogged and confined her for several days in the stocks.'

## Whipping in the United States of America
In 1656 Mary Fisher and Ann Austin, members of the Society of Friends, landed at Boston after a perilous voyage from England, only to receive a most unfriendly reception. The two Quakers were faced by a large and hostile crowd obviously opposed to everything that they thought the Quakers represented, and within minutes the two women were 'stripped stark naked, in such an immodest manner as modesty will not permit me to describe'. Tied to a cart's tail, they were publicly whipped before being forced to re-embark on the ship which had brought them.

Other members of the Society followed later, imbued with the same zealous spirit, only to be persecuted by the New England Puritans. Accounts of their sufferings written in 1702 tell how

Mary Tomkins and Alice Ambrose were cruelly ordered to be whipped at a cart's tail through eleven towns at one time, ten stripes on their naked backs, which would have amounted to one hundred and ten in the whole, and on a very cold day, they were stripped and whipped through three of the towns, the priests looking on and laughing, and through dirt and snow, sometimes half leg deep.

Lydia Ward was stripped from the waist upwards, tied to a fence post, with her naked breasts to the splinters of the post, and there sorely lashed, with twenty or thirty cruel stripes. Ann Coleman was whipped within an inch of her life, the knots of the whip splitting her breasts, and Edward Wharton was flogged so severely that peas might lie in the holes that the knots of the whip had beat into the flesh of his arms and his back, and his body was swelled and very black from the waist upwards. Thomas Newhouse was stripped and fastened to a gunwheel, where he was given ten stripes, and then on three occasions whipped at the cart's tail.

A century later, others were being mercifully flogged, not because of the spiritual message they brought but simply because they were slaves, shipped from Africa to work in the plantations of the southern States of America. That physical punishment was countenanced by the authorities is evidenced by an Act of Legislature in 1740 which stated

In case any person shall wilfully cut out the tongue, put out the eye or cruelly scald, burn, or deprive any slave of any limb or member, or shall inflict any other cruel punishment, *other than by whipping, or beating with a horse-whip, cow-skin, switch or small-stick* (my italics), or by putting irons on, or confining or imprisoning such slave, every such person shall for every such offence, forfeit the sum of one hundred pounds current money.

It must have been gratifying for the slaves to know that the Government at least disapproved of tongue removal, blinding or amputation, if nothing else.

Traditional type whips were used, sometimes followed by the application of red pepper to the wounds to intensify the pain. As, however, an excess of scars could lower a slave's value on the market, the more ingenious of the Southern gentlemen perfected the art of cobbing. Instead of the whip, a wooden paddle was used, in which holes had been drilled. This weapon left few marks on the flesh and, if anything, caused more pain because on the downward stroke the holes permitted the air trapped between paddle and flesh to escape more quickly, the paddle thereby travelling the faster.

As related by the world-famous author Harriet Beecher Stowe, slaves held prisoner in gaols such as that in New Orleans were subjected to brutal whippings on the slightest pretext, many delivered by other negroes. The victims, male and female alike, would be stretched on a board, their thumbs bound together and tied to one end of the board, their feet to the other.

Naked below the waist-strap that held them immovable, they would then have to endure fifty, even a hundred lashes before being released. And although slavery was declared illegal in 1865 by Abraham Lincoln, it still lingered in the more isolated plantations for many years afterwards.

Whipping, far from lingering, continued to thrive. In 1851, negroes found on the streets of Boston after dusk were taken into custody and received thirty-nine lashes of the whip, these being administered by a police officer, who was paid fifty cents for his or rather their pains.

This particular number of lashes, thirty-nine, also mentioned as being the maximum permitted in Jamaica, was in accordance with the Law of Moses in the Old Testament Book of Deuteronomy, chapter 25, verses 2 and 3, which states 'And it shall be, if the wicked man be worthy to be beaten, that the judge shall cause him to lie down, and to be beaten before him, and to receive a certain number according to his fault. Forty stripes he may give him, and shall not exceed; lest if he should exceed, and beat him above these with many stripes, then those who judged him should seem vile unto thee.' So rather than 'seeming vile', the judiciary stayed on the safe side and restricted the penalty to thirty-nine lashes.

Where offenders were already in prison, such limits did not apply, of course. In the Sing Sing penitentiary of the nineteenth century, the instrument most feared by recalcitrant convicts was the cat-o'-nine-tails. As if the searing impact of its wire-tipped leather thongs were not punishment enough on an inmate's bare back, the subsequent and far from soothing caress of the salt-water sponge on the broken flesh finally drove the lesson home.

Similarly, in San Quentin prison, inmates were whipped while strapped to a ladder secured at an angle to the wall. Unlike the practice in British gaols, in which those being flogged had their necks and kidneys protected by pads, San Quentin convicts were stripped naked for the whip, thereby having to risk serious injury.

The end of flogging by the cat came in 1880, but other instruments took over. If an ordinary baton did not subdue a violent prisoner, a two-foot length of hose, corded at one end to provide a non-slip handle, weighted at the other end with an insert of lead, certainly did. Sharp-edged paddles taught the inmates of Ohio State Penitentiary to be penitent, and their compatriots in North Carolina heeded the persuasive powers of the leather strap.

By the 1940s, corporal punishment had been all but abolished from American prisons, though in view of the simmering violence constantly pervading such institutions, it is hardly surprising that instruments other than those purely of restraint lurk in the background, to be wielded when necessary.

# 10
## Spectator Sports

Although a world away from such crimes as treason, conspiracy and murder, minor offences committed against society at large had nevertheless to be dealt with. Little more than a century and a half ago, before the days of railways and cheap transport, villages and towns were closely knit communities in which most people knew everyone else. So when someone transgressed the accepted social or moral code, what better retribution to exact than a punishment that everyone could see?

The name of the game was Getting One's Come-uppance while the neighbours watched. Ridicule was a powerful medicine as well as a deterrent, so a wide range of shame-inflicting restraints were at the disposal of the local magistrates, the choice being determined by the nature and seriousness of the offence.

### The Stocks
These were perhaps the most widely used punitive device, some also being utilised to secure offenders awaiting trial. Many stocks still survive on village greens, though now regrettably they are only olde worlde artefacts rather than a threat to wrongdoers such as vandals and lager louts.

Portrayed in Anglo-Saxon books, stocks were in constant use for many centuries, changing little in design. They were of simple construction, consisting of two sturdy uprights fixed in the ground, having grooves down their inner surfaces in which were slotted two solid timber boards, one above the other. Each plank had semicircular notches in it, positioned so that when aligned with the other, the notches formed holes which encircled the culprit's ankles.

With the upper plank locked in position by a padlock, there was no escape for the victim until he or she was released by the beadle, sergeant-at-mace, or other appointed official.

Situated as they were in the centre of the village or town, the unhappy occupant of the stocks was inevitably the focus of attention, not least by those who relished his or her discomfiture. A target for jibes and taunts, if nothing more injurious, the victims could do little to retaliate, or even defend themselves. This was of course the whole purpose of the punishment, literally to make a laughing-stock of them by exposure to the scorn and opprobrium of the others in the community.

The authorities considered it so important that villages should have stocks that Acts decreeing this were passed in 1351, 1376 and 1405, the latter further declaring that the absence of stocks would downgrade a village to the status of a mere hamlet.

Larger towns had more than one set of stocks, and in 1503 Sir William Capell, Lord Mayor of London, ordered that every ward in the City should be equipped with them. Those by the Tower of London were commented on by the sixteenth-century historian Machyn: 'At St Katheryne beyond the Toure the ale wyfe at the Syne of the Rose, a taverne was set up for ettyng of rowe flesh and rostyd bowth – and four women was sett in the stokes all nyght till the hosbandes dyd feyche them hom.'

In 1497, Westminster Hall stocks gripped the ankles of Perkin Warbeck, the impostor who claimed to be one of the murdered Little Princes, and he, like them, ended his days in the Tower. Even Henry VIII's high and mighty Cardinal Wolsey was similarly secured at Limington, near Yeovil, in 1500, for drinking unwisely at the village feast.

At the other end of the social scale, the newspaper *The Scotsman* reported on 2 April 1834 that a Kelso woman convicted of stealing clothing from a hedge was placed in the stocks, and the novelty of the spectacle attracted large crowds. Another delinquent, William Allen, found guilty of abusing his wife on a Sunday – evidently not a crime on a weekday – spent twenty-four hours in the stocks on market day. Another such offence, he was warned, would lead to his being banished from the town.

Beggars were always a prime target, as evidenced by a statute in 1426 which decreed that, for a first offence, such vagrants were

Two young boys in the stocks

The whipping post

The drunkard's cloak, also known as the Spanish Mantle, was the seventeenth and eighteenth centuries' punishment for the lager louts of the day

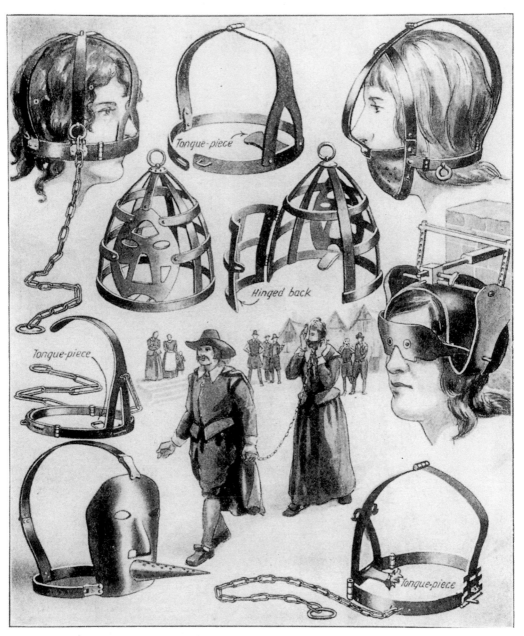

Some variations of the scold's bridle

The picquet, also known as the picket.

Martyr roasting on the gridiron

*Opposite* Leg-irons and whipping stocks at Newgate Priso

Torture of the pulley

A Czech executioner
wearing his working apron
(detail from an altar-piece
dating from 1430–40)

A disembowelling (detail
from an engraving dated
1592)

A convict with his thumbs tied in preparation for the sentence of death

to be kept in the stocks for three days and three nights, on bread and water only, and then expelled from the town. A second offence would earn them a longer sojourn – no less than six days and nights in the stocks, on a similar diet.

However, this punishment was somewhat mitigated by a later statute dated 1504 which reduced it to only one day and night for a first offence and three days and nights for a second offence – a humanitarian measure indeed.

Wood stealers, ladies of ill repute, card sharps and gamblers were all candidates for the stocks, as were those who refused to assist with the harvest. Sunday drinkers in the town of Skipton, Yorkshire, had to be extra cautious, for while the church service was in progress, the churchwardens would visit the inns looking for those who preferred holding tankards rather than hymn books.

The wardens were led by the beadle, resplendent in his gold-trimmed coat and cocked hat, and carrying his staff of office. Anyone found imbibing ale would be locked in the stocks until midday, though occasions arose when the wardens themselves yielded to the temptations of their task and finished up drunk!

Resisting arrest was also punished by a spell in the stocks. The offender had to go to church during morning prayers and publicly apologise for his actions. He was then taken out and set in the stocks until the end of the evening prayer, and the punishment was repeated on the next market day.

Great houses and colleges had their own set of stocks for servants and students, and prisons used them for restraint. Stafford Gaol was able to cope with multiple disobedience by having a set of stocks ten yards long.

In 1705 Beatrix Laing, who lived in the town of Pittenweem, Fife, was accused of witchcraft. After her resistance had been broken by harsh and cruel treatment, she was put in the stocks, then imprisoned for months in solitary confinement before being driven out of town.

Some stocks required the culprit to sit on a bench, others to sit on the ground. A few had extra attachments to grip the victim's wrists and neck, while others raised the ankles in the air. Occasionally, stocks were situated inside the town's gaol. John Dalaber was punished in 1528 by being locked into 'a great pair of very high stocks, in which I sat, my feet being almost as high as my head. And so my masters departed, locking fast the door and leaving me quite alone.'

The duration of imprisonment in the stocks was of course part of the sentence imposed by the magistrates. John Gambles of Pudsey, Yorkshire, was reported in the *Leeds Mercury* of 14 April 1860, of having lived up to his name by gambling on a Sunday, an offence for which he was secured in the town's stocks for six hours.

Even as recently as 1825 a set of stocks on London Bridge was still in use, and the last recorded case in England was that of rag and bone man Mark Tuck, who was found drunk and disorderly in the parish church at Newbury on Monday 10 June 1872. A crowd of hundreds gathered the next day to witness his discomfiture as he sat facing the church with his ankles locked in the stocks. His exclamations of relief as the church bells chimed each passing quarter of an hour were drowned by shouts of derision from the crowd, and it was not until four hours later that he was released.

The plight of anyone secured in such a device was exacerbated the longer one had to stay there. Even apart from the unwelcome attentions of the audience, the delicate question of how to deal with nature's demands was ever present. In Germany a possible solution was included in a description of stocks installed in the gaol in Nuremberg. It was explained that 'the sanitary arrangements provided with the machine show that some of those who were locked in it suffered for days on end. It was customary to put such patients (!) on short rations.'

In Trinidad a variation on the standard-pattern stocks was employed. Used as an alternative to flogging female prisoners, its two uprights were over six feet in height, with an adjustable crossbar to secure the woman's wrists high above her head. A lower crossbar gripped her ankles in such a way that only her toes touched the ground, thereby suspending her for long periods only by her wrists, a torture not dissimilar to the Gauntlets of an earlier chapter.

## The Pillory

Also known as the Stretchneck, the pillory was anciently described as 'an engine made of wood, designed to punish offenders by exposing them to public view and rendering them infamous'. As an instrument of judicial punishment the pillory, like the stocks, was of simple construction, well within the capabilities of the average village carpenter.

It consisted of a wooden post with its end sunk into the ground, or more usually mounted on a platform. Fixed to the top of the post were two horizontal boards, the upper board being hinged at one end to the lower one. Each had three semi-circular holes cut in it which matched up when the upper board was lowered.

The culprit stood directly behind the post, the upper board was then lowered so that his or her head was trapped in the central, larger hole, wrists being similarly pinioned in the two outer holes. Appropriately enough, the device's name was derived from a Greek phrase meaning 'to look through a doorway'. Thus secured, the victim could neither withdraw his head nor his hands, and such were the distances between the holes that it was also impossible for him to reach his mouth with his hands, so that he was incapable of feeding or drinking without assistance. Worse, he was unable to protect his face and head from any assault directed against him.

The device had been on the statute-books since 1269, enacted during the reign of Henry III, and Lords of the Manor claimed the right to erect their own pillory, together with a ducking stool and a gallows, on their estates.

Pillories were considered so essential by the authorities that villages not having one risked forfeiting the right to hold a market – a serious loss of trade in those days. And once towns and villages had installed pillories, culprits were quickly found. In 1364 John de Hackford caused public alarm and consternation by declaring that 10,000 men were assembling to murder the councilmen of London. For that he was sentenced to be imprisoned for a year and a day, and every three months he was to be marched through the streets to the pillory preceded by two trumpeters, there to stand without hood or girdle, barefoot and unshod, with a whetstone hung by a chain about his neck, and a notice 'False Liar' on his chest.

Later that century, in 1385, Alan Birchore, a maker of bow-strings, brought four dozen of his products to London and sold them. When they were tested in practice they were found to be faulty 'and to the people's manifest peril'. To put the safety of the King's Realm in such jeopardy could not be tolerated, and Birchore was secured in the pillory at Cornhill for one hour, the faulty strings being burnt in front of him.

Many other offences were punishable by a sojourn in the pillory. Among the people at risk were those who bought goods at fairs and resold them at a higher price, those who cornered the market and so gained a monopoly, and others committing similar dubious transactions.

From such heinous crimes, the penalty of the pillory was widened to include 'those who sold putrid meat, stinking fish, rotting birds, and bread with pieces of iron in it to increase its weight'. Purveyors of faulty goods were also liable, as were innkeepers whose spirit measures contained a layer of pitch in their bases, gamblers who used loaded dice and coalmen whose sacks were shorter or narrower than permissible. Merchants who bought or sold goods after the curfew, cutpurses and witches, even itinerant vagrants who obtained money by sleight of hand, faced the penalty. In short, pillories all over the country were much in use, especially in the larger towns where commerce and trade flourished. London, although much smaller in those days, nevertheless boasted pillories at Westminster and the Royal Exchange, Charing Cross and Temple Bar, Tyburn of course, and one at the Maypole in the Strand.

Two men who paid for their audacity by being locked in the Tyburn pillory were William Duffin and Thomas Lloyd. Not content with escaping from the Fleet Prison, they actually delayed their departure in order to nail an impudent notice to its massive gates, advertising 'This prison to let, and peaceable possession will be given by the present tenants on or before 1 January 1793'.

With the passing of time, pillories became more elaborate in design. Some had a circular platform near the top of the post so that six or more victims could be pilloried together. The posts of others were used as whipping posts, with two pairs of stocks positioned at the base.

Village humour never being far away, one unfortunate occupant explained sarcastically to an enquirer that he was not really being pilloried but was 'celebrating his nuptials with Miss Wood', and that his friend, then being flogged by the beadle, was in reality dancing at his wedding!

Some pillories were raised high above the ground on a lofty pole for greater prominence. One of this type was built in Manchester, Lancashire, a document dated April 1625 recording 'the jurye doth order that the constables for this yeare, att the charges of the inhabitants, shall cause to bee erected and set vp a sufficient gibbett or pilorye for the vse of this towne, in some convenient place about the Markett Crosse, to be done before the xxiiijth daye of August next'.

Not all pillories were situated in the centre of towns, of course. In 1813 an innkeeper in Rye, Sussex, was found guilty of assisting a French prisoner of war, General Philippon, to escape. For his treachery, the man was pilloried at a rather more appropriate site, the pillory itself being moved and re-erected on the beach so that its occupant would have to face in the direction of France while enduring the abuse of the crowd.

Exposed to all weathers, some pillories deteriorated over the years, and this was never more true than when one such device got into such a bad state that under the weight of an occupant, the footboard collapsed, leaving him hanging by his neck and wrists. When eventually released he took legal action, sued the council for negligence, and won his case.

Even worse than a stretched neck befell Thomas Scott, whose punishment was reported in the *Morning Herald* of 28 January 1804:

The enormity of Scott's offence, in accusing Captain Kennah and his servant of robbery, having attracted much public notice, his conviction that followed the attempt could not but be gratifying to all lovers of justice. Yesterday the culprit underwent a part of his punishment; he was placed in the pillory at Charing Cross for one hour. On his first appearance he was greeted by a large mob with a discharge of small shot such as rotten eggs, filth, and dirt from the streets,

155

which was followed up by dead cats, rats etc. which had been collected in the vicinity of the Metropolis by boys earlier in the morning.

When he was taken away to prison, in which place he was sentenced to serve twelve months, the mob broke the windows of the coach and would have proceeded to violence, had not the police officers been at hand.

As in that case, punishment by pillory was often only part of the sentence. In 1543 Dr London, Warden of New College, was so determined that a group of heretics should face retribution, that he manufactured false evidence to get them convicted.

For that offence he was removed from office and was forced to ride on a horse, seated facing backwards, a figure of ridicule, with a notice in his hat proclaiming him a detected perjurer. His uncomfortable journey took him through Windsor, Newbury and Reading, in the market places of which he had to stand in the pillory, to be pelted by the mob. Imprisonment in the Fleet Prison followed, the insanitary conditions there bringing about his early death.

The injuries inflicted by missiles were not all that the victim had to suffer, as Timothy Penruddy discovered in 1575. Found guilty of forging the seal of the King's Bench Division, he was sentenced to stand in the pillory in Cheapside on two successive days. And to make sure that he did not even attempt to withdraw his head, the court ordered that on the first day one of his ears was to be nailed to the wooden framework, his other ear being similarly attached on the following day.

And when Lady Jane Grey was proclaimed Queen of England, an apprentice who voiced his disapproval too loudly was pilloried, both his ears being nailed to the structure so thoroughly that the organs had to be amputated in order to free him. Had he only held his tongue for nine days, he would have retained his ears as well!

Sometimes things seemed to go from bad to worse, as in the case of James Nayler, a Quaker who claimed to be the Messiah. Selecting just about every penalty listed in the statute-book, the court sentenced him to be pilloried at Westminster for two hours displaying an account of his crimes, then whipped through the streets by the hangman to the Old Exchange. After another session in the pillory there, his tongue was to be bored through with a hot iron and a letter 'B' for blasphemer branded on his forehead.

He was then to be sent to Bristol, his home town, and paraded on horseback through the streets, facing his mount's tail, to be whipped in the market place. As if that were not enough, imprisonment in the Bridewell Prison, London, was to follow where, it was emphasised, he was to be deprived of pen, paper and ink. A salutary lesson indeed.

In the days when horses were the major motive power, there was considerable shame and humiliation in having to face the wrong way when astride, and it was a spectacle obviously enjoyed by the crowds that thronged the medieval streets. For insulting the daughter of James I, Edward Floyde was not only forbidden ever to bear arms as a gentleman again, but was in addition sentenced to be pilloried at Cheapside with the inevitable paper displayed to inform onlookers of his offence, to be whipped by the hangman, fined £5,000 and imprisoned in Newgate for life, and was also 'set on horseback, with his face to the horse's tail, holding the tail in his hand'. One wonders at the horse's reactions!

Perhaps the classic case of a multiple punishment involving a pillory was that meted out to Titus Oates in 1685. Oates was the instigator of the Popish Plot, in which prominent Catholics were accused of plotting murder and massacre, and so much credence was given to the testimony of Oates and his followers that at least sixteen innocent men were executed for high treason, among them Dr Oliver Plunkett, Catholic Primate of Ireland, Viscount Stafford and five Jesuits.

When the falsity of the accusations later became apparent, Oates was brought to trial and found guilty of perjury. Sir George Jeffreys, the Lord Chief Justice, then announced the sentence:

First the Court does order that, for a fine, you pay one thousand marks upon each indictment. Secondly that you be stripped of all your Canonical Habits. Thirdly, the Court does award that you do stand upon the pillory and in the pillory, here before Westminster Hall gate, upon Monday next, for an hour's time, between the hours of ten and twelve, with a paper over your head (which you must first walk with round about to all the courts in Westminster Hall) declaring your crime.

Fourthly, upon Tuesday, you shall stand upon and in the pillory at the Royal Exchange in London for the space of one hour, with the same inscription. You shall also upon the next Wednesday be whipped from Aldgate to Newgate. Upon Friday you shall be whipped from Newgate to Tyburn, by the hand of the common hangman.

And as annual commemorations, that it may be known to all persons as long as you live, we have taken special care of you for an annual punishment. Upon 24 August every year, as long as you live, you are to stand upon the pillory and in the pillory, at Tyburn, just opposite to the gallows, for the space of one hour between the hours of ten and twelve. You are to stand upon and in the pillory here at Westminster Hall every 9 August, in every year, as long as you live. You are to stand upon and in the pillory at Charing Cross on 10 August every year during your life, between ten and twelve. The like over against the Temple Gate on the 11th. And on 2 September you are to stand upon and in the pillory for the space of one hour at the Royal Exchange, and to be committed close prisoner as long as you live.

This I pronounce to be the judgment of the Court, and I must tell you plainly, if it had been within my power to have carried it further, I should not have been unwilling to have given judgment of death upon you, for I am sure you deserve it.

The prolonged whipping inflicted on Oates was horrific in the extreme, endangering his life, and the annual pillory attendances continued until 1688, when the penalty was annulled.

There is little doubt that throughout the centuries of the pillory, nothing more excessive than shame and indignity was intended to be the outcome, and not the violence that was only too often directed against the culprit. Yet so hated were some of those who were being pilloried, so bloodthirsty the brutal mobs who congregated at the pillory, whipping post or stocks, that even fatalities were not unknown.

When Charles Hitchen, a City Marshal, was pilloried for a minor offence, the crowds, having little love for one of his authority, broke through the cordon of Hitchen's colleagues and delivered such a veritable fusillade of cobble stones, broken bottles and brickbats that 'when released he was ready to expire'.

Other felons fared even worse. In the 1750s two men, James Egan and James Salmon, together with John Berry and Stephen M'Daniel, inveigled susceptible youths to steal valuables for them. Egan and company then denounced them to the authorities and claimed the rewards, their dupes being promptly executed.

This system was operated a number of times with much lucrative success, but eventually the gang was apprehended and put on trial at the Old Bailey. They were all found guilty and the *Newgate Calendar* reported:

> The court sentenced Berry and M'Daniel 'to stand on the pillory once at the end of Hatton Garden in Holborn, and once at the end of King Street in Cheapside; Egan and Salmon to stand once in the middle of West Smithfield, and the second time at the end of Fetter Lane in Fleet Street'.
>
> Egan and Salmon (the *Calendar* continued) were taken to Smithfield amidst a surprising concourse of people, who no sooner saw the offenders exposed on the pillory than they pelted them with stones, brick-bats, potatoes, dead dogs and cats, oyster shells and other things. The constables now interposed but, being soon overpowered, the offenders were left wholly to the mercy of an enraged mob. The blows they received occasioned their heads to swell to an enormous size, and by people hanging on to the skirts of their clothing, they were nearly strangled. They had been on the pillory about half an hour when, a stone striking Egan on the head, he immediately expired, and Salmon was so severely wounded that it was thought he would never recover.

Another who died while undergoing 'harmless' humiliation in the pillory, was John Waller. He was also a bounty hunter who fell

159

foul of the law and on 17 June 1732 was pilloried in the unsavoury slums of Seven Dials, St Giles, in London. There the efforts of the beadles and constables failed to protect him, and he was the target of the mob's vicious attack as they pelted him with stones and rotten cabbages for over an hour.

Finally the hooligans dragged him from the pillory and threw him to the ground, where he was trampled to death. Inexorably the Law took its ponderous course, and a few months later two men, Dalton and Griffiths, were arrested and charged with Waller's savage murder. Not for them the pillory, though, for both were hanged at Tyburn.

In complete contrast, there were times when the pillory *aficionados* had their heroes as well as their villains. Daniel Defoe, author of *Robinson Crusoe*, penned a few pamphlets to which the authorities took exception. He was sentenced to be imprisoned during the Queen's pleasure, fined £200, and to stand three times in the pillory at Temple Bar and Cheapside.

If his political opponents had hoped that he would suffer abuse or violence from the crowds, they were sadly disappointed, for instead of hurling brickbats, they threw roses and, clambering on to the platform, they garlanded the pillory and its pleasantly surprised occupant with more flowers.

Men of course did not have the monopoly of the pillory. In those days there was no argument about equal opportunities; if a woman was guilty, she was eligible, and in she went. To accommodate members of the fairer sex, there was a version of the pillory called the Thewes, probably consisting of a shorter post and smaller neck and wrist holes, those eligible for this model being common scolds, shrews, and ale wives guilty of purveying short measures.

Witches of course were always at risk. The Lancashire County records of 1612 describe how Margaret Pearson, found guilty of witchcraft, was sentenced 'to stand in the Pillorie in open market at Clitheroe, Whalley, Padiham and Lancaster, four market days, with a notice upon your head in great letters, declaring your offence, and there you shall confess your offence and afterwards remain in prison for one year without Baile'.

In *A Survey of London*, John Stow reported that in 1556 a procuress was pilloried at Cheapside 'for the supplying of harlots to citizens, apprentices and servants', and a year later a woman was similarly punished for beating her child.

Nor did the courts bother unduly about spoiling a woman's looks, for as Stow describes, 'In the year 1560 a maid was set in the Pillory for giving her mistress and her household poison. Besides the shame of the Pillory, one of her ears were cut, and she was burnt on the brow (branded). And two days after, she was set again on the Pillory, and her other ear cut. And but some few days after, another maid was set on the Pillory for the same crime; and her ear cut, and burnt on the brow.'

If the hangman didn't mutilate women, the mob did. As in the case of Ann Morrow, a woman who impersonated a man three times in order to marry other women. So merciless was the rabble surrounding the pillory, that she was blinded by the stones thrown at her.

It was inevitable that sooner or later a woman in the pillory would be killed, and on 30 April 1731 it became reality. Mother Needham, an infamous procuress with a criminal record stretching back over ten years, was sentenced to stand on the pillory in St James's Street, London. Despite being protected, the mob, hundreds strong, broke through the cordon and stoned her so severely that she died from her wounds two days later.

As with all similar public punishments, the pillory was eventually phased out. After nearly 600 years of subjecting men and women to degradation, the pillory was destined for the woodpile by Act 56 Geo.III 138, passed in 1816, which substituted a fine for those crimes previously punishable by the pillory, except for that of perjury.

The exception must have been regretted by those inclined to trifle with the truth while under oath, not least by Peter James Bossy who was found guilty of that offence and pilloried on Tower Hill on 22 June 1832, the last man to be so punished.

## The Barrel Pillory

The pillory might have been abolished on land, but certainly not at sea. Among the many punishments meted out by the tyrannical captains of the nineteenth-century Royal Navy was that of the Barrel Pillory. As its name implies, it consisted of a barrel placed on the quarter deck in full view of the crew and any visitors to the ship, in which any less-than-able seaman had to stand for several hours.

A dunce's cap adorned his head and, in typical pillory-style, a notice proclaiming his misdeeds was nailed to the front of the barrel for all to see.

## The French Pillory

As in England, so most French towns had their pillory, though of a rather more elegant construction. It generally consisted of a two-storey octagonal tower, within the upper room of which was a circular multi-pillory, capable of accommodating several culprits at once. Their pinioned heads and hands were visible through the large unglazed apertures in the sides of the chamber, and rather than put the watching crowds to the trouble of walking round the tower, the better to inspect the victims, the upper part of the building was made to rotate, in much the same way as did medieval windmills.

The responsibility for the Paris pillory was that of the city's executioner, and in fact the historic document appointing Charles Sanson to that official post in 1688 not only detailed his duties and emoluments, but also specified that his entitlements would include 'the use of the house and residence of the "*Pillori des Halles*" (the Market Pillory) with its purlieus and dependencies'. Living under the shop, rather than over it, as it were.

Culprits were displayed therein during three successive market days, and every half-hour one of the executioner's assistants would appear, to crank the upper chamber round a bit further, evoking a fresh outburst of taunts and jeers from the crowd at the appearance of a 'new' victim. As usual their offences were advertised by notices hung about their necks. Blasphemy, forgery, fraud, bigamy, cheating at cards, and keeping a brothel were among the more prevalent crimes.

As elsewhere, being pilloried was sometimes only part of their sentences. Those awaiting transportation to one of France's penal colonies, or destined to serve a prison sentence, were first shown in the pillory. One case which attracted much attention early in the last century was that of Mme Morin and her sixteen-year-old daughter Angelique Delaporte who, having been plunged into debt by the unscrupulous machinations of a man named Ragouleau, took drastic steps to avenge themselves.

Luring Ragouleau to a lonely house in the country, they threatened to shoot him if he refused to clear their name. The man got away and the two women were put on trial. Despite their plea that they never intended to harm the man, they were sentenced first to the pillory and then to twenty years' hard labour.

Executioner Henri Sanson escorted the widow and her daughter to the pillory in the Halles and apologised as he secured their wrists and necks. Such was the publicity of the trial that seemingly all Paris was there to watch the spectacle, but so strong was public support for the pair that only shouts of sympathy and encouragement greeted the ladies.

After an hour in the pillory they were led away to serve their imprisonment in full. The public may have felt compassion for them, but the authorities certainly did not, for when finally released in 1832, Mme Morin was sixty, and Angelique was thirty-seven years old.

Not all French pillories were identical, of course. That situated in the market square at Orleans was a cage, six feet high by two and a half feet wide, in which the prisoner had to stand. The cage revolved on a pivot, and members of the public were free to turn it round in order to see the victim from all sides, so that he or she could not avoid their jibes or missiles.

## The German Pillory

Built to the same pattern as the English pillory, the German model was a common feature in most towns. And just as in other European countries, being pilloried was only part of the punishment.

In Nuremberg in 1585 Barbara Ludtwigin was accused not only 'of being incontinent with six other people', but also 'blasphemed so horribly against the Almighty that a galley and two small ships could have been filled with her profanity'. For that she was pilloried and whipped out of town.

Another wanton *Frau*, Ursula Grimin, suffered even worse punishment for being a procuress and prostitute. Not only was she flogged through the streets to the pillory, but while there the executioner branded her on both cheeks. Then she too was whipped from the town.

## The Chinese Canque

As early as the seventeenth century the Chinese decided to dispense with the post on which the pillory was mounted and instead allow their criminals to go about their daily tasks, as far as they were able, while wearing a two-foot square collar of heavy timber resting on their shoulders.

Also known as the *Tcha*, its two halves had a semi-circular hole in each, and were locked about the felon's neck in the presence of the magistrate at the beginning of the sentence, the duration of the punishment depending on the crime committed.

Across the join of the two halves were notices stating the man's crimes, these also serving to indicate whether or not the collar had been opened. Some models had holes through which the occupant's wrists were secured, though these were too far from his head to permit him to feed himself.

The captains of Royal Navy vessels operating in eastern waters evidently witnessed the punishment of the Canque, and not only adopted it as a punishment measure themselves, but also increased its pain factor by having weights of up to sixty pounds attached to its upper surface, the amount varying with the crime and the captain's temper at the time.

## The Jougs

In Scotland, and to a lesser extent in England, those citizens who failed to attend church or even worse disrupted its services were subjected to an hour or more in the Jougs, also known as the Bregan and the Bradyeane. An iron collar would be locked about the offender's neck, then attached by a chain to the church porch or market cross, the wearer thereby being the object of ridicule and disgrace.

Other equally minor crimes carried the same penalty. Henry Machyn, in his sixteenth-century *Diary*, noted 'The 30th day of June 1553, was set a post hard by the Standard in Cheap, and a young fellow tied to the post with a collar of iron about his neck, and another to the post with a chain, and two men whipping them about the post, for pretended visions and opprobrious and seditious words.' And in 1574 David Leys, having struck his father, was sentenced to two hours in the jougs and afterwards paraded through the town, while in Dumfries, Bessie Black, found lacking in virtue, had to stand in the jougs at the market cross for six successive Sundays, for all to see.

Not all such penances ended harmlessly, however. In 1541 John Porter was arrested for the crime of reading the Bible, and was taken to Newgate Prison. He was left in the jougs there and was subsequently found dead; apparently he had fainted and been strangled by the collar.

## The French Carcan

A version of the jougs, the *Carcan* was a collar which was riveted about a criminal's neck by the executioner. He was then led, hands either tied behind his back or to the tailboard of the executioner's cart, to the market place where the collar would be attached by a chain to a post.

As usual, the length of time wearing the *carcan* varied with the offence. For instance, blasphemy carried a penalty of six hours exposure to public abuse and scorn.

## The Cage

Those arrested nowadays usually spend the night in the cells of the local police station, but in earlier times they were penned in the Cage. These were simply lock-ups, positioned strategically in the town, where disturbers of the peace could be held pending appearance before the magistrates the next day.

Larger towns had more than one cage, and in seventeenth-century London there were two on Tower Hill and another not far away, on London Bridge, where 'a woman accused of heresy found herself carried across the Bridge to the Cage wherein she was deposited and told to "coole her selfe there" '

A cage for a different purpose was built to house the Countess of Buchan in 1306. Because of her fervent support of Robert the Bruce, King Edward sentenced her to be incarcerated within a large cage erected in one of the turrets of Berwick Castle. She was attended by her own servants, but freedom was always to be denied her.

## The Drunkard's Cloak

The seventeenth and eighteenth centuries' answer to the lager louts of the day was the Drunkard's Cloak, also known as the Spanish Mantle. It was simply a barrel with the base removed and a hole cut in the top through which the culprit's head emerged. Two further holes low down in the sides allowed his or her hands to protrude, in order to take some of the barrel's weight off the shoulders. Scratching the nose, however, was quite out of the question.

The enforced retention of the barrel would seem to have been achieved by a lockable collar around the offender's neck, and while wearing it, the occupant would be led through the town by the beadle.

In a book by Ralph Gardener, published in 1655, he describes 'men driven up and down the streets with a great tub or barrel over them, with a hole in one end to put through their heads and so cover their bodies and shoulders, down to the small of their legs. This is the new-fashioned cloak, and so they make them march to the view of all beholders, and this is the punishment for drunkards and the like.'

Across the Channel they were very popular, if only with temperance societies. In Holland, Dutch drunks were doubtless grateful for the buoyancy of the contrivance, should they fall into a canal, and John Evelyn, in his *Diary*, cited the case of an erring Dutch woman and her punishment: 'A weighty vessel of wood, not unlike a butter-churn, which the adventurous woman that hath two husbands at one time is to wear on her shoulders, her head peeping out at the top, and so led about the town as a penance for her incontinence.' And when John Howard, the reformer, visited Denmark in the 1770s, he remarked that 'Some of the lower forms of criminals are being punished by being led through the city in what is called the Spanish Mantle. This is a kind of heavy vest, something like a tub, with an aperture for the head, and irons to enclose the neck. I measured one in Berlin, one foot eight inches diameter at the top, two feet eleven at the bottom, and two feet eleven inches high. This mode of punishment is particularly dreaded, and is one cause that night robberies are never heard of in Copenhagen.'

## The Scold's Bridle

One of the scourges of medieval life, if not of later centuries, was the scold, or nagging wife, and so the judiciary, with its usual robust approach to social problems, came up with the solution – gag them. And that's how the Scold's Bridle, or the Branks, as they were also known, came into being.

There were several different designs, but basically the bridle consisted of an iron framework in the form of a helmet-shaped cage which fitted tightly over the head, with eye holes and an aperture for the mouth. At the front, protruding inwards, was a small flat plate which was inserted into the woman's mouth, and the bridle was then locked about her neck.

Some models were quite painless to wear. Others had large tongue plates studded with sharp pins or a rowel, a small spiked wheel, to hold the tongue down. These could cause appalling lacerations if the victim attempted to speak.

Many bridles had a chain attached to the front so that the victim could be led through the streets, to be secured to the market cross or pillory post, and in order to herald her approach some bridles had a spring-mounted bell on the top. A splendid example of this type is on display in the Torture Chamber of the Tower of London.

Ancient houses in Congleton, Cheshire, had a hook fixed to the side of the fireplace, and incessant nagging would provoke the husband to summon the town's gaoler. He would bring the community bridle, which was then fitted on the wife and attached to the hook until the lesson was learned!

Bridles were first used in Scotland in the sixteenth century; the Statistical Account includes the report of a Montifieth woman who was convicted in February 1563 of 'ye presumful abuse and vyc of drunkinness' and was sentenced to be 'brankit, stockit, dukit and banisit ye haile paris' (branked, placed in the stocks, ducked and banished from the whole parish). And on 5 March 1648 Margaret Nicholson of Dumfermline had to stand with the branks on her mouth for two hours before noon on market day, for her common scolding and drunkenness, to be a public example to others.

Similarly, Isabel Lindsay had her tongue held for her, after her astonishing and slanderous outburst during Divine Service in St

Andrew's parish church. Just when Archbishop Sharp was preaching, Isabel had the temerity to stand up and accuse him of having an illicit affair with her when he was a college student.

Such accusations simply could not be tolerated, and she was promptly arrested. Brought before the Kirk-Session, she was sentenced to the only punishment that would suit her offence. She was made 'to appear for a succession of Sundays on the repentance stool in the church, wearing the brank'.

The device soon crossed the border, and many specimens still survive in museums; Lancaster Castle has an excellent example in its collection of prison artefacts. The use of the bridle became widespread; Elizabeth Holborn was branked at Morpeth town cross for two hours on 3 December 1741 for scandalous and abusive language in the town, while Ann Runcorn rued the day she abused the church wardens as they ensured that all the inns were closed during Sunday service. With the bridle on, she was paraded through the streets accompanied by hundreds of spectators and, on her return to Congleton Town Hall, the bridle was removed in the presence of the mayor, magistrates, constables, churchwardens, and assembled citizens.

It was always considered advisable to brank witches for, their tongues being held down, they could no longer chant or recite the magic spells by which they could change themselves into small animals and so escape.

In 1591 Agnes Sampson was accused of collaborating with John Fiennes in raising a storm which would drown King James on his journey to Denmark. Tortured in the pilliwinks, she was subjected to the witches' bridle, this being a particularly vicious version which, in addition to having spikes on the tongue piece to press on the tongue and palate, had other prongs pressing sideways against the cheeks.

Being unable to speak, it is hard to see how Agnes could have confessed even if she had wanted to, but eventually she admitted to every wild accusation, and was consequently taken to Edinburgh's Castle Hill and suffered the same ghastly fate as had John Fiennes – she was tied to a stake and burned to death.

There were even worse variations of the bridle than the one endured by Agnes Sampson. William Andrews in his book *Old*

*Time Punishments*, published in 1890, described a fearful version in Ludlow Museum:

> The powerful screwing apparatus seems calculated to force the iron mask with torturing effect upon the brow of the victim; there are no eyeholes, but concavities in their places, as though to allow for the starting of the eye-balls under violent pressure. There is a strong bar with a square hole, evidently intended to fasten the criminal against the wall or perhaps to the pillory.

That model would seem to have been designed, not so much for nagging wives, but as a device to keep a felon's head immovable while being extensively branded.

Not that men escaped the indignity of wearing a bridle. James Brodie, a blind beggar, was sentenced to death for the murder of his young guide, but caused so much commotion in prison that he was silenced by the branks. He was executed at Nottingham on 15 July 1799. And any citizen of Edinburgh found guilty of blasphemy had to wear the bridle. In the year 1560 'David Persoun, convicted of fornication, was brankit for four hours, and his associate in guilt Isobel Mountray, was banisit the gait'.

At sea, drunken sailors were also quietened, if not by a bridle, at least by a gag. In 1815 Able Seaman Thomas Payne had a piece of wood, seven inches long and one inch wide, forced between his jaws and held in place by cords tied behind his head. His efforts to dislodge the gag were so violent that he dislocated his jaw, and medical attention had to be rendered by the ship's surgeon.

Other naval gagging devices were the pump bolt, the handle of the ship's pump, and a marlin spike also fitted the bill, or rather the jaws. This latter punishment appeared in the diary of Henry Teonge, Chaplain of HMS *Assistance*. Against the date of 29 January 1676, he wrote

> Now we are at the point of Goza, which is a member of Malta, a place of great strength. This day David Thomas and Marlin the cook stood with their backs to the rails, and the Master's boy with his back to the mainmast, all looking one

upon the other, and in each of their mouths a marline-spike, viz. an iron pin clapped close into their mouths, and tied behind their heads; and there they stood a whole hour, till their mouths were very bloody; an excellent cure for swearers.

## The Cucking Stool

Frequently confused with the ducking stool, the Cucking Stool was strictly a dry land instrument of humiliation. It was referred to in the Domesday Book as *cathedra stercoris*, literally a close chair or commode, and originally the victim sat on one outside his or her own house. Later this degradation was mercifully reduced, an ordinary chair replacing the commode, though the offender continued to be an object of derision.

In Leicester in 1467 scolding women were ordered to be seated in the cucking stool and were carried to the four gates of the town. In Cornwall the cucking stool was described as 'a seat of infamy where strumpets and scolds, with bare feet and head, were condemned to abide the jibes of those who passed by'.

By a 1512 statute of Henry VIII, carders and spinners of wool convicted of fraudulent practices, were 'to be set upon the cukkynge-stole', and in 1555 a historian Thomas Wright noted that 'the Scottish queen-regnant enacted that itinerant singing women should be put on the cuck-stoles of every burgh or town'.

This fate also awaited common brawlers, and even Scottish ale wives whose home-brewed beverages were not up to standard. Quoth Sir John Skene in his *Regium Mejestatem*, 'Women who brew ale to be sold, if she makes good ale, that is sufficient. But if she makes evil ale, contrary to the use and consent of the borough, and is convicted thereof, she should be fined or shall be put upon the cuck-stule, and the ale shall be distributed to the poor folk.'

## Riding the Stang

Displaying the victim to the greatest number of people was obviously the main aim of all these 'domestic' punishments, whether pillory or stocks, bridles or cucking stools. Another predominantly mobile penalty was that of Riding the Stang. Oddly enough in such a male-dominated society, this was inflicted on men accused of wife-beating or vicious behaviour, who had to be shown the error of their ways, if not by a court of law necessarily, then at least by their neighbours *en masse*.

Riding the Stang was essentially a noisy procession involving the villagers banging on tin cans and kettles, blowing whistles and sounding horns, and sometimes even accompanied by a trumpeter. At the front, carried shoulder-high, was the offender, straddling a thick pole or a ladder, a figure of scorn to all as the deafening parade passed through the streets.

Later the custom changed, and the man on the stang was a spokesman chosen by the villagers. He carried noise-making implements, usually a stick and a dripping pan, to add to the cacophony. Every fifty yards or so the procession would stop for the spokesman to recite loudly slanderous verses about the offender and his crime.

Effigies sometimes replaced the spokesman, one instance of which was recorded in the *Westmorland Gazette* in October 1893. Villagers expressed their indignation at the offender by riding his effigy on a stang, and a few years before, in 1887, the *Sunderland Post*'s roving reporter described a local incident in great detail: 'Some excitement was caused in Northallerton last night by the celebration of "riding the stang", which is to expose someone guilty of gross moral practices and of breaches of sacred matrimonial rights. Some hundreds of people followed the conveyance, in which two effigies were exhibited, through the principal streets. At intervals a person in the conveyance shouted out in rhyme their object, and to state their intention to ride the stang three nights in succession and on the last night burn the effigies on the green near the church.' The house of the culprit was visited during the parade and, if the offence was very serious, the offender's effigy would be burned before his door.

In the south of England the custom was known as Skimmington Riding. Instead of a spokesman, two characters played the part of the offender and his wife, with one character wielding a saucepan and the other a skimming ladle, much like a Punch and Judy show, except that in this one Judy triumphed! Their dialogue provided a mobile drama, the performance reaching its crescendo at the culprit's house, after which the procession traversed the village. Among the crowd were some with brooms who ominously swept the doorsteps of others similarly suspected of maltreating their spouses.

The custom was country-wide, as a Scottish poem of 1721 shows:

> They frae a barn a kaber raught
> And mounted it wi' a bang,
> Betwisht twa's shoulders, and sat straught
> Upon't and rade the stang
> On her that day.

Wales too had its quota of wife-beaters and philanderers to punish, and there they rode the *ceffyl pren*, the wooden horse. The *Liverpool Mercury* of 15 March 1887 reported that

> the custom intended to operate as a wholesome warning to faithless husbands and wives was revived on Saturday in an Anglesey village near Llangefni. The individual who had drawn upon himself the odium of his neighbours had parted from his wife and was alleged to be persistent in his attentions towards another female. A large party surrounded his house and compelled him to get on to a ladder, carrying him shoulder high through the village, stopping at certain points to allow the womenfolk to wreak their vengeance on him. The amusement was kept up for some time, until the opportune arrival of a sergeant of police from Llangefni, who rescued the unlucky wight.

Riding the stang was still carried on in remote parts of the country as late as the 1890s, having been reported at Sutton, near Hull, in August 1877 and in Hedon in 1889.

## The Wooden Horse

This was the military version of riding the stang, and was aptly described by Francis Grose in his *Military Antiquities Respecting a History of the English Army*, published in 1786.

> The wooden horse was formed of planks laid together so as to form a long sharp ridge or angle, about eight or nine feet

long. The ridge represented the back of a horse, and it was supported by four posts or legs, about six or seven feet long, placed on a stand, made movable by small wheels; to complete the resemblance, a head and a tail were added.

When a soldier or soldiers were sentenced by a court martial, or ordered by the Commanding Officer to ride this horse, they were placed on its back with their hands tied behind them, and frequently, to increase the punishment, had muskets tied to their legs to prevent, as was jocularly said, their horse from kicking them off. This punishment was chiefly inflicted in the Infantry, who are supposed unused to ride.

Military records quote that on 7 June 1731 'a soldier in General Tatton's Regiment was whipt in the Abbey Court for marrying a girl. He who advised them to marry was set upon a Wooden Horse, with six pairs of spurs at his heels.'

The American Army also had wooden horses in its punishment stables. In a book *Curious Punishments of Bygone Days*, published in 1896, the author, Alice Morse Earle, cites the case of a soldier who, having stolen some hens, was made to ride the wooden horse for three days, with a fifty-pound weight tied to each foot. She also reports that, hardly surprisingly, fatalities had been caused by such harsh penalties.

Such was the reputed cruelty of Spaniards and their Inquisition, that many torture devices were attributed to them, the Spanish Chair and the Spanish Bilboes, being but two of them. Another was the Donkey, reportedly used by the Spanish Army and adopted by the Germans. This was akin to the wooden horse but was instead a short stone wall which, tapering to the top, provided a sharp ridge which the miscreant had to straddle. Again weights were tied to the man's ankles for the duration of his punishment.

In France the *Cheval de Bois* was ridden, the one at Besançon being garnished with short spikes along its ridge. And not only were the poilus of the French Army subjected to the military version, but also any prostitutes caught out of bounds in the barracks!

173

## Double Yokes

Not eggs, but another device designed to inflict ignominy on erring couples. Those who neglected the formality of marrying before begetting a family aroused the moral indignation of the worthy burghers of Nuremberg. Accordingly the couple were secured side by side in a wooden yoke and made to carry water up the hill outside the town, Jack and Jill fashion. Swiss couples were similarly shamed, their task doubtless being more strenuous, the hills being steeper.

## French Degradation

Always demanding the highest standards of chivalry from their aristocracy and the conduct pertaining thereto, the French had a strict ritual of retribution when a knight dishonoured the code.

Thirty knights of proven courage met in council and summoned to their presence the nobleman charged with felony. A king- or herald-at-arms pronounced the accusation of treason, or broken faith, and if the charge was proven, he was ignominiously stripped of the titles, functions and privileges with which he had been invested. Then the degradation took place, with much solemnity.

Two scaffolds were erected in public: on one the judges were assembled, surrounded by heralds and men-at-arms; on the other stood the culprit, fully armed, with his shield stuck on a spike before him. He was then stripped of all his weapons and armour, beginning with his helmet; his shield was broken into three pieces; the king-at-arms poured a basin of hot water on his head; and priests sang the service of the dead.

The judges, clad in mourning, then went to the church, accompanied by the culprit borne on a litter. After a *Deo profundis* he was given up to the royal judge to be dealt with by High Justice. On some occasions he was allowed to outlive his infamy, as in the case of Captain Franget, a Gascon gentleman, who had treacherously surrendered Fontarobia to the Spaniards. He was degraded in 1523, but afterwards set free.

The ceremony of degradation was later abandoned, the sentence in itself implying the stigma. It was resumed in 1791, however, under the name of civil degradation, the clause being worded 'The culprit shall be led to the public place, where sits the Tribunal that passed sentence on him. The Clerk of the Court shall address him in these words: "Your country has found you guilty of an infamous act; the Law and the Court hereby strip you of your title of French citizen".'

## Amende Honorable

More injurious to the honour than to the body, this French penalty involved public humiliation of the wrongdoer. Petty thieves, even noblemen, were paraded through the streets in a cart, and husbands who allowed their wives to beat them were led around the town astride a donkey, shamefully facing aft.

Knights were disgraced by having their spurs symbolically broken on a dunghill, and those who had committed an act of cowardice were publicly dishonoured at a formal banquet by having the table cloth cut in front of them. One instance of this occurred at the King of France's own table, the cloth being slashed before William of Hainaut for failing to avenge the murder of his granduncle.

However, it was not always merely a formal punishment. In 1691 Urbaine Attibard, aged thirty-five, wife of Pierre Barrois, poisoned her husband, and for that crime she was sentenced to *amende honorable* and to be taken to the scaffold, there to have her hand struck off. After that she was to be hanged, her body burned, and her ashes scattered to the winds. And the sentence was duly carried out.

## Maritime Measures

When the Royal Navy consisted of sailing ships manned by ill-disciplined seamen who had been forcibly recruited by the notorious press-gangs, and conditions on board were harsh beyond belief, most captains were at best martinets, at worst sadistic tyrants. Operating thousands of miles from their home bases, answerable to no one while on long voyages, many captains devised their own punishments to keep their crews compliant and under control.

Flogging and keelhauling, described in earlier chapters, were among those frequently administered, but some of the more bizarre penalties mentioned by nineteenth-century naval historians were the Spread-Eagle and Carrying the Capstan Bar.

The former required the seaman to position himself in the

rigging, his wrists and ankles wide apart and tied to the surrounding tackle. An hour or more of such seemingly innocuous treatment was in reality a severe punishment, especially when the ship was wallowing in heavy seas.

Carrying the Capstan Bar, as its name implies, involved carrying a heavy beam of timber up and down the decks for up to four hours at a time. An associated penalty was that of being Spread over the Capstan. As described by Captain Butler RN in his *Discourse* of 1634, it consisted of

A capstans barre beinge thrust through the hole of the burrell, the offenders armes are extended to full the length, and soe made faste unto the barre crosswise; haveing sometimes a basket of bulletts or some other the like weight, hangeing his neck upon, in which posture he continues untill hee be made either to confesse some plotte or cryme whereof hee is pregnantly suspected, or that hee have received suche condigne sufferinge as he is suffered to undergoe by the ceinsure of the Captaine.

These punishments were exhausting and no doubt painful, unlike the revolting chastisements reported by Chaplain Teonge in his diary:

24 June 1675, Midsummer Day, and we are calmed still over against the Isle of Wight, and within ken of Portland, though thirty leagues from us. This day two seamen that had stolen a piece or two of beef were thus shamed; they had their hands tied behind them, and themselved tied to the mainmast, each of them a piece of raw beef tied about their necks in a cord, and the beef bobbing before them like the knot of a cravat; and the rest of the seamen came one by one, and rubbed them over the mouth with the raw beef; and in this posture they stood two hours.

Even worse was his entry of 3 August 1678 in which he wrote that seaman Isaac Webb stood tied to the rigging for an hour and had a 'speculum oris' placed in his mouth, for saying to another seaman in the Captain's hearing, 'Thou liest, like the son of a whore'. Delicacy forbids me to define 'speculum oris' in any greater detail – but the object was definitely not a lollipop!

And when midshipman John Hervey was court-martialled for stealing 'two trunk cases of ironware, a case of pictures, a case of Delph ware and a cask of wine' from a captured enemy ship, before the booty could be shared out between the whole crew, he was sentenced to be disrated as a midshipman, to receive seventy-two lashes with the cat-o'-nine-tails, have a halter around his neck, and to clean the ship's latrines for three months.

# 11
## Unusual Torments

It says much for man's inventive spirit that he is not restricted to the more stereotyped methods of persuasion and punishment, but can let his fertile imagination conjure up more ingenious devices, all based on the same premise, that of causing pain or death. With men like these around, torture and execution may be abhorrent and detestable, but never boring or routine.

For instance, there was certainly nothing conventional about punishing criminals with Quagmires or Whirligigs, Barnacles or Bottles. Yet in England during the Middle Ages, quagmires were quite popular among the barons, most of whose estates were equipped with 'drowning pits', in which many an erring serf was sentenced to be submerged.

### The Barnacles
Coercion by the Barnacles is rarely mentioned in the history books, but seems to have resembled a short rod with a noose of cord at one end. The victim's upper lip was pulled through the noose, which was then tightened, and subsequent twisting of the rod resulted in acute agony and eventual mutilation. Its use was probably limited, for with his lip trapped in that manner, it was doubtful whether the victim's incoherent mumblings would have been understood, even if he had been willing to confess.

### Booting and Bottling
This punishment, also known as Cold Burning, was frequently inflicted in the British Army. After being struck by each member of the regimental jury using a boot-jack, the offender would be tied with one arm extended high above his head. Bottles of cold

179

water were poured down his sleeve until he was thoroughly soaked, a punishment resulting in discomfort though hardly a painful one.

## The Whirligig

Yet another penalty designed to cause distress rather than agony was a session in the Whirligig. This device was a six-foot high cylindrical cage mounted top and bottom on pivots so that it could be rotated, and once the offending soldier had been placed inside it, the cage would be spun round at high speed, disorientating the occupant and causing nausea and extreme dizziness. A punishment in the nineteenth century, but a useful adjunct in this century for training would-be astronauts!

## Running the Gauntlet

Among the many military and naval punishments, this one was always highly rated, at least by those in authority. It took different forms, depending on the regiment and service. Even its name varied, from gatloupe, gantlope, to gantlet, words believed to have been derived from the Swedish word *gatlopp*, meaning 'passageway'.

And a passageway it was too, albeit a painful one, for unruly or insubordinate soldiers of the seventeenth and eighteenth centuries were forced to march between two ranks of their comrades, and were struck by each of them in passing. In some regiments the victim was stripped to the waist; in others he was naked, and the weapons wielded by his fellow soldiers varied from cudgels to whips, canes to willow wands.

To ensure that the miscreant did not set up any new battalion record for sprinting, he was preceded by a sergeant holding a pike or halbert, reversed so that its point was directed towards the victim's chest. On reaching the end of the 'passageway', the drums would beat and, depending on the gravity of the offence, the man would have to traverse the ranks four, five, even six times.

The naval version of running the gauntlet was basically the same. The entire ship's crew was assembled in two files around the deck area, facing inward. Each seaman wielded a knittel, a ten-inch long plaited cord with two or three knots in it, and the wrongdoer would have to complete as many as three circuits of the ship's deck.

Hurrying was similarly discouraged, the master-at-arms leading the way with his drawn cutlass pointing at the man's chest, and to thwart any attempt to turn and run, a corporal followed, also with drawn sword. Bringing up the rear was the surgeon's mate, and throughout the punishment the drummer beat the 'Rogue's March'.

Although this punishment generally ceased to be inflicted in the services by the end of the eighteenth century, it still continued in English prisons. Extortion was the name of the game, practised by all levels of authority from the turnkeys to the trusties. A new prisoner refusing to part with his few possessions and having the temerity to complain was called a 'nose', and forced to run between a double file of his fellow felons who lost no time in belabouring him with short ropes or knotted handkerchiefs.

Other countries adopted the Gauntlet, Russian victims being first shaved and stripped to the waist. With wrists tied to the barrel of a musket and the weapon positioned so that the bayonet point pressed against his stomach, the man then traversed the ranks, being struck with whips the while. The maximum of 12,000 lashes as decreed by Peter the Great was hardly a magnanimous gesture – 2,000 blows usually proved fatal.

## The Log

A much less punitive punishment in the British Army, this consisted of chaining a wooden log or an artillery shell to the miscreant's ankle, and except when on guard duty, the log had to be laboriously dragged everywhere for a specified number of hours, making life difficult in the billet, cookhouse and latrine. The French Army also used this method in the nineteenth century, their prisoners being tethered by a *boulet*, a cannon ball, attached to their legs or waists.

## The Bench of Justice

In the penal colony of French Guiana, convicts rather than judges sat on this particular bench. It was a three-inch wide steel shelf along one side of a cage in which the prisoners lived. The offender was made to squat on the shelf as best he could for up to

181

three hours at a time, his arms thrust backwards between the bars of the cage, his wrists manacled together. This punishment inflicted excruciating pain on the muscles of the arms, hips and legs, crippling the felon for days after release from his bonds.

## The Hot Room

Another punishment there was that of being immured in the hot room, a steel cell little larger than a clothes locker. Situated next to the prison boilers, the occupant could hardly breathe in the lung-searing atmosphere, and the punishment was further increased by the blisters caused by contact with the walls and floor of the cubicle.

## Licked by Goats

A bizarre torture practised during France's early history involved securing the victim to a bench, and bathing his feet in salt water. A goat would then be brought in, the animal losing no time in licking the captive's feet! The repeated application of the goat's rough tongue to the sensitive soles of the feet quickly stilled the initial giggles, replacing them within minutes by maddened shrieks for mercy.

## The Rope Saw

During the persecution of the French Catholics by the Huguenots, many were tortured by the Rope Saw. A length of coarse-fibred rope was stretched taut across the room, the naked victim then being dragged head first, backwards and forwards along it, the sawing action rending flesh and tissue alike.

In ancient Persia, real saws were used to punish those accused of witchcraft. The sisters of the Christian Bishop of Salencia were found guilty of casting a spell on the Empress and were put to death by being sawn in quarters, which were then displayed to the Empress in order to lift the malevolent curse.

## Seared by Sulphur

During the witch hunts which obsessed Europe in the seventeenth century, German witches in particular were cruelly persecuted. In addition to the routine strappado and racking, ducking and being put to the thumbscrews, suspects had alcohol poured over their heads and bodies, and the liquid was then ignited to burn all the hair off. Pieces of sulphur were placed in their armpits and set alight, and they were bound to boards covered in sharp bristles.

## Hair Plucking

In the following century German convicts were also rendered hairless, as John Howard discovered when visiting Hanover prison in 1781. There he found that the prisoners would be awakened at two o'clock in the morning and put to the torture, the executioner extracting confessions by pulling handfuls of hair from the victim's head, chest and body.

## Chain through the Neck

In the more exotic parts of the world, more exotic punishments were administered. In China, monks who broke their sacred vows were punished by having a hole burned through their necks with a red-hot iron. A long chain was then passed through the hole and, stark naked, he would be led along the streets, any attempt to relieve the pain caused by the weight of the chain on the open wound being thwarted by the application of a whip carried by another monk bringing up the rear.

## Chilli Powder Torture

Such was the vastness of the Indian subcontinent and the ingenuity of the native mind, that a variety of unusual punishments were used. In one province thieves were tied upside-down, the local magistrate then ordering chilli powder to be packed into their nostrils, the resultant nausea and vomiting occurring within minutes.

## Blown from a Cannon

Death itself came in different forms. In the 1750s, when the French forces in eastern India, under the command of Thomas de Lally-Tollendal, captured the towns of Madras and St David, natives suspected of being spies were blown from a cannon: tied over the muzzle of an artillery piece, which was then fired.

The French were later defeated by the British, and Lally-Tollendal was blamed for the military disaster. Sentenced to death for treason, he was beheaded by a sword wielded by Jean-

Baptiste Sanson, as described in chapter 12.

Long after the French had departed from India, army mutineers continued to suffer the same fate, the last reported case of being blown from a cannon occurring as recently as 1858.

## Trampled by Elephants

Killed at a cannon's muzzle was horrific enough, but even that lacked the nightmarish quality of another Indian punishment, that of being trampled to death by an elephant. One instance occurred in 1814 when a slave, guilty of murdering his master at Baroda, was dragged by the legs behind an elephant which was being spurred on by the bamboo lathis wielded by natives.

Within yards, the murderer's legs were fractured, his hips dislocated, and when the macabre procession eventually halted, the mahout backed the huge beast and ordered it to put its foot on the head of the semi-conscious man, crushing him to death.

## The Death of Twenty-one Cuts

Rather more finesse was shown in Japan, where executioners despatched their victims by means of the Death of Twenty-one Cuts. This entailed the executioner dexterously slicing away pieces of the victim's body, then cutting off the limbs one by one, timing his carving so accurately that by the twentieth stroke, little was left, other than to administer the *coup de grâce*.

## Flaying Alive

Not only Japanese criminals flinched before the knife blade; Turkish pirates and French noblemen were subjected to many more than twenty-one cuts, for they were flayed alive. This was a more leisurely method of execution, the skin being peeled away from the top of the skull first, and then down over the shoulders and torso, though few victims actually survived once the breast bones had been exposed.

French executioner Henri Sanson reported that this method was often resorted to in the past, the Count of Rouci dying in this manner in 1366 for betraying Laon into the hands of the English.

184

## Hanged Alive in Chains

Without doubt, a more lingering death was that of being hanged alive in chains (*Vivum excoriari*). In his book *Account of Germany*, Morryson says: 'Near Lindau I did see a malefactor hanging in iron chains on the gallows, with a mastive dogge hanging by the heels each side of him, as being nearly starved, they might eat the flesh of the malefactor before he himself died of famine; and at Frankforte I did see the like punishment of a Jew'.

That medieval practice survived into the eighteenth century and was widely used in Jamaica and neighbouring islands. The local trade being that of piracy, one such entrepreneur, Captain Calico Jack and his crew, received their just desserts in November 1720, when they were hanged in chains at Gallows Point, Port Royal.

Kingston was also a venue for such executions. Prior to being hanged there, two murderers requested and ate a hearty breakfast, so hearty in fact that one of them survived for a week and the other for nine days, before succumbing to starvation.

## The Third Degree

On the mainland of the United States of America, no Hollywood gangster film worth its salt would fail to mention the persuasive methods applied by the police, known as the Third Degree. Forced to stare into bright lights, deprived of sleep and subjected to continual and repetitive interrogation, the victim would be physically assaulted by his questioners in a number of ways. Blows with a short length of lead-filled rubber hose was the favourite; other less well-known methods being to bend the victim's head back and strike his Adam's apple until blood filled his mouth and throat. Drilling his teeth with a blunt drill without the benefit of any anaesthetic also proved effective in extracting confessions.

## The Spanish Spider

This nasty specimen of the arachnid family was the product of the warped minds of the Inquisitors. It consisted of two iron bars protruding from the dungeon wall, having long curved spikes at their ends. Female heretics would be pulled face-down over these

185

claws, lacerating flesh and severing tendons, often with fatal results.

## Buried Alive

Many of those found guilty by the Inquisition were disposed of by being buried alive. One of the last to be so despatched was Anne van de Hoor, a woman who lived in Malines in the Netherlands. Refusing to forsake her faith, she was buried in the ground up to her chin and, persisting in her defiance, she suffocated to death when her tormentors heaped more earth on her.

## The Cave of Roses

In seventeenth-century Sweden, criminals were not buried alive but were confined in the Cave of Roses – an incongruous name for a cavern which swarmed with poisonous snakes and other reptiles. With little or no chance of survival, many victims died therein, and it was not until 1772 that King Gustaf III had the cave closed down and its slithery occupants doubtless transferred to the local zoo.

## Torn Apart by Horses

Torture by goats, death by snakes or elephants – none were quite as bad as having one's limbs pulled off by bolting horses.

A comparatively rare method of execution, one reported instance in this country occurred in 1238 when a squire broke into the royal residence at Woodstock, Oxfordshire, where Henry III was staying, with the intention of killing the King.

In order to make a fearful example of the would-be assassin, the man was sentenced to be torn limb from limb by horses and then beheaded. His limbs were then to be dragged through the city before being hung on the gibbet for all to see.

Japan used oxen rather than horses when they massacred the Christians in the seventeenth century. At Nagasaki many victims, with each leg tied to an ox, were dismembered when the animals were driven in opposite directions.

But perhaps the most notable case occurred in France when, in 1757, François Damiens attempted to assassinate Louis XV at the Palace of Versailles. Damiens, a tall, middle-aged man of florid complexion with deep-set eyes, stabbed the King but was seized by the guards before he could complete his mission.

Wrongly suspecting that he was but one of a larger conspiracy, the authorities tortured him, tearing his flesh with red-hot pincers and burning his legs by holding them over the flames of the fire, Damiens repeatedly insisting that he had no accomplices.

The result of the trial was a foregone conclusion; a verdict of guilty was unanimous. If the wording of the sentence condemning a man to be hanged, drawn and quartered was considered barbaric, that passed on François Damiens by the French court surpassed any other in sheer savagery.

The Court declares that Robert François Damiens duly convicted of the crime of *lèse-majesté*, divine and human, for the very wicked, very abominable, and very detestable parricide perpetrated on the King's person; and therefore condemns the said Damiens to *amende honorable* before the principal church of Paris, whither he shall be taken in a cart, wearing only a shirt and holding a taper of the weight of two pounds; and then, on his knees, he shall say and declare that, wickedly and with premeditation, he has perpetrated the said very wicked, very abominable and very detestable parricide, and wounded the King in the right side, for which he repents and begs pardon of God, the King, and Justice; and further the Court orders that he then be taken to the Grève and on a scaffold erected for the purpose, that his chest, arms, thighs and calves be burned with pincers; his right hand, holding the knife with which he committed the said parricide, burned in sulphur; that boiling oil, melted lead, and rosin, and wax mixed with sulphur, be poured into his wounds; and after that his body be pulled and dismembered by four horses, and the members (limbs) and his body consumed in fire, and the ashes scattered to the winds.

The Court orders that his property be confiscated to the King's profit; that before the execution, Damiens be subjected to *question ordinaire et extraordinaire*, to make him confess the names of his accomplices. Orders that the house in which he was born be demolished, and that no other building be erected on the spot.

Decreed by Parliament on 26 March 1757.

On the day of execution Damiens, confined within a large leather bag secured at the neck so that only his head protruded, was carried from his cell and informed of the judgment. In accordance with the sentence he was released from his bondage and subjected to further interrogation. Because ordinary and extraordinary questioning had been decreed, his legs were forced into the *brod-equins*, the dreaded boots, and for the next two and a quarter hours he endured the agony as the wedges were driven deeper and deeper, splintering bones and tearing his flesh.

Out at the execution site everything was going wrong. One of the torturers, Soubise, detailed to obtain the necessary lead, sulphur, wax and rosin, had got too drunk to buy the commodities, and even if he had got them it would have been impossible to boil the oil or melt the lead, because the wood for the fire was too damp to ignite.

Understandably the Criminal-Lieutenant was enraged at such inefficiency and reprimanded Gabriel Sanson, the older executioner. After threatening to send him to prison for a fortnight, he handed over the responsibility to Gabriel's nephew, the eighteen-year-old executioner Charles-Henri Sanson.

The young man hastily sent his assistants to the local shops for the vital ingredients, while Damiens sat on the scaffold steps until all was ready for his frightful ordeal. At long last the punishment began, with the victim's right arm being secured to an iron bar. Carrying a chafing dish, the executioner approached Damiens, and for three minutes the blue flames of the burning sulphur seared the flesh of the half-fainting man's hand.

Giving him no respite, an assistant, Andre Legris, then proceeded to bring the red-hot pincers from the blazing fire and, while the vast crowd watched in fascinated horror, Damiens' chest and limbs were torn with the smoking tongs.

Oil and lead, wax and rosin were poured into the open wounds until, his erstwhile brown hair now white as snow, Damiens was carried down the scaffold steps and his limbs tied to the four horses purchased earlier for the sum of 432 livres.

The executioner and his staff whipped the animals into action, the helpless victim's limbs being pulled from their joints as the horses wildly galloped away. So resistant were Damiens' sinews and muscles that finally the horses had to be caught so that the

188

executioner could complete the dismembering with a knife.

So horrific was the spectacle that one onlooker, the worldy-wise Italian, Casanova, wrote in his *Memoirs*: 'I watched the dreadful scene for four hours but was several times obliged to turn my face away and to close my ears as I heard his piercing shrieks, half his body having been torn away from him.'

To have been hanged, drawn and quartered would have been infinitely preferable.

# 12

# The Ultimate Punishment

To be executed by having one's head removed by cold steel was considered an honourable death by the Normans, in as much in keeping with one's rank as being slain in battle by the sword or the battleaxe. So this method of being punished for one's crimes was introduced into this country by William the Conquerer in 1076, for the benefit of aristocrats only, the first knight to be so despatched being Waltheof, Saxon Earl of Huntingdon, Northampton and Northumberland. The instrument used was a sword, and this type of weapon continued to be used in Scottish executions for many years to come.

## The Axe

In England the sword was soon superceded by a weapon which resembled the battle-axe in name only, for the 'heading axe' was a crude and ill-balanced implement little better than a heavy, unwieldy chopper.

To get some idea of its dimensions, the historic example on display in the Tower of London has a sixteen-and-a-half-inch-wide blade which broadens to a convex cutting edge ten and a half inches long. Thirty-six inches in overall length, this clumsy weapon weighs seven pounds fifteen ounces and kills, not with a clinical cutting action, but by crushing its way through the vertebrae, not unlike a very blunt chisel.

Another axe, held on the inventory of the old Newgate Prison in the last century, had a nine-inch cutting edge, its shaft was an inch and a half thick, and it weighed about eleven pounds. Axes of these dimensions and lack of balance required considerable skill and accuracy by the wielder, qualities not noticeably possessed by the average executioner, whose vital concentration was in any case distracted by being the cynosure of the vast numbers of execution *aficionados* packed tight around the scaffold.

The awareness that one's swing is being critically analysed by thousands of spectators is one which nowadays is experienced only by internationally acclaimed golfers. To a dedicated executioner, and even more to the victim prone in front of him, a sliced shot had results too horrific to contemplate, as James, Duke of Monmouth, found out to his cost in 1685. 'Pray do your business well,' he exclaimed to Jack Ketch, the public executioner. 'Do not serve me as you did my Lord Russell. I have heard that you struck him three or four times; if you strike me twice I cannot promise not to stir.'

Monmouth should have saved his breath, for 'the butcherly dog Ketch did so barbarously act his part that he could not, at five stroaks of the ax, sever the head from the body'. After the third stroke the executioner threw down the axe and offered forty guineas to anyone who would finish the job. This sum was probably that given to him by Monmouth, such 'gifts' being traditionally handed to executioners as an incentive to strike with precision.

However, the now enraged mob threatened to storm the scaffold and kill Ketch unless he took up the axe again, and so the desperate executioner did so, only to find that, after two further blows, decapitation was still not complete. Hastily taking a knife, he severed the strip of skin still connecting the head to the torso as the crowd, now clamouring for his blood, attacked the scaffold. Had it not been for the strong cordon of soldiers present, Ketch would surely have died even more violently than had his mutilated victim.

After the execution the rarely enacted but always gruesome custom took place, whereby the corpse was taken away and the head was then sewn back on to the body for inspection by members of the Court. The artist Sir Godfrey Kneller took the opportunity to paint a portrait of the dead Duke, which was later hung in the National Portrait Gallery.

The essential accessory to the axe was of course the Block. Originally just a section of an oak log, it soon evolved into a purpose-hewn component. Rectangular in shape, it was scooped out midway along each of the longer sides at their upper edges. One scoop was wider than the other, allowing the victim to push his or her head as far over the block as possible, thereby positioning the neck immediately over the flat area between the two scoops. The victim's chin rested in the smaller scoop, the head being poised above the waiting basket of sawdust.

Generally the block was about two feet high and was reinforced by a vertical support immediately beneath the scaffold in order to reduce the recoil of the axe, which otherwise caused the body to bounce convulsively and so spoil the executioner's aim, should further strokes be required.

That more than one blow was frequently necessary was understandable: the back of the neck was a small target; the task one of high, sometimes historic importance; the heavy axe always ponderous; the scaffold boards usually slippery – all weighting the odds against one swift, deadly-decisive blow.

Hardly to be wondered at, then, that Sir Walter Raleigh suffered two blows, as did the Duke of Suffolk, Lady Jane Grey's father. Two strokes were also necessary to decapitate Mary, Queen of Scots, while Robert Devereaux, Earl of Essex, the erstwhile favourite of Queen Elizabeth I, only succumbed after three blows, though it was said that 'the first deprived him of all sense and motion'. One can only hope so.

Some blocks were low, so low in fact that the victim, instead of kneeling, had perforce to lie prone on the scaffold boards, this intensifying his sense of complete humiliation and despair. Charles I had to suffer this indignity, and after having told the executioner, Richard Brandon, to await the signal, he paused a moment, then stretched out his arms. Instantly Brandon responded, 'thus sodenly with one bloe his hed sped from his shoulders' and the King of England sprawled headless on the blood-soaked boards.

After every decapitation it was the executioner's duty to pick up the head by the hair, remove its blindfold if necessary, and display it from each corner of the scaffold, shouting, 'Behold the head of a traitor! So die all traitors!'

This macabre performance was not simply one of sadistic gloating. Lacking national newspapers and television, it was essential that as many people as possible could not only see that justice had been done, but also that it had been done to the right person, this also obviating the possibility of an impostor later emerging to claim the victim's identity and confiscated estates.

The last person to be executed by the axe in England was the Jacobite, Simon, Lord Lovat, on 9 April 1747. But he was not the last to be beheaded by the axe! This seeming anomaly came about when in 1817 three Derbyshire labourers, Jeremiah Brandreth, William Turner and Isaac Ludlum, were accused of leading a revolt to overthrow Parliament, and were condemned to be hanged, drawn and quartered. Reputedly the Prince Regent remitted the quartering part of the penalty, but ordered that they should be beheaded by the axe. Accordingly two axes were made by the local blacksmith, modelled on the one held in the Tower, the blades being twelve inches wide and eight inches along their cutting edges.

The initial hanging took place outside the walls of Derby Gaol before a large crowd which included their fellow rioters. Cavalry and foot soldiers formed a wide circle around the gallows, and nearby was a long bench on which lay the two axes and a knife. A basket stood at one end of the bench together with two sacks of sawdust.

The three ringleaders were brought forward, nooses were placed around their necks, and they were duly hanged, their bodies being suspended for half an hour. The masked headsman, a burly Derbyshire miner, cut them down and, placing Brandreth's body face down on the bench, dealt the neck two prodigious blows, but still required to complete the separation by using the knife.

Holding the head high, he shouted 'Behold the head of the traitor Jeremiah Brandreth!', a spectacle which so terrified the spectators that they fled in panic. The corpses of Turner and Ludlum were similarly maltreated, causing the poet Shelley, who witnessed the butchery, to write a pamphlet condemning the authorities for their callous brutality.

The axe rarely featured in the judicial armoury of other Continental countries, most of whom favoured the sword. Ireland's last recorded occasion was that of Father John Murphy, executed in 1798 for supporting the rebel cause, while in eighteenth-century Sweden, women were beheaded by the axe, the scaffold on which

194

they knelt being afterwards set alight at all four corners, to be consumed together with the body.

## The Rope

Watching the axe descend on the neck of a noble lord was a rare delicacy for scaffold devotees, an event equivalent, in soccer parlance, to a Wembley cup final. At other times they had to content themselves with the minor league fixtures of the day, the hanging of common criminals, these nevertheless being well-attended and popular occasions.

In an age when there was little or no entertainment as we know it, and poverty and disease made life cheap, an execution anywhere in the country was a diversion to look forward to. A wide range of offences, from shoplifting to murder, carried the death penalty. Even rare offences, such as the one noted by Stow in his *Annals*, incurred capital punishment: 'On 26th day of Septembar in anno 1564, beying Tweseday, ware arraynyd at ye Gyldehalle of London four persones for ye stelynge and receyvynge of ye Queen's chamberpot, combe and lokinge glasse . . .'.

Most towns had gallows, bringing to mind the doubtless apocryphal story of the shipwrecked mariner who, on being washed up on a shore, saw some gallows and promptly fell on his knees to thank God that he was in a Christian country. Nor were these devices merely Olde Worlde ornaments, for over 72,000 people were executed during Henry VIII's reign alone.

And just as nowadays London is reputed to have the best cinemas and theatres, so in earlier days it boasted the best hangings, many of them multiple events and so well worth attending.

The vast majority of criminals were hanged at Tyburn, at what is now the junction of Edgware Road and Oxford Street, adjacent to Marble Arch. A stone set in the central road island there bears an inscription to that effect but, should the unwary investigator not heed the traffic, yet another tombstone would be engraved 'Died at Tyburn'!

Tyburn Fields originally consisted of 270 acres of rough ground, flat except for a row of elms bordering a little stream called the Ti, or Ty, bourne. The elms were significant because in Norman mythology the elm was the tree of justice.

It is estimated that over 50,000 people died a violent death at

Tyburn, but as few written records were made or considered worth keeping, the real total may be considerably higher.

Those destined for Tyburn Tree, as its gallows were known, were brought either from the Tower or from Newgate Prison. Reportedly the first execution to take place there was in 1196 when William FitzOsbert, 'William Longbeard', was found guilty of sedition. His hands tied behind him, he was 'suspended by his feet from the neck of a horse and drawn through the midst of the city to the gallows near the Ty-bourn'.

Because this primitive method of dragging the condemned felon the three miles to Tyburn through the mud and filth of the cobbled highway frequently resulted in the premature death of the victim and the consequent fury of a crowd denied their entertainment, an ox-hide was eventually provided by the management. This amenity was later replaced by a rough hurdle or sledge, the victim thereby arriving more or less alive.

In the early part of the twelfth century the gallows consisted merely of two uprights and a crossbeam, capable of accommodating ten victims at a time. Obviously this could not cope with the crime rate and in 1220 Henry III ordered that a further gallows be constructed at the site.

Once there, the doomed men and women were forced to mount a ladder and the rope about their necks was tied to the beam above. After a prayer or a speech, one by one they would be 'turned off', i.e. the ladder was turned so that they swung in the empty air.

In due course the procedure was speeded up by the use of a horse and cart, one large enough to transport a number of prisoners together with their coffins, the hangman of course, plus a clergyman or two. The English language was thereby enriched by such phrases as 'in the cart' and 'gone west', the direction of Tyburn from the two places of imprisonment.

The advantages were immediate, for the cart not only allowed the crowds lining the route to get a better view of the condemned prisoners but, once halted beneath the gallows, it then served the purpose of a launch pad. Up to ten victims at a time could be roped to the beam and then a quick smack on the horse's flank delivered by the hangman would ensure the rapid departure of the cart, hanging the ten simultaneously. The cart method held sway in more ways than one for centuries, until superceded by the trap-door system described later.

Gallows were further improved when, on 1 June 1571, the Triple Tree was brought into use. Also known as the Three-Legged Mare, this was a triangular gallows with three uprights joined to each other by crossbeams, making it possible to hang twenty-four malefactors at once. As befitted such an important innovation, its first victim was not any ordinary footpad or highwayman, but a celebrity from the Tower of London. The Harleian manuscripts state 'the first daye of June 1571 the saide John Story was drawn upon a herdell unto Tyborn, wher was prepared for him a newe payre of gallows made in triangular manner'.

The fixed gallows continued to be used for two centuries, and were replaced in 1759 with portable ones which were assembled when needed and afterwards returned to store. On at least one occasion, in 1776, when the cart contained gallows-birds of different religions, two Jews were hanged on one beam, five Christians on the other.

But regardless of the type of gallows, the scene on hanging day was unchanged. Every window, every balcony and rooftop was packed; the whole arena was jammed with thousands of spectators who had spent many hours waiting, drinking, fighting and making merry. Grandstands were filled to capacity by those who could afford to buy a ticket from the proprietors, who were known as Tyburn Pew-openers. Just as ringside seats for a boxing match cost more when a championship fight is staged, so the grandstand owners raised their prices at the hanging of a famous or infamous felon. One owner, Mother Proctor, made a commercial killing, appropriately enough at the execution of an earl, Lawrence Shirley Ferrers. So great was the demand for a good vantage point that she reaped a profit of £500.

But private enterprise was always risky. Mammy Douglas, the owner of the stands in 1758, increased the prices from 2s to 2s 6d for the hanging of Dr Henesey, found guilty of treason. Despite protests the customers paid up, but their discontent turned to fury when, just as the doctor was about to be turned off, a messenger arrived with a reprieve! A riot ensued in which the stands were wrecked, and the efforts to substitute Mammy Douglas for the doctor were only narrowly frustrated.

Usually, however, the crowds waited patiently, listening for the distant roar which heralded the approach of the hanging procession, a roar much as one might hear on a State occasion today when the royal cavalcade is approaching. On Tyburn days however, the already heavily charged atmosphere seethed with a bloodthirsty undercurrent of feverish excitement, growing louder and louder like a spark travelling along a touchpaper, to explode in a frenzy as the cart actually came into view and stopped beneath the gallows. 'Hats off! Hats off!' would come the cry, not as a mark of respect for those soon to die, but so that the spectators' view would not be blocked by the headgear of those at the front.

The condemned prisoners were given a hearing as they made their defiant or apologetic speeches, interspersed with jeers or applause, music-hall fashion, depending on the crowd's mood or the victim's star quality. Then, as the assistant hangman swarmed up the 'tree' to attach the ropes, singing broke out, usually including Psalm 51 'Have mercy upon me, O God'. Amid an atmosphere now almost tangible, the victims were made ready. Where a solo hanging was involved, the condemned person gave the signal by raising his bound hands and pulling his cap down over his eyes, but with a multiple event no individual decision was practicable. Caps were pulled down, the cart was jerked away, and the victims were left swaying in unison until they expired.

Until about 1870 the rope was tied with a hangman's knot to form a running noose, and the victim died of strangulation as the weight of the body kept the noose tight. The saying 'Hemp is a herb of suffocating quality' was never more true, for death came slowly, up to twenty minutes elapsing before breathing stopped. As a concession, the executioner would permit the victim's friends or servants to hasten death by pulling the felon's legs or thumping his chest while the jeering mob kept up a torrent of abuse at the hangman for thus shortening the performance, casting doubt on his sobriety or parentage.

Eventually the cart was dispensed with and instead the victim stood on a trap-door. It was known as 'the drop' and when it was introduced on 5 May 1760, the Tower supplied its first candidate, Earl Ferrers, sentenced to death for murder.

The gallows now stood on a scaffold, or platform, part of which, about a yard square, was raised eighteen inches above the rest of the boards. This hatch was covered with black baize and, when operated, was designed to fall until level with the boards.

As Tyburn did not hang a lord every week, there was an immense crowd watching as the earl stood at the hatch. When the release was operated, design defects immediately became obvious, for the victim's toes still touched the lowered hatch; but as one observer recounted, 'The hangman, Thomas Turlis, pulled his legs and he was soon out of pain and quite dead in four minutes.'

The body was allowed to hang for another hour while the sheriffs and friends sat eating and drinking on the scaffold but it was quite clear that, as death came after some four minutes rather than the usual twenty, the new method was considerably more humane. Despite this, Tyburn reverted to the previous procedure, probably because of the difficulties encountered by the Home Office back-room boys in perfecting the drop, and the cart was used until 7 November 1783 when, following the hanging of a robber, John Austin, the execution site was transferred from Tyburn to the area in front of Newgate Prison.

The Tyburn Tree, no longer needed, was broken up and its timbers, together with those of earlier gallows, were sold to the landlord of a local tavern for use as barrel stands in his cellars. Some fragments are still preserved as holy relics by the nuns of the Tyburn Convent situated nearby.

The choice of Newgate as the new execution site was a shrewd one. Most of the victims were already imprisoned there and so the macabre procession along the crowd-lined route, together with the necessary traffic diversions, were eliminated. The smaller area available outside the prison also reduced the number of spectators to more manageable proportions.

A further innovation coincided with the move to Newgate, and this was the re-introduction of the drop. Its hatch was now ten feet long and eight feet wide, large enough for the ten malefactors who were the first to be hanged there on 9 December 1783. Regrettably the drop was still a short one, and this inadequacy was to go unrectified for over ninety years. Doubtless the authorities considered that four or so minutes' strangulation wasn't too unmerciful; the criminals were after all enemies of society.

The last man to be hanged in public was Michael Barrett, a Fenian who attempted to free his imprisoned colleagues Burke and Casey by dynamiting the walls of Clerkenwell Prison. In the explosion many people were killed and scores injured. His executioner was William Calcraft who throughout his long career as a hangman scorned to use any rope much longer than three feet in length, and so Barrett was virtually strangled to death when the trap-doors opened beneath his feet outside Newgate Prison on 26 May 1868.

The drop, from then on situated within the prison precincts, continued to be perfected, not without some bizarre mistakes, one at least resulting in decapitation caused by too long a rope. Several improvements were introduced, the inefficient hangman's knot being replaced by a metal eye through which the rope slipped quickly and smoothly, and the noose itself became almost user-friendly, being lined with soft leather.

Not only were new techniques devised, but executioners of intelligence and humanity were selected for the task. By careful calculations involving the victim's weight, age and fitness, the correct length of rope could be established, death coming instantly by the severing of the spinal cord rather than strangulation, this is many cases occurring within twenty seconds of the condemned person leaving the cell. The act ceased to be one of vengeance wreaked in public, becoming one of necessary extermination in private.

The twentieth century saw fewer hangings than before, all behind prison walls, and in 1964 the death penalty was abolished except for offences under the Treason Act of 1351. The last criminals to be hanged were Peter Anthony Allen and Gwynne Owen Evans, condemned for murder. Tried at Manchester, they were executed at 8a.m. on 13 August 1964, Allen at Liverpool, Evans at Manchester.

## Hanging in Ireland

In that country condemned felons were usually executed at the prisons where they had been confined. Rather than line the route to another scaffold location, the townsfolk assembled outside the prison. This building had a doorway cut in the wall well above ground level, usually at third-storey height. Level with this entrance, or rather exit, was a hinged platform with a sliding bolt holding it horizontal, while above the doorway a beam projected, to which a pulley was attached.

Once the felon had been ushered out on to the platform and the noose from the pulley positioned around his neck, prayers were said by the priest while watched by a sea of upturned and expectant faces. Prayers over, all but one then vacated the platform. The hangman promptly withdrew the bolt, allowing the platform to drop down against the wall with a terrifying crash which reverberated through the town, the noise being accompanied by a long drawn out gasp from the crowd as the felon swung twitching helplessly above their heads.

Not every Irish execution ended with a fatality however for as reported in the *Gentleman's Magazine* of February 1767:

One Patrick Redmond having been condemned at Cork, to be hanged for a street robbery, he was accordingly executed, and hung upwards of twenty-eight minutes, when the mob carried off the body to a place appointed, where he was, after five or six hours, actually recovered by a surgeon, who made an incision in his windpipe called bronchotomy, which produced the desired effect. The poor fellow has since received his pardon, and a genteel collection has been made for him. It is recorded that the man had the hardihood to go to the theatre the same evening.

## Hanging in France
In France's pre-guillotine days, the red tunic worn by the public executioner was embroidered in black with the gibbet and a ladder, indicative of his trade. Most towns had their own permanent gallows, stone pillars rather than wooden posts supporting the crossbeams from which the victims were suspended. Depending on their social rank, some Lords of the Chateaux were entitled to have a larger number of pillars than others, by implication allowing them to hang more criminals caught on their estates, literally a status symbol with a vengeance.

But, as befits a capital, the city gallows of Paris boasted no fewer than ten pillars, erected on a hilltop just outside the city. This eminence, known as Montfaucon, was situated north of the city, near the main highway leading to Germany, and was crowned by a platform forty-five feet long by thirty feet wide, reached by a stone stairway guarded by a heavy door. The pillars, thirty feet high and constructed of blocks of stone one foot thick, stood equidistant round three sides of the platform and were linked with double beams, both halfway up and at their tops. Attached to the beams were iron chains three and a half feet in length to which the hanging ropes would be tied.

As in England, the French criminal was transported to the gallows seated facing backwards in the hangman's cart, that position delaying understandable panic until the very last minute. Once at the dreaded destination, however, the victim had to dismount, as it was probably not possible to hang him by driving the cart out from under him because of the raised platform.

The executioner then placed two nooses called *tortouses* about the victim's neck, thereby reducing the risk should one rope snap, together with a third rope called a *jet*. Each pillar had a long ladder permanently fixed to it, similar to those attached to factory chimneys, and this the executioner awkwardly scaled backwards, dragging the victim up after him until he could secure the *tortouses* to the hanging chains. Astride the crossbeam, he then jerked hard on the jet, pulling the felon off the ladder so that the nooses tightened under the felon's weight.

Due to the height of the crossbeams above the ground, the English method of expediting the felon's demise by pulling on his legs was not possible, but the problem was solved by the hangman who, with professional agility, clambered down until he was able to stand on the victim's bound wrists, stirrup-wise, jerking down until the victim expired.

The corpses were left suspended for some considerable time on this awe-inspiring monument to Justice, food for the countless numbers of carrion crows which flocked to the hill. The cadavers of other criminals who had been boiled, quartered and beheaded were also suspended from the beams in wicker baskets or sacks of leather, their rotting remains eventually being removed and thrown in the deep pit situated in the centre of the platform.

## Hanging in Germany
As mentioned earlier, hastening the end of a criminal's life did

202

not always meet with the approval of the watching crowds. At an execution in Germany in 1620 the hangman, in turning the victim off, saw the ladder topple to the ground, leaving him marooned on the crossbeam. Instead of keeping his nerve and calling for assistance, he pressed down on the victim's head, probably with his foot, in order to bring the execution to a speedy conclusion. The crowd, infuriated either by the hangman's callous action or the prospect of a curtailed entertainment, rushed the scaffold, and only the rapid action of his assistant in replacing the ladder saved the executioner from being hanged on his own gallows.

This unfortunate mishap occurred at Nuremberg which, as in Paris, had its gallows erected just outside the city boundaries. Built in 1441, the structure consisted of high wooden posts connected by the inevitable crossbeams. The platform was also used for other judicial punishments such as Breaking on the Wheel, of which more anon. As in France, the bodies of those hanged were left swinging from the ropes, prey to the crows, the remains being later thrown in the gallows pit.

A visitor to the Prussian capital in 1819 gave an account of an execution there, which was published in *The Percy Anecdotes* shortly afterwards.

The executions take place about a quarter of a mile from the gate of Orianesberg. A triangular gibbet is raised in the centre of an extensive plain, commanding a view of the city; attached to this gibbet is a stone platform, lightly railed in with iron, so as to admit of all that takes place being distinctly viewed by the spectators. A large grave was dug in front of it. The area was cordoned off by a detachment of lancers formed in hollow squares, and enfiladed round the execution place by an inner square of the infantry guard.

About half an hour before the appearance of the criminal, twelve persons, executioners, officers of police, and two little boys as assistants, mounted the scaffold and fixed the strangling cords. At length the buzz of the surrounding multitude, the flourishing of naked sabres and the galloping of the officers, announced the slow approach of the criminal upon a hurdle drawn by six horses.

On his approach the word of command flew through the

203

ranks, arms presented, drums beat, and colours and lancers' flags were raised until he had mounted the scaffold. Never, continued the narrator, never shall I forget the one bitter look of imploring agony that he threw around him, as almost immediately on stepping on the scaffold, his coat was rudely torn from his shoulders.

He was then thrown down, the cords fixed round his neck, which were drawn by the executioner until strangulation was almost commenced, or at least until dislocation of the neck was effected.

Another executioner then approached, bearing in his hands a heavy wheel bound with iron, with which he violently struck the legs, stomach, arms and chest, and lastly the head of the criminal. I was unfortunately near enough to witness his mangled and bleeding body still convulsed. It was then carried down for interment, and in less than a quarter of an hour from the beginning of his torture, the corpse was completely covered with earth. Several large stones which were thrown upon him hastened his last gasp; he was mangled into eternity.

More recently, hanging history was made when, in 1946, after a last meal of tinned German sausage, cold meat, potato salad, bread and tea, ten leaders of the Nazi Party, convicted war criminals, were executed at Nuremberg by Master Sergeant John C. Woods of the US Army. Woods, aged forty-three, from San Antonio, Texas, was no stranger to the task, having hanged 347 men during his fifteen years service as US Army executioner.

## Hanging in Austria
Here, hangings took an unusual form, in that the victim stood on a small platform, his back to a post. A noose attached to a high hook was placed round his neck, and another rope was tied round his ankles, this latter passing via a pulley situated at the bottom of the post below the platform.

At a signal, the platform was jerked out from under the victim's feet, and the pulley was rotated, pulling the felon downwards and so increasing the noose's strangling effect on his neck. And if the desired result did not come quickly enough, the hangman, rather than standing on the man's bound wrists, French-style, or pressing on his head, German-style, climbed up and jumped on his shoulders.

## Hanging in the USA

A similar pulley-assisted procedure was used earlier this century in a few prisons in the United States of America. The rope from the noose passed over a pulley; the other end was attached to a heavy weight balanced on the edge of a drop. Upon the weight falling, the resultant tightening of the rope jerked the victim off the ground with, hopefully, sufficient impetus to fracture the cervical vertebrae and cause instant death.

Although the more conventional method involving trap-doors had been used by most States, their numbers had dwindled until by 1989 only three – Washington, Montana and New Hampshire – retained hanging as capital punishment. And as no executions had been performed for about twenty-five years, problems arose when triple murderer Charles Campbell elected to die by the rope rather than by lethal injection, for there was no one with the necessary expertise to officiate.

In the old days it would not have mattered, but the spokesman for Walla Walla Jail in the State of Washington pointed out that hanging was a problem involving many calculations such as momentum and inertia. A modern hangman, he said, needed to know the body weight to rope length ratio, to estimate the height and weight of the prisoner, to calculate the proper drop and tie the correct knot. Well, it never bothered Jack Ketch.

A wide search was instituted, reaching as far as South Africa, a country experienced in that method, while advertisements in American papers brought replies from scores of eager volunteers, including many from women. Eventually an American, a male, was selected and, having performed the duty satisfactorily, received the sum of £900, plus expenses.

In all the execution methods considered so far, only one person has been directly responsible for the deed, that being the executioner himself. However, during the last century, San Quentin Prison in California employed a technique which incorporated a 'blame-free' factor for those directly involved, in much the same way as members of a firing squad salve their consciences by

205

believing that the round they had fired could have been one of the blank cartridges issued.

After the hooded victim had been placed on the conventional trap beneath the beam, and the noose placed round his neck, the prison warden would signal to three guards positioned behind a screen, out of sight of reporters and members of the public. Each of the guards would immediately cut a cord, only one of which would release the trap, none thereby knowing whether he was personally responsible or not.

## Hanged, Drawn and Quartered

The worst possible crime in the eyes of the State was high treason, and this applied not only to those who plotted against king or country, but also to courtiers who dallied with the king's wife, as in the case of Anne Boleyn in 1536. It was appropriate that such crimes should merit the worst possible punishment. To be hanged by the rope or decapitated by the axe for committing 'ordinary' crimes was drastic enough, but high treason invoked the ultimate atrocity of being butchered *before* death – the penalty of being hanged, drawn and quartered.

The wording of the penalty requires some explanation as different interpretations have been made throughout the ages. The generally accepted meaning was that the traitor would be hanged and cut down while only half-strangled. A long incision would be made in his stomach, and his bowels extracted and burned in front of him; that is, he would be 'drawn' as is a chicken before cooking. Next he would be decapitated and quartered, his head and limbs being severed for display purposes.

However, some confusion exists over the meaning or position of the word 'drawn', because the sentence of the court decreed that the prisoner should be 'drawn on a hurdle or sledge' to the place of execution, as below:

> That you be carried to the place from whence you came, and from thence you shall be drawn upon a Hurdle to the Place of Execution where you shall be hanged by the Neck and, being alive, cut down; Your Privy Members shall be cut off and Bowels taken out, to be burned before your face, your Head severed from your Body and your Body divided into

four quarters, and they to be disposed of at the King's Pleasure. And the God of infinite mercy have mercy upon your Soul.

More precisely, then, the details of the punishment were drawing, partial hanging, disembowelling, beheading and quartering. No matter how it was expressed, it was an appallingly inhumane death, although on rare occasions mercy was shown whereby deserving cases and those of noble birth were allowed to hang until dead before being butchered.

There was no mercy however for Messire Willame le Waleys (William Wallace), the Scottish hero and patriot who, long a thorn in the side of the English, was finally captured in 1305 and 'drawn at the tail of a horse through the streets of London to a very lofty gibbet erected for him upon which he was hung with a halter'. Afterwards he was taken down half-dead, disembowelled, and his intestines burned in the fire. His head was then cut off and set on a pole on London Bridge, the first one to be displayed there, and his four quarters were hung on gibbets at Newcastle upon Tyne, Berwick, Stirling and Perth.

Another of the many who suffered this ghastly fate was Sir Thomas Blount, deputy Royal Naperer (Keeper of the King's Linen) and fervent supporter of Richard II. When Richard was deposed by Henry IV, Sir Thomas was accused of plotting against the new king and so the dread sentence was passed upon him. And, according to a contemporary historian,

Sir Thomas Blount was hanged, but the halter was soon cut and he was made to sit on a bench before a great fire; and the executioner came with a razor in his hand and knelt before Sir Thomas, whose hands were tied, begging him to pardon his death, as he must do his office.

Sir Thomas asked, 'Are you the person appointed to deliver me from this world?' The executioner answered, 'Yes, sir, I pray you pardon me.' And Sir Thomas kissed him and pardoned him his death. The executioner knelt down and opened his belly and cut out his bowels straight from below the stomach and tied them with a string, that the wind of the heart should not escape, and threw the bowels into the fire. Then the executioner knelt down before him, kissed him in a humble manner, and soon after his head was cut off and he was quartered.

After quartering, the head and limbs of such victims were par-boiled, this part-boiling being necessary to preserve them for as long as possible when displayed on London Bridge and over city gates. The treatment was carried out in as barbaric a fashion as was the execution. The *Annals of Newgate* relate how the hang-man brought the heads in a dirty bucket and, picking them up by the hair, tossed them around playfully before putting them in a big pan and parboiling them with bay-salt and cumin seed, the purpose of the latter ingredient being apparently to make the remains unpalatable to the seagulls.

The last head to be set up on the Bridge was that owned by William Stayley, a Roman Catholic banker and goldsmith. Accused of treason in 1678, he was duly hanged, drawn and quartered, but because of a petition raised by his friends, the authorities agreed that his dismembered remains could have a decent burial. However, at his funeral service, held in St Paul's Church, Covent Garden, the singing of Masses attracted so much attention that the King ordered the grave to be opened up, the corpse's quarters to be displayed over the City gates, and the head spiked on London Bridge.

The aftermath of the Monmouth Rebellion – when Judge Jef-freys' Bloody Assizes exacted retribution by executing over 330 rebels in the West Country in 1685 – resulted in similar gory scenes. An eyewitness's lurid account, as quoted by Sir Edward Parry, describes how some places 'were quite depopulated, nothing to be seen but forsaken walls, unlucky gibbets and ghos-tly carcases. The trees were loaden almost as thick with human quarters as leaves; the houses and steeples covered as close with heads as at other times with crows or ravens. Nothing could be liker hell; caldrons hizzing, carkases boyling, pitch and tar spark-ling and glowing, blood and limbs boyling and tearing and man-gling, and Jeffreys the great director of all.'

The sheriff wrote to the Mayor of Lyme Regis in Dorset, order-ing him to build gallows and provide nooses to hang the prisoners 'with a sufficient number of faggots to burn the bowels of the traitors and a furnace or caldron to boil their heads and quarters, and salt to boil them with, half a bushell to each traitor, and tar to tar them with, and a sufficient number of spears and poles to fix and place their heads and quarters'.

The penalty of being hanged, drawn and quartered was not legally abolished until 1870, although it had not been carried out for many years previously. One of the last cases in which the actual words of the sentence were spoken occurred in 1781, when Francis Henry de la Motte was found guilty of passing details of British shipping to the French. Like the enemy spies of the twentieth century, he was held in the Tower of London and after six months' imprisonment was taken to Tyburn, where he suffered a traitor's fate.

Mercy was shown, however, and he was allowed to hang for fifty-seven minutes before being cut down and beheaded. He was then disembowelled and, after his heart had been thrown into the fire blazing near the scaffold, his body was buried in St Pancras churchyard in London.

## The Sword

In the courthouse of medieval Nuremberg, condemned prisoners would plead, 'Please, as a favour, let me be beheaded!' Such was their trust in the dexterity and skill of their German executioners, that the sword was infinitely preferable to slow strangulation by the rope. And sometimes their cry would be heeded.

The accuracy of the executioner was matched by the superb quality of his weapon. Measuring about three feet in length and weighing four pounds, the average sword had a two-inch wide blade with parallel cutting edges and a rounded tip. Seventeenth-century specimens on display in the Tower of London are engraved with appropriate mottoes: 'Whenever I raise the sword, I wish the sinner everlasting life', and 'The judges check evil, I carry out their capital punishment'. They also bear grim portrayals symbolic of the profession, those of a gibbet and a wheel.

On the scaffold, the executioner gripped the sword with both hands, swinging the finely balanced weapon horizontally, sometimes two or three times in order to gain the necessary momentum before delivering the lethal blow to the back of the victim's neck. No block was used, a downwards stroke being impractical, as the sword would encounter the block before striking the victim.

Despite the appalling trauma of the moment and the terrifying swishing sound of the whirling blade, it was essential that the kneeling or standing victim remained absolutely still, for to flinch or sway would result, not in instantaneous oblivion, but in mutilation beyond belief.

That the weapon could gain considerable kinetic energy was very much in evidence when, in 1645, one executioner removed not only the felon's head but, the victim having raised his hands, neatly amputated them as well!

The procession to the scaffold was similar to that in other countries: the condemned man, preceded by two mounted constables, walked or rode in a cart with the magistrate and a priest. Notorious criminals had the ignominy of being dragged on an ox-hide, but members of charitable organisations were permitted to walk alongside him and support his head to protect it from the cobbles' impact.

*En route* the man would be given a 'heartening draught', probably containing a tranquillising drug. At the scaffold the executioner waited to greet the cortege and to give the traditional warning to the crowd, that anyone interfering with the due process of the execution, or seeking to avenge the lawful deed, would incur the court's grave retribution.

The victims were mostly male; only women committing the most serious crimes were beheaded. In such cases women, due to their stature and temperament, were allowed to sit in a chair to be decapitated, the heads of those guilty of infanticide being nailed above the scaffold as a warning to all.

In England the only woman to be beheaded by the sword since Norman times was, of course, Queen Anne Boleyn. There being no executioner competent with such a weapon, a French headsman was brought from Calais (then still an English possession). The princely sum of one hundred crowns was given 'for his rewarde and apparail', the latter consisting of a tight-fitting black suit, a half mask and a high, horn-shaped cap. One stroke of the sword was sufficient, and the head, its eyes and lips still moving convulsively, was placed with the body in a makeshift coffin, and buried within the Tower of London.

Not all French executioners were so adept however. In 1677 the founder of the dynasty of French headsmen, Sanson de Longval, needed three strokes to behead Mme Tiquet, guilty of conspiring to murder her husband. In a later century the head of criminal de Thou fell only after the eleventh blow.

In complete contrast Charles-Henri Sanson wielded his sword so accurately when executing the Chevalier de la Barre in 1766 that the victim's head remained balanced on his shoulders. Rumour has it that Sanson murmured quietly, 'Shake yourself – it's done!'

But not even Charles-Henri was infallible. His heavy sword, thirty-three inches long, with '*Justicia*' engraved on one side of the blade, the Wheel on the other, only wounded Thomas Arthur de Lally-Tollendal, slicing into the victim's jaw and cheek, the impact knocking him to the scaffold boards. Instantly an assistant seized the unfortunate noble by the ears and, in order to save the situation, Sanson's elderly father Jean-Baptiste hastily took the sword and dispatched the badly injured man with one blow.

On 4 June 1568, Count Egmont, Prince of Gavre, was executed in what was then the Spanish Netherlands but now is Belgium. Dissenting from Philip's Catholic policy, he was accused of treason and condemned to death. In the picturesque Place in Brussels, guarded by 3,000 Spanish soldiers resplendent in their uniforms of yellow, blue and scarlet, the Count mounted the scaffold. As was the custom, he carried over one arm the cloth which would soon cover his lifeless body.

After prayers he knelt on a cushion and drew his cap over his eyes. The executioner unerringly swung his sword, then retrieved the head. It was impaled on a lance and taken to Madrid, there to be displayed as evidence of Philip's methods in dealing with traitors.

In Holland, the sword was also the judicial weapon of execution until capital punishment was abolished in 1870. Denmark and Switzerland employed the same method – even Swiss women were beheaded in the eighteenth century.

## The Guillotine

Until 1789 many different methods of execution were in use in France but this did not pose a problem until the 'Equality' aspect of 'Liberty, Equality, Fraternity' became a social issue. Public attention was then directed to the inequality of those methods. Why should only the aristocracy have the privilege of dying swiftly by the near-merciful sword, while the *hoi polloi* suffered slow strangulation on the rope or had their limbs shattered on the wheel? Everyone knew that the sword literally had the edge over other instruments of execution: fashioned by craftsmen skilled in the manufacture of fighting weapons, deadly accurate when wielded by practised hands, delivering a blow so instantaneously lethal that it was virtually painfree. Why shouldn't *all* criminals be executed by the sword, and do away with the other methods?

But these criteria were based on the victim remaining motionless, and on single rather than multiple executions. A queue of felons waiting at the scaffold would quickly become imbued with terror, and would at least flinch when their turn came, thereby deflecting the executioner's aim. And with more than one victim to be beheaded, repeated impacts of the sword's cutting edges on the bone and tissue would quickly blunt the weapon, making it virtually useless. So how could an executioner, even with more than one sword, possibly cope with large numbers of criminals? It would be physically impossible.

For the solution, who better to turn to than Henri Sanson, last in the line of renowned executioners? Writing in 1876, he said,

> On 21 January 1790 the following decree was published: 'In all cases of capital sentence, the punishment shall affect a single form, whatever the nature of the crime. The criminal shall be decapitated, and the execution shall take place by means of a special apparatus.'
>
> This machine, which was to bear the name, not of its inventor, but of Dr Guillotine, who had improved it, was 'The Guillotine'. This zealous citizen, impelled by a humane sentiment which merely aimed at abridging decapitation and depriving it of much of its physical suffering, had only perfected a machine known in Italy since 1507 under the name of 'Mannaia'. When Dr Guillotine proposed this form of death to the Constituent Assembly, he was much laughed at, but his suggestion was ultimately adopted.
>
> The machine was constructed in the following manner and

it has been but slightly altered since; on a scaffold from seven to eight feet high, two parallel vertical bars are made fast at one end and their top part is united by a strong cross-bar. To this cross-bar is added a thick iron ring, in which is passed a rope which holds and retains a ram. This is armed with a sharp and broad blade, which gradually becomes broader on all its surface in a triangular configuration, so that instead of striking perpendicularly, it strikes sideways, so that there is not an inch of the blade that does not serve.

The ram weighs from sixty to eighty pounds, and its weight is doubled when it begins to slide down. It is enclosed in the grooves of the vertical bars. A spring makes it fast to the left bar; a band of iron descends along the outside of the same bar, and the handle is locked to the ring with a padlock so that no accident is possible, and the weight only falls when the executioner operates it.

To a vertical weigh-plank, strong straps are fastened, by which the criminal is attached under the armpits and over the legs, so that the body cannot move. As soon as the weigh-plank pivots down, the head, falling between the bars, is supported by a rounded cross-bar (i.e. semi-circular), and the executioner's assistant lowers another rounded cross-bar on to the neck, the head being thus gripped within a perfect circle which prevents it from moving in any way. This precaution is indispensable, in regard to the terrible inconveniences of fear.

The executioner then touches the spring and the blade descends. The head then falls into a basket of bran, and the body is pushed sideways into another wicker basket lined with very thick leather. The whole affair is done so quickly that only the thump of the blade when it slides down informs the spectators that the culprit is no longer of the living. *Viola!*

Tradition has it that Louis XVI suggested replacement of the original convex or crescent shaped blade by a triangular one for increased efficiency, a fact that was confirmed when the King himself died beneath the falling blade nine months later.

This decapitating machine, cynically nicknamed '*La Veuve*', the Widow, was capable of accurately severing heads as fast as they could be offered up, and it came along just in time to deal with the multiple executions dictated by the French Revolution. No swords could have coped with the sheer weight of numbers involved. At the height of the Terror, Charles-Henri Sanson and his assistants guillotined 300 men and women in three days, 1,300 in six weeks, and between 6 April 1793 and 29 July 1795, no fewer than 2,831 'hated aristocrats' mounted the steps on to the blood-slippery boards of the scaffold.

There, each in turn was swiftly strapped to the vertical weigh-plank, the bascule, which then pivoted horizontally and slid forward to bring their head down in between the two uprights. The lunette, the iron crescent, slammed down, so pinning the victim's head immovable. And even as he or she 'looked through the little window', the blade hurtled along its grooves, its cutting edge thudding into the socket beneath the now severed head, which then fell into the waiting basket. So rapid was the operation, so practised was Sanson's team, that it had been known to dispatch twelve victims in thirteen minutes!

As the decades passed, the guillotine was improved and modified. The 'family picnic basket' was replaced by a hygienic bucket; spirit levels on the framework prevented the blade from jamming in its descent; shock absorbers reduced the bounce of the heavy block, and a transparent screen protected the executioner's assistant from being drenched with the blood that spurted from the headless stump.

Unlike England, where executions in public ceased in 1868, the French crowds continued to assemble around their scaffolds for a further seventy or more years, the last occasion being on 16 June 1939 when the murderer Eugen Weidmann was decapitated. As it is likely that such scenes will never be witnessed again in public, a more detailed description is considered worthy of inclusion.

Eugen Weidmann, a ruthless and brutal killer, murdered three men and two women, the motive being robbery. After extensive investigations by the police, he was finally cornered and in the struggle that ensued, he shot and wounded a police inspector. At his trial in March 1939 he was found guilty and sentenced to death.

The night before the execution, workmen under the supervision of the public executioner Henri Desfourneaux assembled the guillotine on the roadway outside St Peter's Prison in Versailles, the hammering clearly audible to the man in the condemned cell. So too were the sounds of music and laughter from the local bars and cafés which stayed open all night to cater for the crowds already starting to gather for the big event.

Early the next morning the chaplain and prison officials came to Weidmann's cell. After the necessary formalities and prayers, the back of his collar was cut away and the hair trimmed from his neck. The traditional cigarette and a mouthful of rum was offered and accepted, then Weidmann's wrists were tied behind his back and his ankles were hobbled. Slowly he was escorted out into the daylight to where the guillotine stood.

Barriers kept the noisy crowds back as the prisoner was secured to the bascule, the vertical plank, but it was not until it had been pivoted into its horizontal position that it was realised that the board had not been correctly adjusted for the victim's height, the man's neck not lining up precisely with the slot into which the blade would fall. Too late to rectify the situation, the assistant quickly seized Weidmann's hair and ears, pulling him forward as far as was possible, though his chin still rested in the slot.

Even as the lunette, the iron collar, dropped into place, pinning the victim's neck down, executioner Desfourneaux acted; the weighted blade descended, accelerating until, passing through its victim, it struck the block with a crash that reverberated around the square, the impact shaking the whole structure.

As the blood jetted against the protective shield, the severed head fell into the waiting receptacle, and in the silence that followed, a faint sigh could be heard as the last breath of life was expelled from the lungs of the headless corpse prostrate on the guillotine.

Before the workmen could sluice the pavements and scatter sand, women in the crowd had rushed forward, to soak their handkerchiefs in the rivulets of blood flowing into the gutters. So outraged were the authorities at scenes like this, and the general air of festivity, that within a week a decree was issued, confining all future executions to the precincts of prisons.

As Sanson said, Dr Guillotine's device was not original. Decapitation by machine had taken place in France as early as 1631 when Marshal de Montmorency was executed at Toulouse by means of a sliding axe. Sixteenth-century German engravings portrayed similar machines, as did Italian pictures, Genoa in particular employing the *Mannaia*. This consisted of a framework mounted on a scaffold, the axe positioned between two perpendicular slip-boards. The culprit knelt, his head on a block, and the executioner released or cut the rope, beheading the victim in the traditional manner.

It is equally possible that the good doctor derived his inspiration from having read about other decapitating machines such as the Halifax Gibbet or the Scottish Maiden.

## The Halifax Gibbet

'From Hull, Hell and Halifax, Good Lord deliver us', was a beggars' prayer quoted by the poet John Taylor in the sixteenth century. Hull was feared 'as a town of good government, where beggars meet with punitive charity', Hell was self-evident, and 'Halifax is formidable for a law whereby thieves taken in the act of stealing cloth are, without any further legal proceedings, beheaded with an engine known as the Gibbet'.

In the fifteenth century Halifax was merely another isolated hamlet in the West Riding of Yorkshire, consisting of only fifteen houses. However, the rise to pre-eminence of the great cloth manufacturing trade under the Tudors brought Halifax to the forefront and by 1556 its population had increased by more than 500 new households.

This being a cottage industry, each little manufacturer of a few pieces erected in the open a wooden framework called a tenter over which the cloth was stretched tightly to dry without shrinking (hence the words 'on tenterhooks'). These frames stood in rows out in the fields surrounding the town, making it easy for wandering thieves to hack a length or two off and sell in neighbouring villages.

It was obvious that the only deterrent was the fear of terrible consequences, and so the ancient prerogative of the Lord of the Manor was revived as their authority to administer justice, not by a judge or a magistrate, but by the bailiff of the town together with sixteen local residents as jurors.

Any thief caught with goods 'valued by four constables to the value of thirteen pence halfpenny or more' was sentenced to death. And as the Common Law of England at that time decreed that stealing to the value of twelve pence carried the death penalty, the leeway of a penny ha'penny showed just how lenient the people of Halifax were prepared to be.

Why they did not adopt the methods used elsewhere in the country such as the axe or the rope is not known. Instead they came up with a head-removing machine which they christened the Halifax Gibbet. Actually the word 'gibbet' was somewhat of a misnomer, a gibbet being the structure from which the body of a hanged man was suspended, usually at a crossroads, as a deterrent. But as the Halifax beheading engine was a 'one-off', the inhabitants applied an existing name of equally sinister significance, rather than invent a new word.

Mounted on a platform four feet high and thirteen feet square were two timber uprights fifteen feet in height, joined by a transverse beam at the top. In the grooves on the inner surfaces of the uprights ran a square block, having an axe blade keyed into its lower surface.

The blade, seven pounds twelve ounces in weight, measured ten and a half inches long by nine inches wide, and the block was held at the top of the frame by a wooden pin, to which was attached a long rope passing over a pulley.

Executions were carried out on market day – Tuesday, Thursday, or Saturday – when the greatest number of participants could be expected, and the crowds gathered to watch as the felon was made to kneel down and position his neck between the uprights. It was then that democracy really came into its own for, dispensing with the services of a paid officer of the law, the operating rope extended into the crowd, as many people as possible taking hold of it. Those out of reach stretched out their hands towards the rope, in implied concurrence with the penalty being exacted.

Countless hands pulled the rope, withdrawing the pin and so allowing the blade to descend on the neck of the wrongdoer, no one person therefore being directly responsible for the execution. Should the stolen item have been a cow or similar animal, the beast would be tied to the end of the rope and, driven away, would bring about the end of the would-be thief.

The first reported use of the Gibbet was in 1286, female as well

217

as male heads rolling on to the boards, for the records show:

> Ux. (wife of) Thom. Robarts de Halifax beheaded 13 July 1588
> Ux. Peter Harrison, Bradford, decoll. (decollated, truncated) 22 February 1602
> Ux. Johan Wilson decolla 5 July 1627
> Sara Lume, Halifax, decolla 8 December 1627
> Ux. Samuel Hall, on account of many thefts, beheaded 28 August 1623

George Fairbanke, 'an abandoned scoundrel, commonly called Skoggin because of his wickedness', should not go without mention, nor should Anna, his alleged daughter, for 'both of them were deservedly beheaded on account of their manifest thefts on 23 December 1623'.

It was last used in 1650 when John Wilkinson and Anthony Mitchell were caught stealing sixteen yards of russet-coloured kersey, nine yards at least of which was worth nine shillings. As their loot also included two horses, the bailiff's verdict was a foregone conclusion, and the Gibbet blade was released by the crowd on 30 April of that year.

Some time afterwards the structure was dismantled, but a fine replica now stands on the original platform, and the blade itself, known to have beheaded at least forty-nine miscreants, is on display in the Piece Hall Pre-industrial Museum in the town.

## The Scottish Maiden

The proud burghers of Halifax unfortunately neglected to patent their admirable machine and so it was, in 1565, that James Douglas, Earl of Morton, Regent of Scotland, passed through the town, noticed the gibbet and thought it a gude idea. Back in Edinburgh he put his carpenters to work, eventually to unveil the Scottish Maiden, a name probably derived from the Celtic *moddun*, the place of justice.

It was made of oak and consisted of a single horizontal beam five feet in length on which were mounted two upright posts ten feet in height, each being four inches wide, three and a half inches thick, with bevelled corners. The posts were twelve inches apart and were braced by lengths of timber attached to the ends of the base beam and secured to the upright posts four feet from the ground.

The tops of the posts were fixed into a cross rail two feet in length, the posts themselves having copper-lined grooves on their inner faces, in which the axe slid. This blade consisted of a plate of iron faced with steel, measuring thirteen inches in length and ten and a half inches in breadth, sharpened at its edge and weighted at its upper side with a seventy-pound square block. As with other similar machines, it was released by means of a rope and pulley.

The kneeling felon positioned his throat on a crossbar three and a quarter feet from the base, and a transverse bar, hinged to one upright, was lowered to press against the back of his neck, making it impossible for him to withdraw his head.

It was sited in Edinburgh's High Street near the City Cross, and was operated, not by the local residents as in Halifax, but by the public executioner. Over a hundred victims were executed by the Maiden, not least the very man who had introduced it into the country! Accused of involvement in the murder of Darnley, the Queen's husband, the Earl of Morton was duly decapitated, his head being spiked on the Tollbooth nearby.

The device was dismantled in 1710, the blade and component parts now being exhibited in the Medieval Department of the National Museum of Scotland, in the city where the Maiden brought so many men to their knees.

## Death by Burning

To be consumed by flames was primarily the sentence imposed on heretics. Not as a punishment as such but, being considered guilty of having the 'wrong' religion, the flames would prepare them for the fires of hell that awaited them.

Dr John Hooper, Lord Bishop of Gloucester, was burned to death in that city in 1555, watched by over 7,000 spectators. Clad only in a shirt, he was secured to the stake by an iron hoop about his waist, and bundles of reeds were heaped about him. As the flames rose higher, 'his face turned black and his tongue swelled so that he could not speak, yet his lips went till they were shrunk to the gums; and he knockt his breast with his hands till one of his arms fell off, while the fat, blood and water dripped off the fingers of his other hand. Soon his nether parts were consumed and his bowels fell out . . .'.

This ghastly penalty was also suffered by witches and women guilty of murdering their husbands. Several people perished at King's Lynn in Norfolk where, in 1515, a wife was burned in the market place for murder, as was Margaret Read, a witch, in 1590. Two more witches suffered within the next few years and in 1791 the same market place witnessed the burning of a servant girl for helping a murderer.

One of the worst instances occurred at Lincoln in 1722, when Eleanor Elsom was found guilty of petty treason, of killing her husband. With her clothes and limbs thickly smeared with tar, she was forced to wear a tarred bonnet, then was dragged, barefoot, on a hurdle to the execution site near the gallows.

After prayers she stood on a tar barrel positioned against a stake, to which she was secured by chains. A rope ran through a pulley attached to the stake, and a noose at its end was placed around her neck. When ready, the executioner pulled hard on the rope, strangling her as the pile of wood was lighted. The flames roared upwards fiercely, but it was half an hour before the body was totally consumed.

This barbaric method of executing women was in fact devised out of consideration for the female sex! Where the penalty for a man was to be hanged, drawn and quartered, it was considered publicly indelicate to butcher a woman in this way, so she was burned instead, the sentence being that she should be 'taken from hence to the place whence you came, and thence to the place of execution, on Saturday next, where you are to be burned until you be dead; and the Lord have mercy on your soul'.

Often the executioner's pull on the rope brought death before the flames took hold, or the stool on which she stood would be jerked away, with the same result. Some victims were allowed to have small bags of gunpowder hung about their necks and waists to speed their demise, but even with merciful aids such as these, errors occurred at times.

Catherine Hayes, having killed her husband, was sentenced to be burned at Tyburn on 9 May 1726. As soon as the rope had been placed about her neck the fire was started, but it burned so rapidly that, on trying to pull the rope tight, the executioner had his hands badly scorched and had to retreat. It was impossible to quench the flames in order to tighten the noose, so more faggots were quickly thrown on the fire to hasten the end of the burning, struggling woman.

Nor was gunpowder infallible. Where the faggots had not been piled high enough to reach the victim's legs, considerable time could elapse before the exploding powder brought blessed relief. In England most witches were hanged, but in Scotland the penalty was fire. William Coke and Ali on Dick, guilty of practising witchcraft in Kirkcaldy, were burned to death on 19 November 1633, the following expenses being incurred:

> For ten loads of coal to burn them . . . £3.6.8
> For a tar barrel . . . 14.0
> For towes (tinder) . . . 6.0
> To him that brought the Executioner . . . £2.18.0
> To the Executioner for his pains (!) . . . £8.14.0
> For his expenses here . . . 16.4
> For one to go to Tinmouth for the Laird . . . 6.0
> Total . . . £17.1.0

Things were rather cheaper in Canterbury a century earlier, as the corporation records show: 'Paid 14s 8d, the expense of bringing a heretic from London, for one and a half load of wood to burn him, 2s, for gunpowder 1d, and a stake and a staple, 8d, total 17s 5d'. Officials and the general public watched such executions, of course, and sometimes the Church was represented. The parish records of Glamis for June 1679 states: 'Na preaching here this Lord's Day, the minister being at Cortachy burning a witch'.

Not even a title could save a woman from being accused of witchcraft, for when Lady Glamis was charged with poisoning her husband and consorting with the Devil in 1535, she was put to the flames. Nor were these isolated cases. In 1597 in Aberdeen, no fewer than one warlock and twenty-three witches were burned in public. In Charles II's reign, the law stated that witches 'were to be worried at the stake and then burned'. 'Worried' meant tormented by the crowd, of course, and not their state of mind!

Sometimes the Witch's Bridle was used. Far from being a scold's bridle, this consisted of an iron ring nine inches in diameter, with a hinged opening enabling it to be locked around the witch's throat. The ring was then attached to the stake by means of a chain and, if mercy was to be shown, the stool on which she stood was pulled away, strangulation hastening her end.

As usual, executioner and victim were often the targets of the mob's abuse. On 5 July 1721 Barbara Spencer was found guilty of counterfeiting coins of the realm and, when taken to be burned at Tyburn, she was given time to pray. But, as reported in the *Annals of Newgate*, she then 'complained of the dirt and stones thrown at her by the mob, which prevented her from thinking sedately on her future. One time she was quite beaten down by them.'

So the inhuman penalty which started when St Alban died at the stake in AD 304, took its terrible toll, not ceasing until 18 March 1789 when Christian Murphy alias Bowman, a woman guilty of coining, became the last person to die in that manner. A year later the law was altered, so that after 5 June 1790, women were no longer burned alive but were hanged instead.

## Burning on the Continent

French heretics were put to the flames by means of the *Estrapade*, described in an earlier chapter. This method, introduced in the sixteenth century by Francis I, involved the victim, his arms bound behind him, being hoisted by his wrists and dipped up and down over the fire until the signal was given to consign him to the flames.

In later centuries a more conventional method was adopted, employing the stake and kindling. The fuel consisted of alternate layers of wood and straw surrounding the stake, to about six feet in height. Through an opening the victim, clad only in a sulphur-soaked shirt, would be led, there to be bound to the stake.

When the entrance had been closed up with more kindling, it would be ignited on all sides simultaneously, but occasionally mercy was shown by strangling the victim first or positioning a pointed iron bar level with the victim's chest, the executioner pushing it forcibly after lighting the straw.

As elsewhere on the Continent, witches were the prime target, Judge Remy proclaiming that he had sentenced no fewer than 800 of them to the flames. At Bamberg in Germany 600 died, 900 in one year in the bishopric of Wurtzburg, while in other parts of the country, the bodies of those who had committed suicide were tied to the stake and similarly despatched. Switzerland too burned their criminals, the last woman dying in that way as late as 1782.

## Burning in Spain

In Spain the Inquisition had developed the fearsome penalty to a fine art, execution by fire being the climax of the *auto da fé*. The procession, comprising Dominican friars, Jesuits and officers of the Inquisition, preceded by trumpets and kettle drums, escorted the victims to the place of execution. The incorrigible heretics wore the *san benito*, a yellow tunic with a picture of themselves on it, burning in flames fanned by devils, while the tunics worn by those who had just repented bore pictures in which the flames pointed downwards. As a special favour the latter were strangled before the fire was lighted.

All the victims had a rope around their necks and carried a large yellow wax candle. On their heads they wore a three-foot high, pointed hat, the *coroza*, and those victims thought likely to shout protests or divulge secrets were gagged.

On arrival at the execution site each was chained to a high stake, the priests proclaiming that 'They leave them to the Devil, who is standing at their elbow ready to receive their soul and carry them with him into the flames of hell as soon as they are out of their bodies'.

At that the vast crowd shouted 'Let the dogs' beards be made (singed)', and clumps of burning furze, on long poles, were repeatedly thrust into the faces of the helpless heretics, scorching them black, while the crowd roared its approval. After a while more furze was heaped around the base of each stake, the rising heat slowly roasting the heretics to a hideous death.

Such was the implacable obsession and power of the Inquisition that no fewer than 13,000 people were burned alive between 1481 and 1517, a further 19,382 perishing in the flames by 1808.

## *Death by Drowning*

Not surprisingly, those incurring this penalty in England were seafarers. Richard I, *en route* to Palestine, commanded that any man killing another on board ship would be tied to the corpse and thrown into the sea, while in the fourteenth century a man convicted of treason by the Court of Admiralty was bound to a stake in the River Thames during two flows and two ebbs of the tide. Two centuries later it was reported that 'pirats and robbers by sea are condemned in the court of admeraltie, and hanged on the shore at lowe water marke, where they are left till three tides have overwashed them'.

Even worse penalties awaited those who gave away royal secrets for, as threatened by the Admiral of the Humber, 'any member of the court who discloses or discovers (uncovers) anything of the King's secret council while trying cases before them shall suffer punishment prescribed by the law; that is, their hands and feet bound, their throats cut, their tongues pulled out and their bodies thrown into the sea'.

## Drowning in Germany

In Germany adulterous women were buried alive, but this provoked such violent objections by the outraged public that in 1513 such women were put to death by drowning. At Nuremberg this took place on a wooden jetty on the River Pegnitz, from which the felon, tied in a sack, was pushed in and held under by the executioner's assistant wielding a long pole.

On one occasion a woman managed to free herself and swam to the shore, begging for mercy, but this availed her little, for justice had to prevail, and she was returned to the depths.

Scenes like this again wrought anger among the populace and so the penalty was once more changed, drowning being replaced by beheading.

## Drowning in France

After that country's Revolution, *noyade*, execution by drowning, was carried out on a vast scale during the massacres committed by the Revolutionary Government on their French brethren in the Vendée. The inhabitants of this western region of France, through which flows the River Loire, were predominantly of farming stock and though in sympathy with the revolutionary aims, could not accept the Paris decree that henceforth the Catholic clergy, who had always led, educated and guided them, would be appointed, not by Rome and the Pontiff, but by the State.

Such was the resistance shown by the Vendeans that Representative Carrier ordered the army into the area, to crush the defiance by all means in his power. The guillotine, although being widely used, he said, was too slow; and as shooting the rebels meant expending powder and ball, they adopted the plan of putting certain numbers of them in big boats, conducting them to the middle of the river and there sending the boats to the bottom – a 'vertical deportation' as it was cynically called.

Two of Carrier's aides, Lamberty and Fouquet, had the task of getting the plan, and the boats, under way. Prisoners young and old, many of them priests, were herded on board the rickety vessels. One man asked for a drink of water, only to be told by his captors that there was no need, for 'soon you will be drinking out of the big cup'.

On 23 December 1793 one of the many horrifying atrocities which took place was described by an eye-witness in Henry Jephson's *The Real French Revolutionist*, published in 1899.

Two barges, laden with people, stopped at a place called Praire-au-Duc. There I and my comrades witnessed the most cruel carnage that could possibly be seen. More than 800 persons of all ages and both sexes were inhumanly drowned and cut to pieces. I heard Fouquet and his satellites reproach some among their own people that they did not know how to use their own sabres, and he showed them by his own example how they ought to use them. The barges did not sink to the bottom quickly enough, so they fired with their guns at those who were still above the water. The cries of these unfortunate victims only seemed to increase the energy of their executioners.

I wish to observe that all the individuals who were drowned this night were previously stripped naked as one's hand. In vain the women besought that they might be left their chemises; but the drowners laughed at their tears and joked about the figures of their victims, with horrid comments according as they were young or old. Their rags, their jewels, their belongings were the prey, and what one can scarcely believe is, that those who thus despoiled them, sold these spoils the next day to the highest bidder.

Later Lamberty, chatting to his generals, pointed to the Loire and commented '2,800 brigands are already in the national bath'. More *noyades* took place, at Nantes, at Angers and elsewhere, tens of thousands of Vendeans being killed by drowning, the guillotine or the firing squads, until the Terror receded from the region. Belated justice brought Carrier and his brutal henchmen to the scaffold, but the pitiful victims of the Loire *noyades* were beyond resuscitation.

## Boiled to Death

Rarely has one person had an Act of Parliament directed against him by name, but this is precisely what happened to one man in 1513.

'Richard Roose' it ran 'of his moste wyked and dampnable dysposcyon dyd caste a certayne venym or poyson into the yeste (yeast) or barme wyth whych porrage or gruell was mayde for the famyly of the Byssopp of Rochester and others'. The poison not only affected seventeen members of the household, but also killed one Benett Curwen and Alyce Tryppytt, and because Henry VIII was 'inwardly abhorrying all such abhomynable offences, the sayde poysonyng be adjudged high treason'.

So outraged were the authorities that such an un-English and detestable method should be used, that 'it requyreth condigne punysshemente, to wit, that the sayd Richard Roose shalbe therfore boyled to deathe withoute havynge any advauntage of his clergie'. And so Richard was, at Smithfield, on 5 April 1531.

The Act remained in force for sixteen years, during which a poisonous maidservant, Margaret Davy, who did for three families in more ways than one, was boiled, as was another maid at King's Lynn for the same heinous crime.

Generally victims were boiled in a cauldron containing water, though some countries used oil or tallow. The methods varied, from the prisoner being placed in cold water which was then heated up, forced into the already boiling liquid, or suspended from a beam and repeatedly dipped into the bubbling cauldron.

France favoured total immersion after the liquid had been thoroughly heated, though the penalty was abandoned in the seventeenth century and abolished by law in 1791. But that came too late for the executioner of the city of Tours who, on 11

226

February 1488, shouldn't have died, but did, and his prospective victim Loys Secretan, who should have died, but didn't.

Secretan, a convicted coiner, was sentenced 'to be boiled, drawn and hanged in the Place de la Fere-le-Roy', but everything went wrong, when

> the executioner, one Denis, took the said Loys on to the scaffold and bound his body and legs with cords, made him say his 'in manus', pushed him along and threw him head first into the cauldron to be boiled. As soon as he was thrown in, the cords became so loose that he twice rose to the surface, crying for mercy. Which seeing, the provost and some of the inhabitants began to attack the executioner, saying, 'Ah, you wretch, you are making this poor sinner suffer and bringing great dishonour on the town of Tours!'
>
> The executioner, seeing the anger of the people, tried two or three times to sink the said malefactor with a great iron hook, and forthwith several persons, believing that the cords had been broken by a miracle, became excited and cried out loudly, and seeing that the said false coiner was suffering no harm, they approached the executioner as he lay with his face on the ground, and gave him so many blows that he died where he lay.
>
> Charles VIII pardoned the inhabitants who were accused of killing the executioner, and as for the coiner of false money, he was taken to the church of the Jacobins, where he hid himself so completely that he never dared to show his face again.

## Broken on the Wheel

Widely used on the Continent but, as far as is known, never in England, death by the Wheel originally consisted of an iron flanged wheel being placed on top of the spread-eagled victim, the wheel then being repeatedly struck, breaking the bones until eventually the *coup de grâce* was administered to the neck or chest, further blows which brought death.

## The Wheel in France

The French device evolved into one of a large cartwheel mounted horizontally on a short post. On the wheel was secured two lengths of wood in the shape of a St Andrew's Cross, to which the spread-eagled victim was tied. The cross-pieces were hollowed out beneath arms, thighs and shins, so that only the joints of the limbs were supported.

The executioner, using an iron bar three feet long and two inches square, would then strike the limb over each hollow, smashing each arm and leg in two places. After the requisite eight blows, the victim then received the *coup de grâce*. On very rare occasions the *retentum* could be administered, a merciful strangulation with a thin cord, after a certain number of blows had been delivered.

The wheel became so extensively employed that in the 1770s more criminals were broken on the wheel than were hanged. Highwaymen, thieves, murderers, even women were reduced to shattered corpses, their broken limbs hanging as though they were rag dolls when they were lifted off the wheel.

Some died quickly. Others survived longer, like the legendary gang-leader Cartouche who, in 1721, endured eleven crushing blows and lived for twenty minutes from the moment he was tied to the wheel. His accomplices were also executed, and his five mistresses hanged in July 1722.

This brutal method of execution came to an unexpected end when, in 1788, Jean Louschart accidentally killed his father during a family quarrel. So contrite the victim, so supportive the spectators, that before he could be strapped on the wheel, the crowd had rushed the scaffold, broken up the fearsome device and, throwing it into the fire lighted to consume the mangled body, danced in a circle around the charred embers. And on hearing the details, King Louis XVI not only pardoned Jean Louschart but in 1789 abolished the punishment altogether.

## The Wheel in Germany

Germany's wheel was mounted on a tripod so that it could be rotated, enabling everyone to witness the suffering of the felon. The support varied in height, some being raised so that blows could be struck from below as well as from above.

Worse than the French punishment, German regulations demanded that forty blows be struck, the last one directed at the chest or nape of the neck. One would assume, and hope, that the victim would succumb long before that total was reached, though the executioner of Nuremberg had the duty of executing his own brother-in-law on the wheel and, after giving him 'two tweaks with the red-hot tongs, delivered thirty-one blows with the iron bar before despatching him'.

## The Wheel in Other Countries
In the eighteenth century the wheel was used in Denmark, the felon sometimes having his right hand amputated before being tied down. In Holland, criminals were secured to a cross laid on the scaffold, or on a traditional wheel, this practice being employed in Dutch colonies such as Columbo and Ceylon. Even as recently as 1805, five men guilty of murdering a family in the Dutch town of Delft were executed in that manner.

In Belgium the wheel also had its place in judicial punishment. One victim, a young woman who had stabbed her husband, begged 'to be permitted to appear on the scaffold with that decent degree of covering which may screen my naked limbs'. Decency, if not mercy, won the day, the authorities allowing her to wear a jacket and pantaloons of white satin!

## *The Electric Chair*
It was left to the New World to exploit the newly invented electricity beyond that of eliminating oil lamps, to one of eliminating human life. Old Smokey, or the Hot Squat, as it became familiarly known, made its first appearance on 4 June 1888, in New York, the first case being that of William Kemmler, a wife murderer, in Auburn State Prison on 6 August 1890.

By 1906 more than a hundred executions had taken place in the states of New York, New Jersey, Ohio, Virginia, Massachusetts and North Carolina, and between 1930 and 1972 over 3,800 men and women died in the chair.

The chair itself is a heavy high-backed piece of oak furniture fitted with straps which secure the prisoner's head and chest, arms and legs. Once the occupant has been immobilised, an electrode, moistened with salt solution to ensure good contact, is attached to the victim's head and another to the calf of his or her right leg.

A black hood is dropped over the head and a signal is given, whereupon the executioner operates a switch, sending a lethal current of 1,800 to 2,000 volts, 5 amps, through the victim's body for about five seconds, the charge emitting a loud hum through the execution chamber. After being reduced to 500 volts it is increased twice more, this being considered sufficient to extinguish life.

Should there be any doubt, further shocks would be administered, as in the case of Julius Rosenberg and his wife Ethel who, found guilty of spying for the Russians in 1953, were executed in Sing Sing Prison.

Julius Rosenberg, wearing a helmet fitted with the cathode contact and his face screened by a dark leather mask, was the first to be strapped into the chair. At his switchboard in a cubicle ten feet from the chair, executioner Joseph Fancel operated the switch, sending currents surging through the condemned man for three seconds. Two further charges, each of fifty-seven seconds, followed, the doctors duly pronouncing him dead.

The same procedure was then administered to Ethel Rosenberg, but after the third shock, the doctors still detected a weak pulse through their stethoscopes, so faint as to be hardly identifiable, and it was not until two further shocks had been administered, did they consider that life had been extinguished.

The American media always made much of executions, and never more than that of Ruth Snyder who, with the help of her lover, had battered her husband with a lead sash-weight, drugged him with chloroform, then strangled him with picture wire. They even described the last meal she ate: cream of mushroom soup, thick slices of roast chicken with creamy mashed potatoes and gravy. For sweet, Ruth enjoyed strawberry shortcake, then olives, celery and coffee.

Likewise, on 12 January 1928 reporters described in great detail her paroxysms in the electric chair under the impact of the electrical current, her gasps as the air was driven from her lungs, giving rise yet again to assertions that this method of execution was far from merciful.

Yet many learned authorities claim that because the lethally paralysing current reaches the heart and brain faster than the sensation of conscious pain can travel via the nerve centres, execution in the electric chair is painless. They go on to explain that the spasmodic paroxysms, the convulsions of the head and limbs witnessed by reporters and others, are the inevitable muscle contractions after death, in much the same way as dead animals can be made to twitch when a current is applied to them. In the absence of willing volunteers, definitive proof is sadly lacking.

## The Gas Chamber

Another innovation by the United States, introduced in 1924, this takes place in a small airtight chamber containing two chairs bolted to the floor. With the felon strapped into a chair, the executioner in an adjoining room prepares a mixture of distilled water and sulphuric acid and allows it to run into a vat positioned near the chair.

A final check on the chamber's airtightness follows, and the executioner then pushes a red-painted lever, causing a long rod extending into the execution chamber to rotate, thereby lowering two cheesecloth sachets each containing sixteen one-ounce pellets of sodium cyanide into the acid solution. This noxious cocktail generates a gas, prussic acid (HCN, hydrogen cyanide), exposure to a mixture of 300 parts of this per one million parts of air creating a lethal perfume which is fatal though not necessarily instantaneous. Far from it, for in 1960 nine minutes elapsed before the murderer Caryl Chessman was pronounced clinically dead, though the doctor, using the long stethoscope which passed through the wall and was attached to Chessman's chest by a diaphragm, estimated that the man lost consciousness after thirty seconds.

Even more unfortunate were two men executed in 1938, one living for twelve minutes, the other for fifteen minutes, the frantic contortions of their faces being only too shockingly visible because no hoods were worn in the gas chamber, as these would have provided a pocket of life-sustaining air.

## Lethal Injection

Just as one is rendered unconscious prior to a surgical operation, so this method of execution guarantees permanent oblivion in almost the same way, the condemned person being injected with a fatal dose of barbiturates through an intravenous tube inserted into the arm.

Although it has been adopted by several States in America since its introduction in 1980, its first use in 1982 sparked off an intense debate over the ethics of using a medical procedure and medically trained staff to administer what was fundamentally the very antithesis of saving life. The method was last used in March 1992 when a convicted murderer, Olan Randle Robison, was executed in Oklahoma State Penitentiary.

## The Garrotte

Derived possibly from Old French for cudgel, the *garrotte* took its name from the original form of the punishment which involved the criminal first being bound to a post. A rope would be tied around his neck and the post, a cudgel then being inserted between neck and post and twisted, tourniquet-fashion, until strangulation was complete.

This method was improved and, as used in France, Spain and Germany, the felon was seated on a scaffold and secured to a post by an iron collar. A mechanism at the back of the collar was then tightened, driving a screw into the nape of the neck and severing the spinal cord at the base of the brain.

In conclusion one can only say, after studying the gruesome accounts of the sword and the axe, the rope and the guillotine, Old Smokey and the rest, that the authorities of so many countries are to be applauded in abolishing capital punishment. But at the same time let us balance our wholehearted condemnation of executions in general, by remembering the suffering inflicted on innocent members of society, by the very people society has executed.

# For the Record

1076   First recorded execution in England by the axe, the Earl of Huntingdon

1157   Torture reportedly introduced into Denmark

1208   First witchcraft trial in England, Gideon, a sorcerer, acquitted

1231   Earliest legislation on subject of torture in Italy

1241   First person hanged, drawn and quartered in England, William Marise, pirate

1250   Abolition of trial by fire or water in England

1256   First reported use of torture in Spain

1305   First reported head displayed on London Bridge, Sir William Wallace, Scottish patriot

1310   First reported torture in England – Templars

1450   First recorded use of Tower rack

1497   First official mention of torture in Russia

1547   Abolition of boiling to death in England

1612   Last burning alive in England for heresy, Edward Wightman at Lichfield, Staffs.

1640   Last recorded use of Tower of London rack, John Archer, rioter

1640   Use of torture discontinued in England

1649   Greatest number hanged at one time in England, Tyburn, London, 23 men, 1 woman

1650   Last men to be beheaded by Halifax Gibbet, John Wilkinson, Anthony Mitchell, thieves

1652   Last execution by drowning in Switzerland

1678   Last head on London Bridge, William Stayley

1685　Last man executed by the Scottish Maiden, 9th Earl of Argyll

1686　Last hanging for witchcraft in England, Alice Molland

1690　Last recorded torture in Scotland

1697　Last burning alive for heresy in England

1708　Abolition of torture in Scotland

1712　Last trial for witchcraft in England, Jane Wenham, reprieved

1722　Last witch believed to be burned in Scotland

1732　Torture forbidden by law in Sweden

1740　Last reported peine forte et dure (pressing) in Ireland

1740　Abolition of torture in Prussia

1747　Last man executed by the axe in England, Simon, Lord Lovat, Jacobite rebel

1760　First use of trap-door in hanging, in England, Earl Ferrers, murderer

1771　Abolition of torture in Denmark

1776　Last execution by drowning in Austria

1777　Last execution by drowning in Iceland

1783　Last execution at Tyburn, John Austin, robber

1786　Abolition of torture in Italy

1789　Last woman burned in England, Christian Murphy, coiner

1789　Abolition of torture in French Dominions

1790　Abolition of burning in England of women for husband murder

1790　Abolition of torture in Spain

1791　Abolition of death penalty for witchcraft in England

1791　Abolition of whipping for female vagrants in England

1791　Abolition of boiling oil torture in France

1798　Abolition of torture in United Provinces of Holland

1798　Abolition of torture in France

1799　Abolition of torture in Ceylon

1801　Abolition of torture in Russia

1809　Last recorded ducking of scolds in England, Jenny Pipes née Jane Corran

1814　Abolition of beheading in England

1817　Last person sentenced to ducking stool in England, Sarah Leeke (but pool too shallow!)

1817   Last recorded public flogging of a woman in England

1820   Abolition of whipping of women in United Kingdom

1820   Last men to be beheaded by the axe (after death), in England, Cato Street Conspirators

1822   Last man publicly whipped at the cart's tail, a rioter flogged by the hangman through Glasgow streets

1824   Abolition of capital punishment in Finland

1827   Abolition of peine forte et dure in England

1829   Abolition of branding in England, other than military law

1829   Last man hanged for forgery in England, Thomas Maynard

1831   Abolition of torture in Germany

1832   Abolition of hanging for cattle, horse, sheep stealing in England

1832   Abolition of the pillory in France

1832   Abolition of dissection after hanging in England

1832   Abolition of branding in France

1832   Last person to suffer the pillory in England, Peter James Bossy

1832   Last man gibbetted in England (hanged in chains after death), James Cook, murderer

1833   Abolition of hanging for house breaking in England

1834   Abolition of gibbetting in England

1837   Abolition of the pillory in England

1839   Abolition of the pillory in USA (except Delaware)

1861   Last execution for attempted murder in England, Martin Doyle

1863   Abolition of branding in Russia

1864   First murder on a train in England, Franz Muller, executed

1865   Last public hanging in Scotland, Dr Edward William Pritchard

1867   Abolition of capital punishment in Portugal

1868   Last public hanging in England, Michael Barrett, Fenian murderer

1868   First non-public hanging in England, Thomas Wells, Maidstone Prison, Kent

1870   Abolition of capital punishment in Holland

235

1870    Abolition of hanging/drawing/quartering in England
1872    Last person to suffer in the stocks, Mark Tuck, drunk and disorderly
1873    Abolition of torture in Japan
1875    Last execution in Norway
1879    Total abolition of branding in England
1881    Abolition of corporal punishment in British Army except for offenders in military prisons
1888    Abolition of capital punishment in Italy
1889    Electrocution replaced hanging in State of New York
1890    First man to die by electrocution in USA, William Kemmler, murderer, Auburn Prison
1896    Last triple-hanging at Newgate Prison, London
1896    Electrocution adopted by State of Ohio
1898    Electrocution adopted by State of Massachusetts
1905    Abolition of the pillory in the State of Delaware, USA
1905    Abolition of capital punishment in Norway
1906    Electrocution adopted by State of New Jersey
1906    Abolition of hanging of persons under age of sixteen in England
1908    Electrocution adopted by State of Virginia
1910    Electrocution adopted by State of North Carolina
1921    Abolition of capital punishment in Sweden
1930    Abolition of capital punishment in Denmark
1932    Abolition of hanging of persons under eighteen in England
1942    Abolition of capital punishment in Switzerland
1955    Last woman hanged in United Kingdom, Ruth Ellis, murderess
1955    First woman hanged in new republic of India, Rattan Bai Jain, murderess
1964    Last executions in United Kingdom, Peter Allen and Gwynne Owen Evans, murderers

# Select Bibliography

Andrews, W., *England in Days of Old* (Andrews) 1897

Andrews, W., *Old Time Punishments* (Andrews & Co) 1890

Bleakley, H., *Hangmen of England* (Chapman & Hall) 1929

Brooks, V., *Autographic Mirror*, 1864

Burnet, G., *History of his Own Time*, 1828

Claver, S., *Under the Lash* (Torchstream) 1954

Davey, R., *Tower of London* (Methuen) 1910

Evelyn, J., *Evelyn's Diary* (Bickers, Bush) 1879

Ferrier, J., *Crooks and Crime* (Seeley, Service) 1928

Fox, J., *Book of Martyrs*, 1684

Froude, J., *History of England*, 1863

Gallonio, A., *Torture and Torments of the Christian Martyrs* (Fortuna) 1903

Gerard, J., *Conditions of Catholics under James I* (Ed. Fr Morris) 1871

Harper, C., *Half Hours with the Highwaymen* (Chapman, Hall) 1908

Howard, J., *State of the Prisons* (Eyres) 1775

Jackson, J., *Newgate Calendar*, 1818

Jephson, H., *The Real French Revolutionist* (Macmillan) 1899

Lenotre, G., *Guillotine and its Servants* (Hutchinson) 1908

Lingard, J., *History of England*, 1823

Macaulay, T., *History of England*, 1848

Marchant, J., *The Horrid Cruelties of the Inquisition*, 1770

Marks, A., *Tyburn Tree* (Brown, Langham) 1908

Mayhew, H., *Criminal Prisons of London*, 1862

Parry, L., *History of Torture in England* (Low, Marston) 1933

Percy, R. & S., *Percy Anecdotes*, 1820

Sanson, H., *Memoirs of the Sanson Family* (Chatto & Windus) 1876

Schmidt, F., *Hangman's Diary* (Philip, Allan) 1928

Scott, G., *History of Torture* (Werner Laurie) 1940

Stow, J., *England under Elizabeth* (Routledge) 1890

Swain, J., *Pleasures of the Torture Chamber* (Douglas) 1931

Teonge, H., *Henry Teonge's Diary* (Routledge) 1927

Timbs, J., *Romance of London* (Warne) 1865

Younghusband, G., *Tower of London from Within* (Jenkins) 1918


*Archaeologia*, London, 1838

*Calendar of State Papers* (Domestic Series)

*Chronicles of Crime* (Camden Pelham) 1887

Middlesex Session Rolls

Notable British Trials Series

Tower of London Records

*Tyburn Gallows* (London County Council) 1909

# Index